QUANGOS: TRENDS, CAUSES AND CONSEQUENCES

Quangos: Trends, Causes and Consequences

SANDRA VAN THIEL
Erasmus University, Rotterdam

Routledge
Taylor & Francis Group

LONDON AND NEW YORK

First published 2001 by Ashgate Publishing

Reissued 2018 by Routledge
2 Park Square, Milton Park, Abingdon, Oxon OX14 4RN
711 Third Avenue, New York, NY 10017, USA

Routledge is an imprint of the Taylor & Francis Group, an informa business

Publisher's Note
The publisher has gone to great lengths to ensure the quality of this reprint but points out that some imperfections in the original copies may be apparent.

Disclaimer
The publisher has made every effort to trace copyright holders and welcomes correspondence from those they have been unable to contact.

A Library of Congress record exists under LC control number: 2001089782

ISBN 13: 978-1-138-72874-5 (hbk)
ISBN 13: 978-1-138-72872-1 (pbk)
ISBN 13: 978-1-315-19038-9 (ebk)

Contents

List of Boxes   *vi*
List of Figures   *vii*
List of Tables   *viii*

1 Introduction   1

2 Trends   21

3 Theory   51

4 Causes   95

5 Consequences   131

6 Conclusion   205

Bibliography   *235*
Index   *247*

List of Boxes

Box 1.1   The political processes in a democracy as a cascade of principals and agents   3

Box 1.2   Examples of motives of politicians for the establishment of quangos labelled as 'bringing policy implementation closer to the citizens'   10

Box 1.3   Examples of motives of politicians for the establishment of quangos labelled as 'desirability of self-regulation for social groups'   11

Box 1.4   Examples of motives of politicians for the establishment of quangos labelled as 'separation of policy and administration'   11

Box 1.5   Examples of motives of politicians for the establishment of quangos labelled as 'adoption of market-type mechanisms'   12

Box 5.1   Performance indicators used by IB-Groep (based on annual reports and internal reports, 1990-1998)   164

List of Figures

Figure 2.1   Establishment of quangos in the Netherlands, 1900-   23
1993

Figure 2.2   Dutch quangos, 1900-1980   24

Figure 2.3   Bureaucracy and quangocracy in the Netherlands,   26
1900-1990

Figure 2.4   Tasks of quangos at national level in the Netherlands in   30
1993

Figure 2.5   The number of quangos in policy sectors in the   33
Netherlands in 1993

Figure 2.6   Rate of establishment of quangos for eight policy   35
sectors, the Netherlands, 1950-1993

Figure 2.7   Tasks carried out by Dutch quangos in different policy   36
sectors, 1993

Figure 2.8   Accountability requirements imposed on Dutch   41
quangos, 1900-1993

Figure 2.9   Accountability of Dutch quangos by task and policy   42
sector

Figure 4.1   The number of decisions to establish quangos and   108
established quangos, per year, the Netherlands, 1950-
1993

Figure 5.1   Organizational structure of IB-Groep   149

Figure 5.2   Performance of IB-Groep 1990-1997 in output,   158
running costs and commercial activities

Figure 5.3   Quality indicators 1990-1997   161

Figure 5.4   Organizational structure of the ROC   171

List of Tables

Table 1.1 Different types of organizations used by the 8
government for policy implementation, including four
types of quangos

Table 1.2 Motives of Dutch politicians to establish quangos 9

Table 2.1 The number of quangos in the United Kingdom in 1994 27
and 1996

Table 2.2 Random examples of quangos (public bodies) at 29
national level in the Netherlands in 1993

Table 2.3 Expenditures by quangos in the United Kingdom, 32
1978-1995 in millions British pounds

Table 2.4 The percentage of Dutch quangos on which 39
accountability requirements are imposed, 1993

Table 2.5 Accountability of executive NDPBs in the United 43
Kingdom, 1994-1996

Table 2.6 Evaluation of quangos' annual reports, The Netherlands 45
1994-1997

Table 3.1 Expected effects on choice of politicians for quangos as 88
an executive agent

Table 3.2 Expected effects on the efficiency and effectiveness of 89
policy implementation by quangos and on the occurrence
of a performance paradox

Table 4.1 Operationalizations of the conditions expected to 104
influence the choice of politicians for quangos as an
executive agent

Table 4.2 Descriptive statistics of variables in the analysis to 106
explain the number of decisions to establish quangos
in the Netherlands, 1950-1993 (N=44)

Table 4.3 Results of Poisson regression analysis of the number of 109
decisions per year to establish quangos, the
Netherlands, 1950-1993 (N=43, time-lag 1 year)

Table 4.4 Results of Poisson regression analysis on the number of 110
decisions per year to establish quangos, the
Netherlands, 1950-1993 (N=40, time-lag 4 years)

Table 4.5	Results of Negative Binominal Regression Analysis on the number of established quangos, per year, the Netherlands, 1950-1993 (N=43, time-lag 1 year)	116
Table 4.6	Results of Negative Binominal Regression Analysis on the number of established quangos, per year, the Netherlands, 1950-1993 (N=40, time-lag 4 years)	117
Table 4.7	Results of logistic regression analysis of the accountability of quangos, the Netherlands, 1950-1993	120
Table 4.8	Results of the analysis of the number of decisions to establish quangos and the analysis of the number of established quangos	122
Table 5.1	Hypotheses, operationalizations, and methods used in the case studies	142
Table 5.2A	Costs, revenues, personnel and mail IB-Groep, 1990-1997. All costs and revenues are in NLG million, indexed for 1990	154
Table 5.2B	Running costs of IB-Groep, 1990-1997. All amounts are in NLG million, indexed for 1990	155
Table 5.3	Costs, revenues, input and output of the ROC in 1996 and 1997, compared to the national averages of all ROCs	176
Table 5.5	Summary of case study results in terms of the hypotheses about efficiency and effectiveness of policy implementation and about the occurrence of a performance paradox	188
Table 5.6	Degree of support for the hypotheses about the efficiency and effectiveness of policy implementation; case study results	200
Table 5.7	Degree of support for the hypotheses about the occurrence of a performance paradox; case study results	200

1 Introduction

In many western states the preference for policy implementation by core government agencies has changed in favour of alternative arrangements such as contracting out, privatization or the creation of quasi-autonomous non-governmental organizations. This study focusses on the proliferation of these so-called quangos (Barker, 1982). LeGrand and Bartlett (1993:7) predict that, from 1990 on, the provision of public goods and services will be very different than in earlier decades. Under the 'old' system governments owned, funded and provided public services through government bureaucracy. In the 'new' system, although still paying for the services, governments will no longer provide them. Quangos will be charged with this task, operating at arm's length of the government. Instead of a bureaucracy, we will have a quangocracy. This process is labelled quangocratization,[1] by analogy to bureaucratization (Hood, 1984).

Quangocratization can be viewed as one of the most recent stages of state development in the western world. Modern-day government is characterized by the replacement of the central, hierarchical structure with a complex network of organizations with which governments jointly develop, implement and evaluate policies.

This chapter gives an introduction to quangocratization. First, a theoretical perspective is offered on the rise of this phenomenon. Then, I will go into the definition of quangos. Next, the assumptions underlying politicians' preference for quangos are analysed. Some previous research findings are presented as well as some theories on quangos. To conclude this chapter, the central research questions are presented, along with the outline of the book.

State Development and Quangocratization

According to North (1981:20-32), no analysis of state development can be meaningful if no attention is paid to the distribution (i.e., the allocation) of property rights (see also Hardin, 1997). Property rights are broadly defined as the right to use assets and resources in any way actors see fit (Eggertson,

1

1990:33-40). The right to walk about freely, to earn an income, to own a house or land, to be safe from violence in the streets, to get an education, and to speak one's mind all can be considered examples of the rights individuals have in contemporary western societies.

However, the enforcement of rights is not always easy. Take, for example, the right to safety, for which an army and a police force are necessary. Such provisions are difficult, if not impossible, to establish by an individual alone. Also, rights are often difficult to realise for all individuals at the same time, because advantages to one individual may mean a disadvantage to another. *Collective goods*, such as national security, will not be optimally provided by the market, due to two properties of these goods (Mueller, 1989:11). First, jointness of supply, which means that production costs are more or less fixed. Addition of one consumer will not lead to additional production costs. And second, non-exclusiveness which means the impossibility to exclude individuals from consumption of the good.

A well-known example to illustrate the properties of collective goods is national defence (see Stiglitz, 1988:75). The cost of defending a country of one million individuals or a country of one million and one are the same (jointness of supply), and when national defence is successful all inhabitants benefit from it (non-exclusiveness). This example also shows why individuals are not easily prepared to invest in collective goods. If you invest, others who do not invest may benefit as well. You can also acquire these goods without investing in them, therefore, individuals are disinclined to invest. This phenomenon is known as the free-rider problem (cf. Hendrikse, 1993:144) or the problem of collective action (see Olson, 1965; Coleman, 1990:937-938; Ostrom & Walker, 1997). However, no investments means no provision of collective goods and no enforcement of citizens' rights.

One way to solve the problem of collective action is to establish an overarching authority (a 'ruler'; North, 1981), for example, a sovereign or a group of representatives. Today's overarching authority is usually referred to as the government. It acts on behalf of all individuals ('constituents'; North, 1981) and establishes the conditions that enable people to exercise their rights. The following example illustrates this (for more examples see De Swaan, 1989):

> In the Netherlands in the nineteenth century, waterworks and sewerage were initially constructed by private entreprises commissioned by prosperous citizens. However, these citizens found out - although the chance of infection with cholera was reduced - that risks of infection still existed, because the poor were

not connected to the waterworks and sewerage and kept using non-purified water. Therefore, they supported plans of the city council to oblige every citizen to connect to the waterworks and sewerage. The citizens had discovered that besides one's own health national health exists as well. And when national health is bad, one's own health is in danger, in spite of what measures already may have been taken (Ultee, Arts & Flap, 1992:255 [my translation, SvT]).

In the course of time the government's activities have expanded. Modern welfare states provide goods such as education, social security and national health besides the more traditional goods such as national defence and the tax system (Den Hoed, 1992). These goods are not all purely collective goods as they do not always have the two forementioned characteristics. Therefore, they are usually referred to as impure or quasi-collective goods or publicly provided private goods.

Nowadays, in most western democracies citizens pay taxes and give votes to political parties, in exchange for which elected politicians will pass legislation to implement citizens' rights. An executive is charged by the politicians with the implementation of policies. Thus a *cascade of principals and agents* (Moe, 1984:765; Coleman, 1990:146-156; Pratt & Zeckhauser, 1991) is created (see box 1.1). Voters are the principals of politicians (the agent) when they give politicians the right to act on their behalf. Politicians become principals in their turn, when they charge an executive agent with policy implementation.

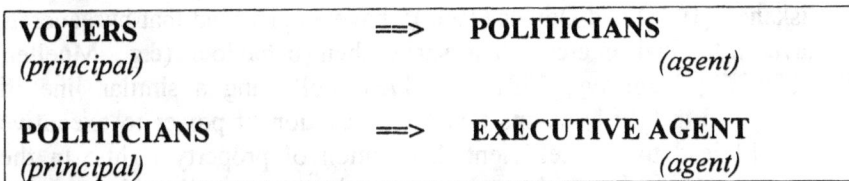

VOTERS	==>	**POLITICIANS**
(principal)		*(agent)*
POLITICIANS	==>	**EXECUTIVE AGENT**
(principal)		*(agent)*

Box 1.1   The political processes in a democracy as a cascade of principals and agents

The relationship of exchange between citizens and politicians, and between politicians and executive agents can be seen as a contractual agreement (North, 1981). The state will seek to maximize the opportunities for citizens to exercise their rights, in exchange for which politicians are given the right to exercise power (e.g. by the use of force). Politicians are also allowed to restrict citizens' use of rights, for instance by attenuation (to avoid damage to the rights of others) and partitioning of rights (i.e., dividing scarce assets or resources) as long as restrictions agree with social norms (Eggertson, 1990). Politicians can transfer part of their rights to an executive agent.

Such differentiation of rights is typical of the development of western democracies. Max Weber labelled it *rationalization of the state* (Ultee *et al.*, 1992:241). As a result of this differentiation, most contemporary western states are characterized by a political system - a democracy - in which legislature and the executive are independent powers, charged with tasks by a constitution (Coleman, 1990:374-375).[2] In most states the executive has developed into a large bureaucracy, which explains why Nonet and Selznick (1978:22) call this stage in the development of western societies the 'bureaucratic' stage.

According to Weber, bureaucracy is the most effective, efficient, and rational form of organization (Van Braam, 1969:157-166; Coleman, 1990:422). Bureaucrats are empowered by politicians to implement policies, but have no rights of production. For example, they do not determine the size of production (input, output), budgets or prices, nor are they allowed to retain surpluses. They are expected to be neutral actors, not acting in their own interest but in the general interest of all individuals, implementing policies that support the enforcement of individuals' rights. This conception of bureaucrats is known as the classical political science perspective (Breton & Wintrobe, 1982:2).

In recent research, however, some scholars - following ideas originated by Niskanen (1975) and Downs (1965) - have emphasized that bureaucrats *do* have individual interests that shape their behaviour (e.g., Mueller, 1989:250-259; Dunleavy, 1991: 147-173). Following a similar line of reasoning, North (1981) claims that the delegation of power to executive agents will lead to an inefficient distribution of property rights. In the absence of competition, citizens have no substitute supplier of collective goods. Exit (emigration to more efficient states) or voice (threating to oppose the ruling authority) are not realistic options for individual citizens. In democracies, tension between dissatisfied constituents and governments will cause political instability, dilution of authority and political pluralism. To maintain its authority and legitimacy, it is the *government* that will initiate institutional reform (North, 1981: 28-32).

North's model can easily be applied to quangocratization. The rapid expansion of the activities and expenditures of government bureaucracy in many western states, especially after the Second World War, raised questions with regard to its legitimacy and effectiveness (see, for example,

Schuyt & Van der Veen, 1990). The drawbacks of bureaucracy as an instrument of rational action, such as inflexibility, red tape and logrolling, facilitated the evolution of western states into a new stage: the post-bureaucratic stage, which is characterized by a diffusion of authority (Nonet & Selznick, 1978:22) and dilution of control (North, 1981). In this stage, the implementation of policies is no longer automatically trusted to core government agencies, but other arrangements such as privatization, contracting out and the setting up of quangos become more popular. These changes are part of what has become known as New Public Management (NPM) or the reinvention paradigm (Pollitt, 1999).

"Effectively NPM has become a generic label for a group of policy and administrative solutions emphasizing competition, disaggregation and incentivization" (Dunleavy, 1994:38). In public sector reforms throughout the western world, a preference for market mechanisms is coupled with a shift from input- towards output-driven management, downsizing, a separation of policy and administration, and an emphasis on customer orientation (Pollitt, 1999). New (types of) organizations, such as quangos, are established to which the government transfers part of its right to implement policies and (some of) the accompanying production rights. As a result, the institutional context of central governments has become more and more complex (Leeuw, 1992). Below I will elaborate more on the political motives underlying these reforms.

Quangocratization can thus be considered as one of the most recent stages in the development of western states. An interesting question in this respect is whether quangocratization is the next step in the process of rationalization[3] as described by Weber in terms of ongoing specialization and differentiation, or whether it is a form of de-rationalization, considering that it replaces bureaucracy, which, according to Weber, is the most rational form of government organization. I shall return to this question in chapter 6. But the first question to be dealt with is: what is a quango?

Definition of a Quango

In this study, quangos are defined as organizations which, as their main task, are charged with the implementation of one or more public policies, and which are funded publically but operate at arm's length of the central government, without an immediate hierarchical relationship existing with a minister or a parent department[4] (Leeuw, 1992). A more precise definition is hard to find, and different researchers and practitioners list different types of organizations as quangos (see, for example, the debate in the United Kingdom between Hogwood [1995] and Hall & Weir [1996] in chapter 2).[5] The debate is complicated even more by all the different terms in use, for example: para-governmental organizations (PGOs; WRR, 1983; Hood, 1984), non-departmental public bodies (NDPBs; Hogwood, 1995), extra-governmental organizations (EGOs; Weir & Hall, 1994; Hall & Weir, 1996), hybrids (In 't Veld, 1995) or 'the grey zone' (Greve, 1996; 1999).

To find a useful solution to the definition problem, it is necessary to acknowledge that there is not just one type of quango. Instead, there are *several* types of organizations that could be classified as a quango. Following this idea, some authors have described a continuum of quangos (see, for example, Loeff Claeys Verbeke [1994:19] and Commissie Sint [1994] on the Netherlands; and Rainey [1997:68] on the USA). Table 1.1 presents the sub-sectional map of quangos that will be used as a guideline in this study (adapted from Greve, Flinders & Van Thiel, 1999).

Table 1.1 shows four types of quangos: (i) contract agencies (cf. the British Next Steps agencies), (ii) public bodies (e.g., the Dutch *zelfstandige bestuursorganen* or ZBOs [Scheltema, 1974; see for more information chapter 2], or the British NDPBs), (iii) voluntary or charity organizations, and (iv) state-owned enterprises (SOEs). Departmental units are listed as a contrast on the right side of the continuum, while on the left side private organizations are listed.[6] Private organizations can be involved in policy implementation through privatization of SOEs, or through contracting out, also known as outsourcing or competitive tendering. In the latter case, public organizations can be involved in the bidding process as well. The position of an organization on the quango continuum need not be constant over time. Quango-drift (Greve *et al.*, 1999:143) can occur; for example, an agency can become a public body or a public body can be privatized.

The typology offers a useful classification for research purposes. It is based on the assumption that the conditions under which an organization operates determine what type of quango it is. Table 1.1 lists three conditions: (i) financial arrangements; (ii) the extent to which ministerial accountability applies and (iii) the control mechanisms for ministers. The type of task is not included as a distinctive condition, because different types of quangos can be charged with similar tasks.[7]

Going through the table from right to left, one will notice the turning point in the middle, where opportunities for politicians to exert influence (control mechanisms, ministerial accountability and finances) decrease and the autonomy of quangos increases. Autonomy is defined here as the ownership of the rights of production, that is who decides about or provides the organization with: goals, tasks, budget, input variables such as labour and capital, output and/or outcome, prices of supplied goods or services, and the production process (including so-called standard operating procedures, information, and technology). The greater the extent to which organizations own such rights, the more they are in control of and responsible for their activities, and the more autonomous they are.

Quangos are *quasi*-autonomous, which means that they are given *some* of the production rights, but not all. Part of the production rights remains the prerogative of the minister of the parent department. There is no uniform arrangement in this matter, as every single quango, irrespective of its type, owns a different set of production rights. Some quangos cannot command their own budget because they receive it directly from the state. Other quangos are allowed to impose fees or levies. Some quangos cannot determine their output, because they are bound by pre-determined numbers of goods or services (output) being laid down in management contracts. Some quangos are free to hire employees while other quangos employ only seconded civil servants from the parent department (see also chapter 2). In general, most quangos receive relative managerial freedom: managing the production process (input, output, procedures) is their own responsibility. The minister is no longer accountable for managerial affairs. The minister does remain accountable for policy matters, the choice of a quango, and supervision of quangos. A limited ministerial responsibility is accompanied by fewer control mechanisms for ministers (Stone, 1995).

Due to the mixed ownership of production rights, quangos are not public organizations in the traditional sense, as, for example, departmental units, although they do belong to the public domain. As stated before, depending on the conditions under which they operate and their degree of autonomy, different types of quangos can be distinguished. Table 1.1 lists some Dutch examples of these types (for more examples see Greve *et al.*, 1999). Most empirical references in this study will be to quangos of the 'public body' type. Now, we turn to the motives of politicians for establishing quangos.

Table 1.1 Different types of organizations used by the government for policy implementation, including four types of quangos (adapted from: Greve, Flinders & Van Thiel, 1999:142)

	Market/Private Sector organizations	State Owned Companies/Enterprises	Voluntary/charity organizations	Public Body	Contract Agency	Departmental Unit
Definition	organization contracted by government	government owns company or majority of shares	bottom-up body given public task and funding	quasi-autonomous organization outside government	quasi-autonomous unit within government	division of government bureaucracy
Finances	through market mechanism	state budget or stock exchange	donations, subsidy	state budget, fees or levying	state budget	state budget
Ministerial accountability	only for terms of contract	limited to strategic and financial decisions	only for terms and the amount of subsidy	only for policy design and regulation	reduced in case of managerial matters	full ministerial accountability
Control mechanisms	contract	market intervention or buying/selling shares	contract	statutes, law	framework document	hierarchical intervention
Dutch examples	Local level waste disposal, co-financed infrastructural projects	Postal and Tele Communications Services (now privatized)	Salvation Army, Red Cross	legal aid, public universities, Water Boards	Service for Immigration and Naturalisation	division of Ministry of Justice, Defence, the Home Office

The Practitioner Theory

Politicians mention different motives for their choice of quangos, that is, *if* they mention one. There seems to be a general lack of justification by politicians for the use of quangos (except in New Zealand; see Boston, 1995). See, for example, table 1.2, which lists the motives for the establishment of quangos in the Netherlands, as mentioned by politicians in the statutes.[8]

It shows that in most cases (53%) no motive is given. If there is, the motives most often mentioned are: an expected increase in the efficiency and effectiveness of policy implementation, bringing the government closer to the citizens by putting policy implementation at arm's length, the desirability of self-regulation by, for example, charging interest groups with executive tasks, and execution of a task by independent experts.

Similar motives are also found in, for example, the United Kingdom (Flinders, 1999a). Next to motives politicians themselves mention, a number of others are thought to play a role, such as the desire to gain additional political support (patronage, i.e. quangos are used to reward political supporters, e.g. by appointing them member of quango boards), to bypass other organizations or governments, to conceal the actual height of government expenditure, and to decrease the 'risk potential' of policy implementation for politicians by limiting ministerial responsibility (Hood, 1988; Hogwood, 1995).

Table 1.2 Motives of Dutch politicians to establish quangos (N=545)

Motive	Number[a]
To increase efficiency	18%
Closer to the citizens	15%
Self-regulation by social groups	13%
Execution by experts	12%
Other motives[b]	12%
No motive mentioned	53%

[a] More than one motive can be mentioned
[b] Other motives are, for example: no state interference is desired; continuation of a historically grown situation; affirmation of independency of executive agents
Source: Algemene Rekenkamer, 1995 (own calculations)

The motives and (implicit) assumptions underlying - and often legitimizing - politicians' preference for quangos are referred to as the practitioner theory. Note that the practitioner theory is not a scientific theory, although politicians might use scientific theories and concepts to explain or justify their decisions (Hoogerwerf, 1984; Van de Graaf, 1988; Leeuw, 1989).

As the lack of (explicit) justification in table 1.2 shows, it is questionable whether there is indeed a coherent set of ideas, a practitioner theory, underlying the creation of quangos. Analysis of the motives of Dutch politicians does show some trends though. The prevalence of certain motives has changed over time (cf. Van Leerdam, 1999). In the 1950s 'self-regulation' and 'bringing the government closer to citizens' are mentioned most frequently, while in the 1970s and 1980s the efficiency and effectiveness motive predominated. This shift in the type of justification can perhaps be explained by the difference in the political and economic situations between those periods.

In the 1950s, Dutch society was highly pillarized. Such a strong (vertical) segmentation of society was possible because co-operation between segments took only place at the top (Lijphart, 1968). The role of the government was limited, in favour of self-regulation and decentralization. The creation of quangos was legitimized accordingly, as the exemplary motives in boxes 1.2 and 1.3 show.[9]

Child Welfare Council (1956)
Established as a quango to guarantee the participation of citizens within the legal district.
Social Security Bank (1956)
It is considered desirable to bring the implementation of social security policies closer to the people concerned.
(Source: Database Algemene Rekenkamer, 1995 [my translation, SvT])

Box 1.2 Examples of motives of politicians for the establishment of quangos labelled as 'bringing policy implementation closer to the citizens'

In some cases, the initiative to establish a quango did not come from the government but from citizens or interest groups (see the last example in box 1.3). In that case, private initiatives were given a legal basis without being incorporated fully into the government bureaucracy. This process is called 'hiving in' (In 't Veld, 1995:10).

The opposite - 'hiving off' - is the placement of departmental units outside core the government bureaucracy. The creation of quangos by means of hiving off is usually motivated by a wish to separate politics and administration, reduce the interference by politicians in the daily operation process, and leave policy implementation to experts (see box 1.4).

Dutch Order of Lawyers (1952)
Voluntary self-regulation by a group of professionals needs a legal basis to ensure that all lawyers will be bound by the same rules of conduct.
Bureau for Registration of Architects (1988)
The government should not support, financially nor organizationally, the execution of a legal arrangement which mainly serves the interests of suppliers and consumers of architects' services.
Foundation to Guarantee the Quality of Calfs (1990)
Businesses within the sector requested establishment of the quango in order to promote and guarantee the quality of meat and feed.
(Source: Database Algemene Rekenkamer 1995 [my translation, SvT])

Box 1.3 Examples of motives of politicians for the establishment of quangos labelled as 'desirability of self-regulation for social groups'

Fund to stimulate Dutch Cultural Broadcasting Productions (1988)
Aim is to improve a certain degree of autonomy for the board to undertake activities and to develop simple procedures for swift decision-making.
(Source: Database Algemene Rekenkamer, 1995 [my translation, SvT])
Land and Registry Office (1994)
Establishment was considered necessary to ensure economic, efficient and continuous control without immediate political intervention.
(Source: *Rapportage Doorlichting Zelfstandige Bestuursorganen*, 1997 [my translation, SvT])

Box 1.4 Examples of motives of politicians for the establishment of quangos labelled as 'separation of policy and administration'

This separation of policy and administration became very popular in the early 1980s, as part of a widespread public sector reform. Reform was triggered by economic decline, growing international competition, general dissatisfaction with public sector performance and a change in the political composition of several western governments (Wright, 1994), including the Netherlands.

A New Public Management was developed (Dunleavy, 1994) which, in combination with the rising (neo-liberal) belief in the superiority of the market mechanism, resulted in the adoption by the public sector of market-type mechanisms, such as vouchers and internal markets (LeGrand & Bartlett, 1993), the creation of new public bodies and agencies to perform public tasks, and downsizing of the government through privatization and contracting-out (cf. Pollitt, 1999). In most countries quangos existed already but they were now re-discovered as instruments for public sector reform (Greve *et al.*, 1999), and a means to achieve more efficiency and effectiveness, as is demonstrated by the motives for establishment listed in box 1.5.

Hallmark of Platinum, Gold and Silver Inc. (1986)
A long-term economic profit is expected because a privatized organization will be able to use its available knowledge or expertise for other activitities besides certifications.
Fund for labourmarkets and training in government (1987)
Imitation of similar initiatives in the private sector that have played a stimula-ting and innovating role in the area of improvement of qualifications of indi-vidual employees, research and the educational infrastructure.
Inspection of Weights and Measures (1989)
More autonomy for the former departmental unit can improve economic mana-gement, including the development of fees. This privatization is aimed at at-taining budget cuts, a decrease in the size of government and an expansion of the market.
(Source: Database Algemene Rekenkamer, 1995 [my translation, SvT])

Box 1.5 Examples of motives of politicians for the establishment of quangos labelled as 'adoption of market-type mechanisms'

So, politicians' preference for quangos from the 1980s on stems from a belief in the superiority of the market. Compared to government bureauc-racy, quangos are viewed as market-like, because they can own production rights. Their quasi-autonomy is expected to create incentives to perform more efficiently, for example, because they are allowed to retain surpluses, or have to compete over budgets with other organizations. Moreover, they operate at arm's length, which means away from meddling politicians and presumedly closer to the citizens (and the market). This is expected to lead to a more articulated demand by citizens and a more efficient match of supply and demand (Waldegrave, 1993). The possibility of competition between quangos or with other organizations is expected to rule out other potential inefficiencies.

There are, however, several reasons to doubt the validity of the practitioner theory underlying the establishment of quangos in and after the 1980s. First, putting an organization at arm's length is not the same as getting closer to the citizens, nor does it equal operating in a market. Before, I already discussed the problem of market failure in the case of collective goods. The free-rider problem, i.e. other organizations will not invest in collective goods, means that quangos usually have a monopoly. Citizens have no substitute providers (cf. Van Waarden, 1995). This situation is enforced by the legal monopoly that executive agents have on policy implementation.

Second, the establishment of quangos is, in itself, no guarantee for efficient and effective policy implementation. Several authors have stressed that efficiency sometimes seems to contradict other policy objectives such as equity, fairness, and responsiveness to needs of citizens (Wilson, 1989:131-132; LeGrand & Bartlett, 1993:13-19). The presence of multiple and sometimes conflicting goals may obstruct efficient and effective policy implementation by any executive agent. Moreover, because of the lack of potential bankruptcy for public organizations and the disjunction between costs and revenues (i.e. the absent or unknown relation between taxes paid by citizens and the amount of goods and services received), there is a lack of incentives to perform efficiently (LeGrand, 1991). These problems are typical of the public sector and will not be overcome merely by establishing quangos.

Third, the establishment of quangos creates new problems. As pointed out earlier, executive agents may pursue their own goals rather than those of their principal (Downs, 1965; Niskanen, 1975; North, 1981; Mueller, 1989, Van den Doel & Van Velthoven, 1990; Dunleavy, 1991). To prevent inefficiency, the performance of quangos needs to be monitored or evaluated, regulators are appointed, and so on. In theory, this undermines the idea that less regulation is needed because quangos can operate more autonomously than government bureaucracy (cf. Van Waarden, 1995). In practice, studies on quangos in the UK and the Netherlands show a severe lack of accountability requirements imposed upon quangos (Weir & Hall, 1994; Hall & Weir, 1996; Algemene Rekenkamer, 1995; see also chapter 2). Performance assessment is complicated by the aforementioned conflicting policy objectives and the absence of competitors to compare performance with. I shall return to these problems in chapter 3.

Finally, the claim of the practitioner theory that quangocratization will lead to more efficient and effective policy implementation has yet to be corroborated. Until recently, there has been little interest in quangos and their performance, both among politicians (hence perhaps the lack of accountability requirements; Leeuw, 1995) and academics. So far, there is no evidence that policy implementation by quangos is more efficient or effective than implementation by government bureaucracy (see, for example, Van Berkum & Van Dijkem, 1997; Ter Bogt, 1997). The next section provides an overview of the research on quangos that has been carried out already.

Previous Research on Quangos

In most western states, quangos have existed for a long time (Greve *et al.*, 1999) but have not attracted much attention either from politicians or academics. While the public sector reform in the 1980s has been studied extensively (see, for example, the international comparative studies by Kickert [1997] and Pollitt & Bouckaert [2000], or Rainey's review of public management [1997]), the increase in the number of quangos has not been given much thought. Some studies carried out in the late 1970s and early 1980s, compare the efficiency and/or effectiveness of public and private providers of public services, usually at a local or regional level. However, these studies confined themselves to contracting-out or privatization (see Mueller [1989: 262-265] and Weimer & Vining [1992:195-200] for reviews; and see Naschold [1996] and Boyne [1998] for a discussion). In the mid-1980s a few studies on public bodies were carried out. These studies gave an inventory of the number of public bodies in several western countries and some of their characteristics, such as the tasks they executed, the policy area in which they operated (WRR, 1983; Hood & Schuppert, 1988; Modeen & Rosas, 1988) and the motives underlying their establishment (Boxum, De Ridder & Scheltema, 1989).

Still, it was not until the mid-1990s that the real interest in quangos was triggered, by the publication of some reports that questioned the use of quangos - mainly public bodies - and their accountability (see Algemene Rekenkamer [1995] on the Netherlands, and Weir & Hall [1994] and Hall & Weir [1996] on the United Kingdom). These reports revealed (i) the large number of quangos that existed, (ii) the large amount of money that was spent on them, (iii) the large amount of money spent by them, and (iv) the poor account they provided of their performance. The consequent political debate concentrated mainly on the accountability of public bodies. For example, in the Netherlands, politicians wanted to restore their control of public bodies (*Herstel van het primaat*, 1995), improve legislation and accountability requirements (*Aanwijzingen voor de regelgeving*, 1996; *Rapportage Doorlichting Zelfstandige Bestuursorganen*, 1997) and limit the possibilities for commercial activities (Commissie Cohen, 1997). In the United Kingdom, the debate concentrated on the large scale appointment of former politicians on quango boards (the so-called 'sleaze' debate, investigated by the Nolan Committee).

The reports and following debate also triggered more interest in quangos among academics. Studies were undertaken to describe the new types of organizations that governments used to provide collective goods (Kickert, Mol & Sorber, 1992; Coops, 1995). One of the most famous international examples is the study by Osborne and Gaebler, who list 36 different types of arrangements (1992:appendix A). Other relevant studies are: OECD (1993), World Bank (1997), and Flinders and Smith (1999). In the UK, case studies were carried out on new bodies in the housing sector, education and the national health service (LeGrand & Bartlett, 1993; Pollitt, Birchall & Putman, 1998). In the Netherlands the semi-privatization of public transport was studied (Groenendijk, 1998) and the provision of legal aid (Bulder, Van der Wal, Leeuw & Flap, 1997). Other researchers focussed on the legal aspects of the use of quangos (Boxum, 1997; Goorden, Den Boer & Buijn, 1997), their democratic accountability (Zijlstra, 1997; Gray [forthcoming]), the relationship between quangos and parent departments (Kickert *et al.*, 1998), and the change in organizational culture of hived-off departmental units (Hakvoort & Veenswijk, 1997; 1998).

Even though academic interest in quangos is growing, the definition problem as discussed above continues to complicate comparative studies of different types of quangos, both within and between countries. And despite there now being more information on public bodies, privatization, public-private partnerships (PPP) and contracting-out, knowledge of voluntary organizations and agencies (cf. table 1.1) is still limited (but see Ministerie van Financiën [1998] and *Next Steps Reviews* in the UK). Moreover, attention is still focussed on the position of the government, i.e. on how it should deal with all these new organizations and relations. Little attention is paid to internal matters of quangos and their performance.

So far, researchers have used different theoretical approaches, mainly neo-institutional economics (see, for example, Ter Bogt [1994; 1997],

Künneke [1992] on property rights, and Van Leerdam [1999] on transaction cost analysis). The application of neo-institutional economics to public bureaucracy offers the opportunity to explain why politicians prefer a certain type of organization - be it government bureaucracy or a quango - as executive agent charged with policy implementation, instead of leaving provision of goods and services to the market (March & Olson, 1983, 1984; Moe, 1984; Powell & DiMaggio, 1991; Hendrikse, 1993; Ter Bogt, 1994, 1997; Douma & Schreuder, 1998; Bovenberg & Teulings, 1999).

The common focus in neo-institutional economics is on the efficiency of markets and organizations. For example, transaction cost analysis (Williamson, 1981, 1989, 1995) posits that organizations are established when that is the best way to minimize transaction costs (i.e. the costs of seeking information, bargaining and enforcing a contract). It is argued that if the production of a good requires very specific investments (e.g. to procure specialist knowledge) it is more expensive - hence less efficient - in the market than in an organization. Assuming that quangos are more market-like than government bureaucracy, the application of transaction cost analysis to explain the establishment of quangos is an obvious choice.

Another example is principal agent theory (e.g., Pratt & Zeckhauser, 1991). The basic model of this theory is very simple. A (the principal) enters into a contract with B (the agent), which states that the agent will execute an order for the principal, for which the agent will receive a compensation. Problems can arise when the principal has no information on the performance of or the efforts made by the agent. Monitoring is required to determine whether the agent acts on the terms of the contract and should be rewarded accordingly. Two problems are discerned: 'adverse selection' (will the agent disclose full information *ex ante* on his performance?) and 'moral hazard' (will the agent perform as agreed upon in the contract?). Principals will choose an agent in such a manner that the risk of these problems is minimized. Principal agent theory can therefore be applied to politicians' choice of an executive agent.

A third approach is property rights theory, which investigates the allocation of property rights, for example through contracts, to actors in order to regulate responsibilities and undo externalities (Coase theorem; Jensen & Meckling, 1976; North, 1981; Eggertson, 1990; Künneke, 1992; Hendrikse, 1993:46-50;). It is assumed that if an actor has the right to use, produce and sell a particular good, it will be produced in the most efficient manner, because the actor stands to gain from his own investments. However, as was mentioned earlier, in the case of collective goods rights cannot be assigned exclusively to one individual. Therefore, it was argued, the provision of such goods and the associated rights are taken over by the government. Another application of property rights theory was touched upon in the definition of autonomy in terms of ownership of production rights.

A specification of (neo-institutionalist) economics in the political realm is public choice theory (Mueller, 1989; 1997; Van den Doel & Van Velthoven, 1990; Dunleavy, 1991, based on work originated by Downs [1965] and Niskanen [1975]). The principle of utility maximization is applied to politicians and bureaucrats in order to explain their behaviour, in particular in cases where it leads to inefficiencies in policy development and implementation, such as the oversupply of goods or services (cf. Breton & Wintrobe, 1982).

The most important common element underlying *all* these approaches is the rational actor model (also known as rational choice theory; Coleman, 1990; Lindenberg, 1983). Individuals are seen as self-interested actors whose rational behaviour is aimed at utility maximization, given their preferences and constraints. Thus far, most applications have concentrated on bureaucrats. However, the approaches can also be applied to quangocratization. Minimalize transaction or agency costs and ensure efficient allocation of (production) rights can explain why politicians choose a particular type of executive agent, such as quangos. Moreover, principal agent theory can be used as well to explain the behaviour of an executive agent. Moral hazard and adverse selection are problems that occur in all organizations, including quangos. Therefore, it has been decided to use the rational actor model as the basic framework of this study (see chapter 3 for more details), taking elements from neo-institutional economics and public choice theory to answer the two main research questions posed in the next section.

Research Questions and Outline of the Book

The previous sections have presented two interesting observations, which will be the leading topics of this study. First, it was argued that quangos are replacing government bureaucracy, and that quangocratization is seen as one of the most recent stages of state development in western countries. To investigate to which extent there indeed is such a trend, chapter 2 will describe quangocratization in the Netherlands between 1900 and 1993. Some international comparisons will be made, albeit limited by the lack of data.

However, this study intends to go beyond description. It also seeks to explain the increase in the use of quangos. To ascertain the causes of quangocratization it is necessary to determine under which conditions politicians choose quangos as executive agent, rather than government bureaucracy. Therefore, the first research question of this study is:

[Research question 1] Under which conditions do politicians choose quangos as executive agents, rather than government bureaucracy, for the implementation of policies?

The practitioner theory will *not* be used to explain quangocratization. It is not a scientific theory, but rather a legitimization by politicians of their actions. Moreover, the practitioner theory as described is merely my interpretation of the motives mentioned by politicians, and in more than half of the cases no motive whatsoever was mentioned (cf. table 1.2). It is therefore an incomplete theory. Finally, the primary focus of the practitioner theory is on (the expected performance of) quangos rather than politicians themselves, which makes it less suitable to explain behaviour of *politicians*, the aim of this study. Based on these considerations, I have decided to construct a theory about politicians' choice for quangos as an executive agent, using the rational actor framework as mentioned before. Chapter 6 will confront the results of this study with the practitioner theory.

The second interesting observation in this chapter concerns the claim of the practitioner theory that policy implementation by quangos is more efficient and effective than implementation by government bureaucracy. Several doubts with regard to that claim were presented already. The review of previous research showed that we still know very little about quangos, in particular when it comes to their performance. Quango performance lies therefore at the heart of the second research question:

[Research question 2] Under which conditions will policy implementation by quangos be more efficient and effective than implementation by government bureaucracy?

To find an answer to the two research questions specified, in chapter 3 a theoretical model will be given of (i) the choice of politicians for quangos and (ii) the performance of quangos. As stated before, the model will be based on the rational actor model, using concepts from neo-institutional economics and public choice theory. From the model, hypotheses will be derived that are tested in chapters 4 and 5 respectively, using a combination of quantitative research methods (regression analysis) and qualitative ones (case studies).

Chapter 6 summarizes the main findings of this study on the trends, causes and consequences of the increased number of quangos. Results of the testing of the hypotheses are discussed and confronted with the practitioner theory. But before that, we turn to chapter 2, which describes trends of quangocratization.

Notes

1. To describe the establishment of all kinds of autonomous organizations some academics use the term 'autonomization'. While this term implies more autonomy, this need not always be the case. Kickert *et al.* found that in a number of cases autonomization actually led to less autonomy because of increased restrictions and regulations placed on an organization after it was put at arm's length of the government. This was labelled the 'myth of autonomization' (Kickert *et al.*, 1998:161).

2. There is yet another independent power: the judiciary. This third power falls outside the scope of this study.

3. Blau and Meyer (1987:183-184) ended their book on bureaucracies with a discussion on the diffusion of the multi-divisional organizational form (M-form) in the private sector. Blau and Meyer considered this diffusion an example of rationalization, which they believed public sector organizations could never adopt, because of the absence of a real market mechanism in the public sector. However, the similarities between the establishment of quangos and the creation of holdings (parent departments) and divisions (quangos) can be said to prove Blau and Meyer wrong.

4. The parent department is the department responsible for the policy sector in which an organization is operating.

5. Advisory councils are generally not considered to be quangos.

6. The ultimate contrast at the left side of the continuum would be that the government leaves the provision of goods or services entirely to the market, and is no longer responsible. As the table lists only examples of organizations used to implement policies, that ultimate contrast is not included here.

7. Another important condition could be the distinction between public and private law (cf. Loeff Claeys Verbeke, 1994). Quangos on the right side of the continuum are more often based on public law, while on the left side of the continuum private law predominates. As this dimension only holds for countries with a system of administrative law, it is not included in table 1.1.

8. Here, data are used on Dutch ZBOs (cf. public bodies in table 1.1) which were collected by the Netherlands Court of Audit (Algemene Rekenkamer, 1995).

9. Not all exemplary motives for the establishment of quangos relate to the time period mentioned. This is caused by two methodological problems. First, a lack of data, because in 53% of the cases no motive was mentioned. And second, the listed date of establishment is not always the original date, due to mergers of many quangos in the 1980s (see also chapter 2).

2 Trends

The purpose of this chapter is to give a description of the proliferation of quangos in the Netherlands.[1] The main focus will be on public bodies (cf. table 1.1) at a national level, in particular the so-called *zelfstandige bestuursorganen* (ZBOs). Data were provided by the Netherlands Court of Audit (NCA), which carried out a survey among all ZBOs in 1993 (Algemene Rekenkamer, 1995).[2]

Information on other types of quangos or at lower levels of government is often incomplete or absent. Privatization has not occurred often in the Netherlands, partly because there have never been that many state-owned enterprises. Two examples are: the postal service (KPN) and the Dutch State Mines (DSM). Dutch contract agencies have been established only after 1994. In 1998 there were 21 agencies assigned with, among others, the prison service, demographic records, meteorology, granting subsidies, and immigration (*Miljoenennota 1999*). No systematical collection of information has been carried out on quangos at provincial and local government level in the Netherlands.[3]

Some data are available on the number of quangos in other countries, such as the United Kingdom (Weir & Hall, 1994; Hogwood, 1995; NAO, 1995; PERC, 1996; Hall & Weir, 1996; Flinders & Smith, 1999) and Denmark (Greve, 1996; 1999). Information on quangos in other countries, like Sweden, Finland, Australia and New Zealand, has been found (Hood & Schuppert, 1988; Modeen & Rosas, 1988; Wistrich, 1996; 1999), but is less complete or outdated. References are made where appropriate.[4]

As said before, this chapter describes quangos, i.e. ZBOs, in the Netherlands. Attention is paid to their number, some of their characteristics and the policy fields in which they operate. When available, information on other countries is used as a comparison. Then I move on to investigate the accounts quangos give of their performance. First, accountability requirements are studied using the NCA survey. Next, the content of the accounts given by quangos are studied, for which data were provided by the accountancy and consultancy firm Arthur Andersen (1995; 1996; 1997; 1998). The chapter is concluded with a summary of trends in quangocratization in the Netherlands.

Quangocratization in the Netherlands

The Number of Quangos

In 1993, the NCA counted 545 quangos in the Netherlands, of which over 40% were established after 1980 (Algemene Rekenkamer, 1995).[5] Figure 2.1 shows the rate of establishment.[6] It is important to note that quangos are sometimes established as clusters, i.e. more than one quango is charged with the same task. These quangos may operate in different regions. The NCA survey contains 23 clusters, which account for 406 organizations, and 139 'single' organizations. Figure 2.1 shows how often a decision was taken to establish (a cluster of) quangos, and the number of established organizations that resulted from these decisions. In the case of a cluster, one decision will have led to several quangos being established.[7]

Figure 2.1 shows that the number of quangos has increased over time, with spurts in the 1950s, the 1970s and the 1980s. The growth of the number of quangos in the 1950s and the 1970s is mainly caused by the establishment of clusters of quangos (e.g. social security). The increase in the 1980s is primarily the result of an increase in the number of single quangos. To put it differently, the number of *decisions* to establish quangos was largest in the 1980s.

Historical comparison The NCA survey investigated only quangos that were in existence in 1993. The data are therefore left-censored. Quangos that were established but abolished again before 1993 are not included, which makes it impossible to draw conclusions on the average life span of quangos.

A historical comparison was made between a study by the Scientific Council for Government Policy (SCGP) on almost 650 para-governmental bodies (WRR, 1983) and the NCA survey (limited to the time period 1900-1980). The results are shown in figure 2.2. Because the SCGP uses a broader definition, the number of quangos in the two studies differs, with a 62.5% overlap (400 odd organizations).

Of the approximately 245 non-overlapping number of organizations in the SCGP-study 75 are not public bodies but government sponsored enterprises or agencies, about 150 organizations have merged or transformed into other (clusters of) quangos[8], and 20 odd organizations have ceased to exist, are inactive or were never established The 'mortality rate' of quangos is thus estimated to be 3%. The average lifespan of the 20 organizations is 30 years.

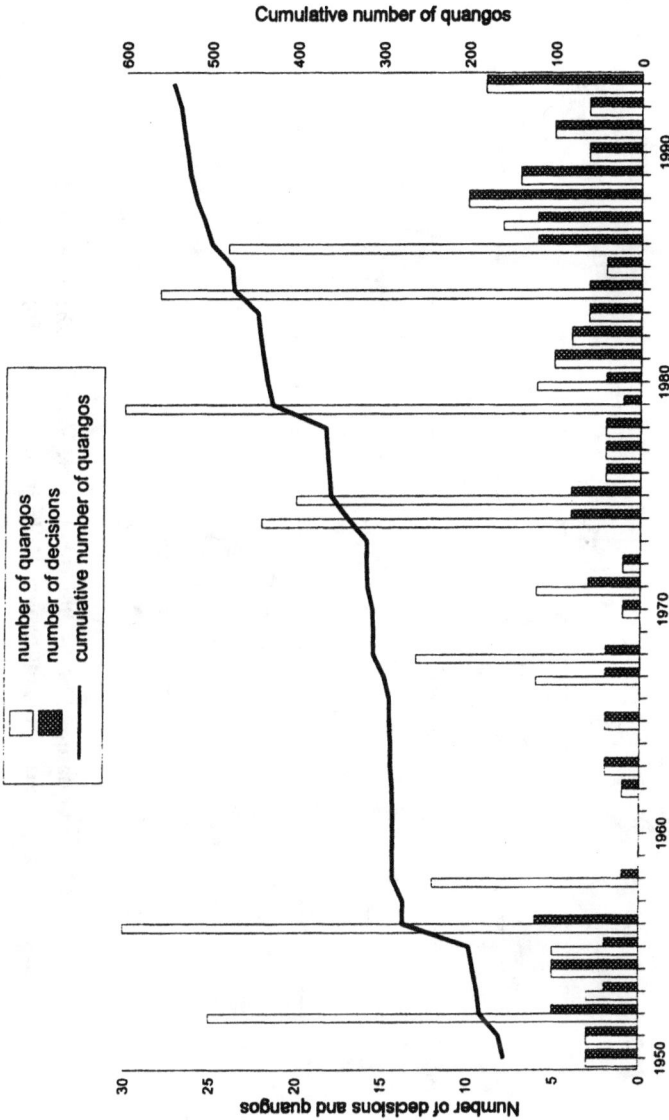

Figure 2.1 Establishment of quangos in the Netherlands, 1900-1993 (*Source:* Algemene Rekenkamer, 1995 [own calculations])

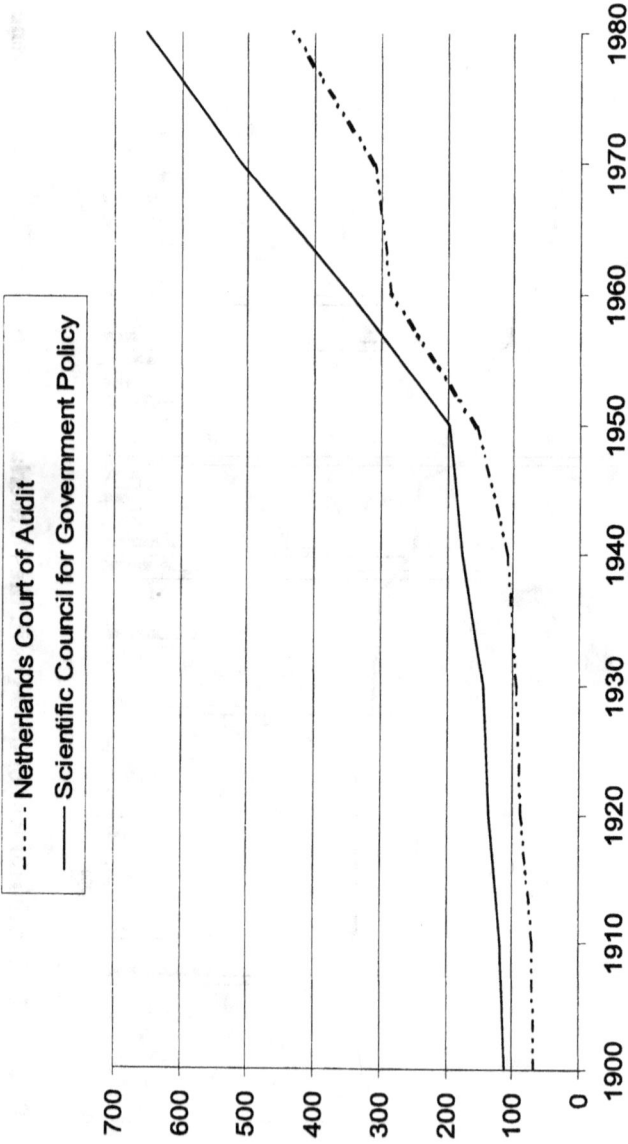

Figure 2.2 Dutch quangos, 1900-1980 (*Sources:* WRR, 1983 [own caluclations]; Algemene Rekenkamer, 1995 [own calculations])

So, only few quangos are abolished but their existence can be discontinued if they merge with other quangos. Still, most quangos have a long lifespan (cf. Kaufman, 1976). Apparently, quangos are 'here to stay'.

Comparison with bureaucratization It seems logical to expect an increase in the number of quangos to coincide with a decrease in the size of goverment bureaucracy, particularly when departmental units are hived off. In fact, one of the objectives of public sector reform, which led to the establishment of large numbers of quangos, was to downsize government bureaucracy. Figure 2.3 compares the trends in quangocratization and bureaucratization. Bureaucratization is indicated by the number of departmental units (taken from Carasso, Koopmans, Raadschelders & Voermans [1994], based on the Dutch State Directory), the number of civil servants in the national administration (taken from Van der Meer & Roborgh, 1993:69) and government expenditures (taken from CBS, 1998a, indexed for inflation, index 100=1990; CBS, 1998b).

Figure 2.3 shows that both quangocratization and bureaucratization have grown over time, which is probably the logical consequence of an expanding and increasingly 'asymmetric' society (see Coleman's [1982] description of a society with an increasing number of corporate actors). It was not until the 1980s that the number of departmental units decreased, but without a decline in the number of civil servants or government expenditures occurring as well. Therefore, there is no immediate evidence to support the claim that quangocratization has led to a substantial decrease in the size of government bureaucracy as was assumed by the practitioner theory described in chapter 1.

International comparison of the number of quangos Most data on quangos in other countries used here relate to the United Kingdom. There is little agreement among British researchers on the definition of quangos. Hogwood (1995) and the British National Audit Office (NAO, 1995) use a very restricted definition. They list only public bodies, in particular executive NDPBs, as quangos, adding up to a total of 228 in 1995. Researchers of the Political Economy Research Centre (PERC, 1996) use a broader definition, which includes public bodies, contract agencies and some privatized organizations. They list 904 public bodies, comprising of 607 NDPBs (283 advisory; 322 executive; 2 others), 107 Next Steps agencies, 72 tribunals, and 118 other organizations.

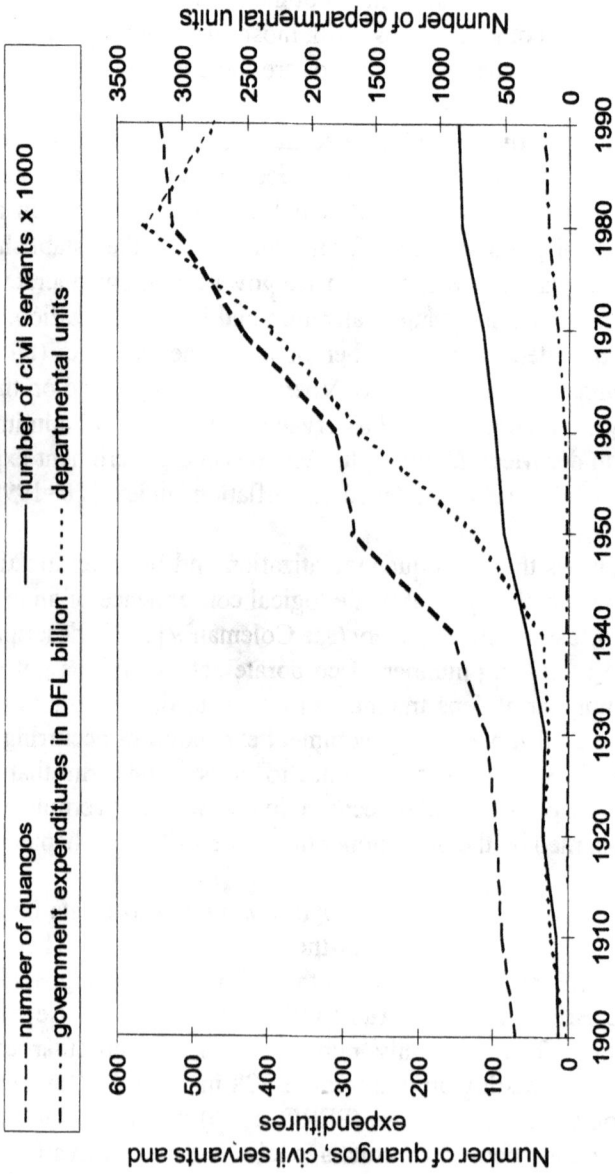

Figure 2.3 Bureaucracy and quangocracy in the Netherlands, 1900-1990 (*Sources*: Carasso *et al.*, 1994; Algemene Rekenkamer, 1995 [own calculations])

The broadest definition is used by Hall and Weir (1996). Besides public bodies (NDPBs), they include local quangos into their count, as well as privatized organizations in the National Health Service, grant maintained schools, and housing associations. Hall and Weir's count is displayed in table 2.1. They estimate that the number of quangos will increase to over 7,000 within a few years (see also Weir & Hall, 1994).

Table 2.1 The number of quangos in the United Kingdom in 1994 and 1996

	1994	1995
Executive Non-Departmental Public Bodies	358	309
National Health Service Bodies	629	788
Advisory Non-Departmental Public Bodies	829	674
Other organizations, such as grant maintained schools, police authorities and housing associations	4,534	4,653
Total quango count	**6,350**	**6,424**

Source: Hall and Weir (1996:5)

Data on the number of quangos in other countries are scarcer. Most counts are estimates only, and are often incomplete because due to lack of information. For example, Greve (1996; 1999), reporting on Danish quangos, finds some 4,189 organizations (contract agencies, public bodies, state-owned enterprises). There is no information, however, on the number of voluntary and private organizations charged with public tasks. Rosas and Suksi (1988; 1994) report some 40 quangos in Finland (public bodies and state-owned enterprises), using a strictly legal definition. The number of quangos in Sweden is not reported in a consistent manner. In the 1980s, there existed approximately 300 quangos at national level (public bodies, voluntary organizations and state-owned enterprises; Tarschys, 1988). There are, however, many more local quangos for which no estimate is given. Wistrich (1996; 1999) found some 3,115 quangos in the New Zealand Official Year-book (state-owned enterprises, advisory quangos and public bodies [Crown entities]). She does not provide an estimate of the number of local quangos, however.

Characteristics of Quangos

Quangos are characterized by a large diversity in their legal basis, tasks, way of financing, *et cetera*. Table 2.2 gives some Dutch examples, taken from the NCA survey.

Legal basis Most quangos (on average 90%) are established by law, although this is more often the case for quangos based on public law than private law (e.g. foundations). More than half of the Dutch quangos (55%) are public law organizations. The law underlying the establishment of a quango, referred to as the statute in this study, is often incomplete. In one third of the cases (35%) no goal has been formulated; in most cases (53%) no motive for the establishment is mentioned; and in 16% of the cases financing has not been stipulated (*source*: Algemene Rekenkamer, 1995 [own calculations]).

Tasks Quangos are charged with different tasks, ranging from supervision to quasi-judicature (categorized by the NCA). Figure 2.4 shows that the most common tasks of quangos are: quasi-judicature (21.7%), judging quality (18.5%), paying benefits (17.2%) and supervision (13.2%). Historically, quangos have been charged most often with the last three tasks, while other tasks such as making regulations, registration, quasi-judicature and advice became popular only after the 1950s.

Ways of financing Quangos can be financed either by the state (60%) or by levying (40%). In the latter case, tariffs can be set by a minister (28%) or by the quango (12%). The NCA survey lists only budgets from quangos that are financed by the state (see also below).

International comparison of characteristics of quangos Information on characteristics of quangos in other countries is limited, but most studies provide some examples of types of organizations concerned. Some British examples were already given in table 2.1. Examples of NDPBs in the UK are: the Health and Safety Commission, Further Eucation Funding Council, police authorities, Arts Council, several museums and the Medical Research Council (taken from: NAO, 1995).

**Table 2.2 Random examples of quangos (public bodies) at national level
in the Netherlands in 1993**

Quango	Task	Legal basis	Esta-blished	Policy sector
Bureaus for legal aid	Advise	Private law	1974	Justice
General Pension Fund for Civil servants*	Paying benefits	Public law	1922	Home Office
State Examinations Committees	Quality judgement	Public law	1971	Education
The Netherlands Central Bank	Supervision	Private law	1814	Finance
Bureau for registration of architects	Registration	Private law	1988	Housing
Council for Air traffic	Research	Public law	1993	Infra-structure
Chambers of Commerce	Advise/co-ordination	Public law	1852	Economics
Chamber for Fishing	Licencing	Public law	1955	Agriculture
Social Economic Council	Making regulations	Public law	1950	Social Affairs
Central Organ for Health Service Fees	Decision-making	Public law	1982	Welfare (Health)
Service Radio Tele-vision Licence Fees	Collection of fees	Private law	1941	Welfare (Culture)

* The General Pension Fund was privatized in 1996

Source: Algemene Rekenkamer (1995)

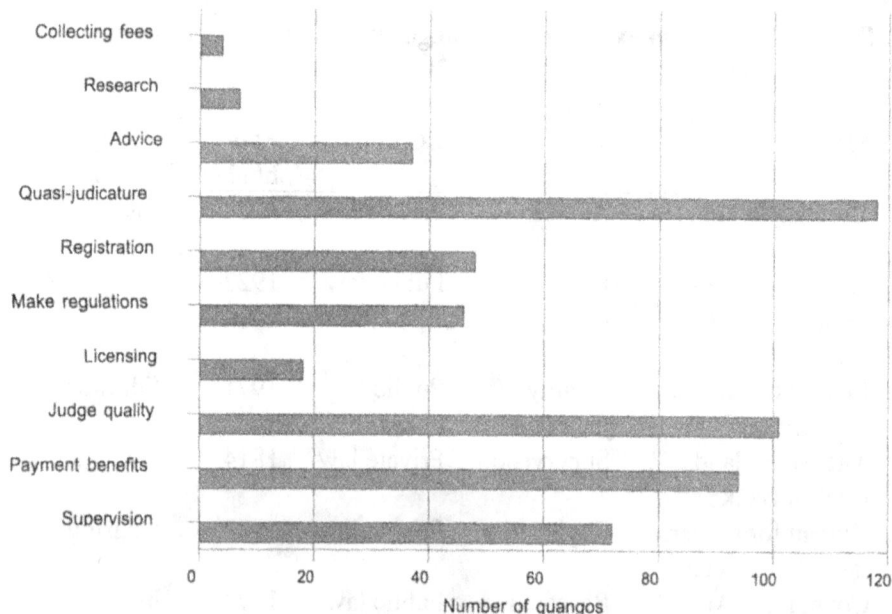

Figure 2.4 Tasks of quangos at national level in the Netherlands in 1993
(*Source*: Algemene Rekenkamer, 1995 [own calculations]).

Greve (1996; 1999) gives some examples from Denmark, such as the National Bank, Copenhagen Airport, the patent office and high schools. In Denmark, quangos are found most often in the sectors of social welfare, health, education, culture and transport (Christensen, 1988). Examples of Finnish quangos are the broadcasting company and the social insurance institution (Rosas & Suksi, 1994). Social security, industry and trade, general administration, and agriculture and forestry are the main fields in which Finnish quangos operate (Rosas & Suksi, 1988). In Sweden, most quangos are found in the sectors of labour, social affairs, industry, telecommunication, education and culture. The regional forestry boards are considered quangos, as is the Swedish bar association and the broadcasting company (Petren, 1988).

Wistrich (1996; 1999), reporting on New Zealand, mentions the postal service, school boards and the Crown health enterprises as examples. Most quangos are found in the fields of education (almost 90%), health and business development. Next to tasks such as issuing grants or subsidies, regulation and quasi-judicature, quangos in New Zealand are also charged with policy development and advisory tasks (e.g., committee on disarmament and arms control). This is relatively unique, as most governments use quangos for policy implementation purposes only.

Budget and Number of Employees

In the NCA survey, information on budgets and the number of employees of quangos is limited. Budgets are listed only if quangos are financed by the state (60% of all cases). Seconded civil servants from the parent department are not listed as employees (30%). Despite these limitations, the NCA has managed to draw a number of conclusions. In 1992, in the Netherlands approximately 130,000 people were employed by quangos and 120,000 by government departments. In the same year, almost NLG 38 billion was spent *on* quangos by the central government, 18% of the total government expenditures in 1992.[9] About NLG 160 billion was spent *by* quangos in 1992 (NLG 126 billion on social security and health insurance). Quango revenues include NLG 38 billion from the State Budget and NLG 122 billion from fees and levying (cf. Algemene Rekenkamer, 1995:15). With the information in the NCA survey it remains impossible, however, to distinguish between expenditures on running costs (e.g. salaries and equipement) and programme costs (the costs of policy implementation, e.g. total of paid benefits).

International comparison of the number of employees and budgets Most international studies give some estimates of the numbers of employees of certain types of quangos. For example, in the United Kingdom 107,000 employees of executive NDPBs were counted (Flinders, 1999b). In Finland the number of employees in public bodies is estimated as 115,000 (Rosas & Suksi, 1988), and in Sweden as 390,00 (Pierre, 1995). Other studies report how the number of civil servants has decreased through the hiving off of units. For example, in New Zealand a decrease of 50% in the number of civil servants is reported (Boston, 1995). In the United Kingdom, nowadays approximately 75% of civil servants works in the 123 contract agencies that have been created since 1988 [*Next Steps Review* mentions 69% in 1995]).

There is much less information on budgets of quangos in other countries, with the exception of the United Kingdom (see table 2.3). In 1993, the British government claimed to spend only 12 billion British pounds on quangos.[10] Weir and Hall (1994), however, estimate that approximately 48 billion British pounds was spent on quangos, which amounts to almost a third of total government expenditures. Table 2.3 summarizes Hall and Weir's findings up to 1995.

After the Conservatives came to office in 1978, quango related expenses increased by almost 45%. The British NAO (1995) found similar figures in 1993-1994. Expenditures amounted to 14,9 billion British pounds on executive NDPBs quangos and 37 billion British pounds on other bodies (health bodies, education, housing associations).

Table 2.3 Expenditures by quangos in the United Kingdom, 1978-1995 in millions British pounds

	1978 1979	1984 1985	1989 1990	1995 1995
Executive quangos	17,940	12,710	14,870	20,840
National Health Service bodies	22,580	27,900	24,260	33,100
Other quangos	1,120	1,180	1,109	6,462
Total	41,640	41,790	40,239	60,402

Source: Hall and Weir (1996:7).

Policy Sectors

Quangos are found in all policy sectors.[11] However, there are large differences between policy sectors, regarding the number of quangos (figure 2.5) and the rate of establishment of quangos over time (figure 2.6).

Most quangos are found in the policy sectors of social affairs, justice, agriculture, welfare, housing and planning, and education, whereas defence and foreign affairs have only one quango each (see figure 2.5). The remainder of this section will deal only with policy sectors in which more than 10 quangos operate.

Figure 2.6 shows the rate of establishment of quangos for policy fields with more than 10 quangos in 1993. In some fields, such as infrastructure and agriculture, a relatively stable pattern is seen, while in other fields, such as social affairs and housing and planning, quangos are established in spurts. In the 1950s and the 1970s such spurts usually concern clusters of quangos.

Besides the rate of establishment of quangos in the different policy fields, there are more differences, for example, in the tasks of quangos, their legal basis, the way they are financed, and the motives underlying their establishment. Figure 2.7 shows the distribution of quangos with the four most frequent tasks, divided along the policy fields in which they operate.

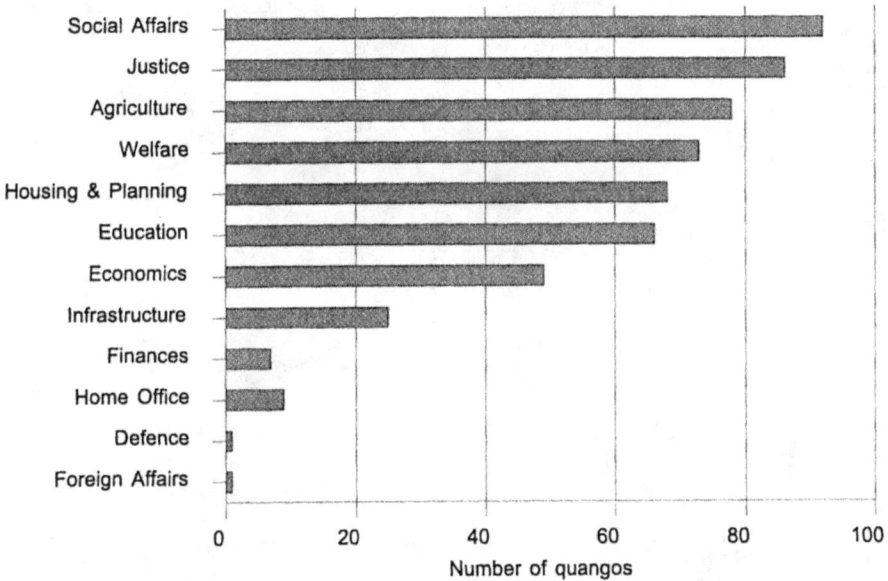

Figure 2.5 **The number of quangos in policy sectors in the Netherlands in 1993** (*Source*: Algemene Rekenkamer, 1995 [own calculations]).

In some fields (agriculture, welfare) a large variety of tasks is carried out by quangos, whereas in others (education, housing) quangos seem to be more specialized. In some policy sectors (housing and planning) most quangos are based on public law; in some (economics) private law is most common; whereas in others (justice, education) there is no preferred legal basis. A comparable situation is found with respect to the financing of quangos; in policy fields such as justice, education, agriculture and housing and planning almost all quangos are financed by the state, whereas in fields such as social affairs and economics quangos are mostly financed by means of levying or imposing tariffs. Welfare is the only policy field with no apparent preferred way of financing.

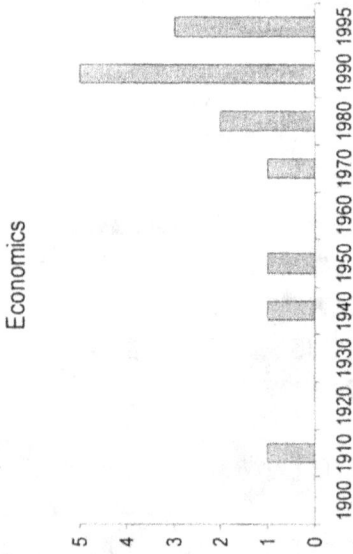

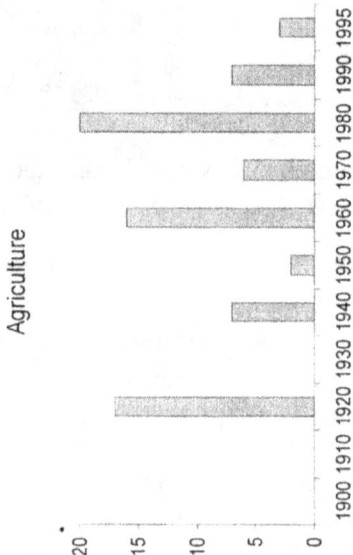

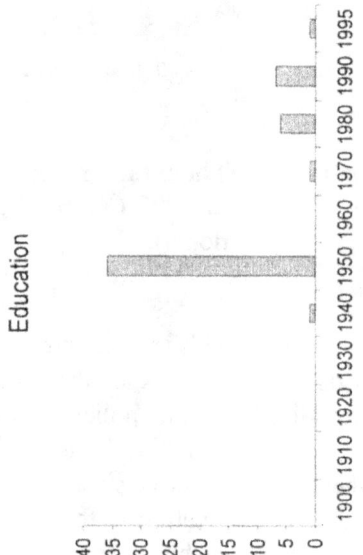

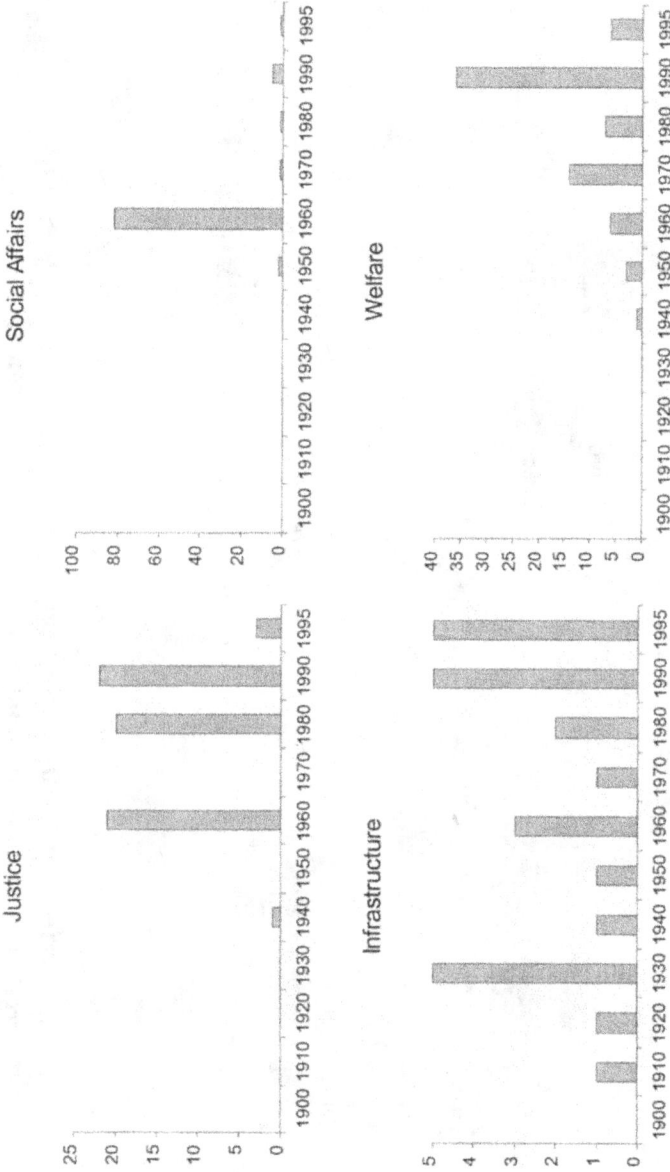

Figure 2.6 Rate of establishment of quangos for eight policy sectors, the Netherlands, 1950-1993 (*Source*: **Algemene Rekenkamer, 1995 [own calculations]**)

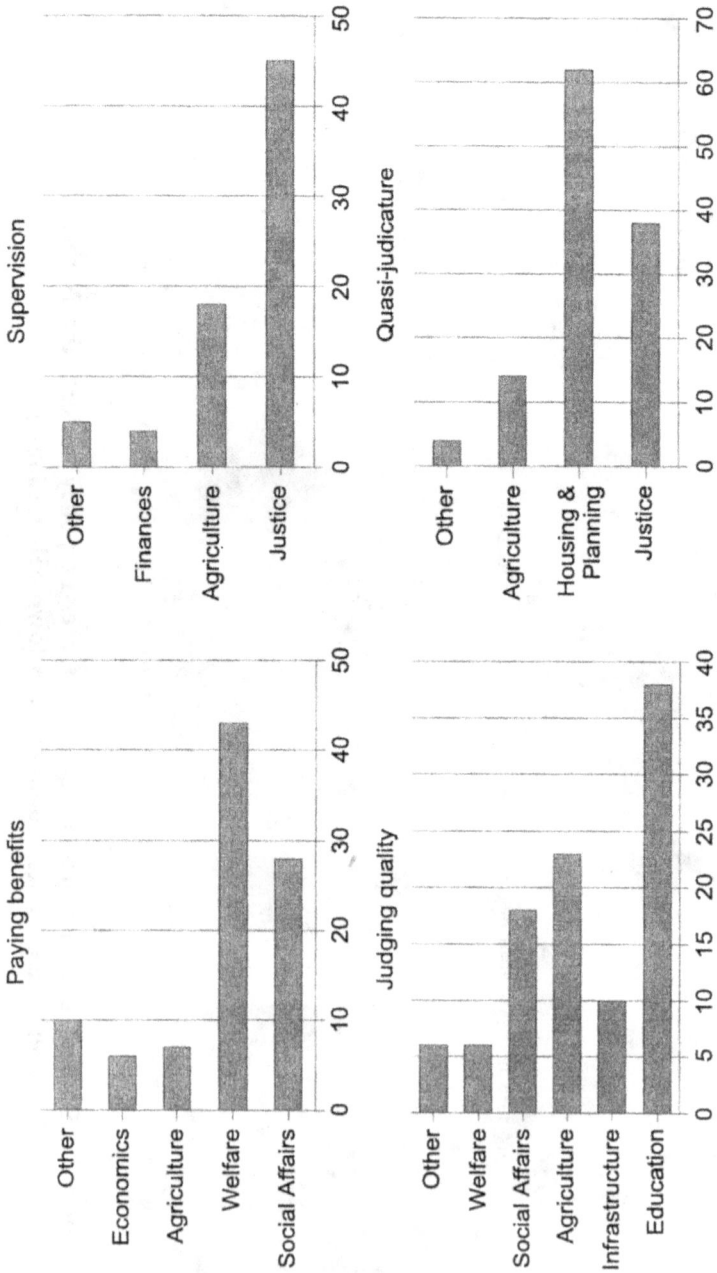

Figure 2.7 Tasks carried out by Dutch quangos in different policy sectors, 1993 (*Source*: **Algemene Rekenkamer, 1995 [own calculations]**)

To sum up, there are differences between policy sectors with regard to quangocratization. Omitting the sectors of foreign affairs and defence (only one quango each), there appear to be two patterns. On the one hand, there are policy sectors in which quangos are established to perform a specific task, such as justice, housing and planning, and education. These quangos are typically established in large numbers at the same time, and often based on public law, with the exception of education. The major motive for establishment of these quangos is efficiency.

On the other hand, there are policy sectors in which quangos are charged with all kinds of tasks. Examples are agriculture, economics, social affairs, welfare and infrastructure. Most of these quangos are based on private law (except in the field of social affairs) and their establishment is based on motives like increasing self-control and getting closer to the citizens (see also table 1.2). The quangos are established in small numbers at stable intervals, except in the case of social affairs.

International comparison of quangos in different policy sectors Some policy sectors in which quangos operate in the UK, Denmark, Sweden, Finland and New Zealand have been mentioned already, as some of the tasks with which they are charged. Most reports do not offer more information than that. Again, the British reports are the most detailed but also very divided about what should be included as a quango. Moreover, apart from the definition problems, not all departments are listed (NAO, 1995; Hall & Weir, 1996; PERC, 1996). Using a restricted definition, it can be said that the most executive NDPBs are found in the policy sectors headed by the Scottish Office, followed by the Department of National Heritage (e.g. museums), the Department of Environment, and the Welsh Office. There is no agreement on the number of quangos in the fields of defence and health.

Accounts of Quango Performance

The previous section showed what kind of organizations quangos are. Now we turn to what quangos *do*. The actual performance of two cases will be described in chapter 5. Here, I shall focus on the accounts that quangos (have to) provide of their performance. Accountability requirements are discussed and the quality and contents of the accounts that quangos give of their performance.

Accountability Requirements

There are two reasons why quangos should account for their performance. First, a large amount of public funds is spent on and by quangos (see before). Quangos are accountable for the way in which these budgets are spent and the results to which this leads. Second, ministers remain responsible for policies even if the implementation is done by quangos. To fulfil his ministerial responsibility, a minister needs information on the performance of quangos and therefore imposes accountability requirements on them.

Accountability has two dimensions: scrutiny and openness to the public (cf. Weir & Hall, 1994). Scrutiny means that external control or evaluation is possible, that is, quangos provide (written) information that can be checked by others such as Members of Parliament, audit offices, or the Ombudsman. Openness to the public is achieved if when actions of quangos are transparent, for example, if board meetings are held in public, or if citizens have opportunities to influence the actions through, for instance, the use of a complaints procedure.

Table 2.4 shows which accountability requirements are imposed on Dutch quangos and their compliance with these demands, i.e. whether the required information is indeed provided.

As most quangos (75%) are subject to the Open Government Code of Practice, scrutiny is usually possible by, for example, the Ombudsman. However, almost 28% of Dutch quangos are not required to publish an annual report, which can be regarded as a minimal level of accountability. In fact, in 18% of the cases no requirements have been made at all to ensure that quangos provide information about their performance. In 54% of the cases the information given is insufficient, according to the NCA (Algemene Rekenkamer, 1995:53-54).[12]

As far as openness to the public is concerned, in most cases (56% and over 80% respectively) public meetings and complaint procedures are not statutory requirements. In 1994, it was determined that all quangos at national level are subject to the General Civil Law, which offers citizens possibilities to settle differences with (public) organizations. However, this does not imply that quangos have a formal complaint procedure. According to table 2.4, only 19.8% of the quangos has to have such a procedure.

Table 2.4   The percentage of Dutch quangos on which accountability requirements are imposed, 1993 (N=545)

Requirements	Stipulated in statutes	Has to be sent to department	Present at dept.
Annual report	72.3%	62.6%	59.6%
Annual plan	-	12.1%	17.4%
Annual account	67.2%	49.4%	55.6%
Audited annual account	45.3%	36.5%	54.7%
Budget	-	44.2%	44.4%
Evaluation report	6.2%	5.0%	42.0%
Performance data	25.5%	24.4%	62.4%
Board:			
- Appointment procedure	93.2%	-	-
- Reimbursement	-	41.3%	41.3%
- Public meetings	44.0%	n.a.	n.a.
Complaints procedure	19.8%	-	30.4%*
Subject to open government code of practice	75.0%	n.a.	n.a.

*   from National Ombudsman survey (own calculations): N = 322
- = no information available; n.a. = not applicable
Source: Algemene Rekenkamer (1995 [own calculations])

Data from a small survey among ZBOs, carried out in 1993 by the National Ombudsman (NOM), confirm that quangos, in particular those in the policy sectors of education, housing and planning, infrastructure, and agriculture have little concern for their clients (own calculations). The NOM survey covered 322 quangos, and although over 75% stated that they had to comply with general legal procedures in case of complaints, in only 30.4% of the cases a formal complaints procedure existed.[13] The number of reported complaints is extremely low. Fifty percent of the quangos in the NOM survey reported that they had had only 1 complaint in every 1,000 contacts with citizens. About 20% of the quangos reported 1 complaint in every 100 contacts. However, as most quangos have no formal complaint procedure, they do not keep a record of the number of complaints.

According to table 2.4, the compliance of quangos with accountability requirements is good. Quangos provide most of the information required and in some cases even more, often in the form of evaluation reports and performance data.

On the basis of the information in the NCA survey on accountability, an accountability scale has been constructed (7 items, Cronbach's alpha .77) ranging from 0 (=no requirements) to 1 (=all requirements). Items included are:

1. providing information; indicated by the requirement to publish an annual report and an annual account (two items);
2. subject to audit or scrutiny; indicated by the requirement to have the annual account audited by an accountant, the minister's right to make general inquiries, and the minister's right to act on neglect by the quango (three items);
3. openness to the public; indicated by the requirements to hold public meetings and to have a procedure for the appointment of board members (two items).

Analysis with the scale confirms the NCA conclusion that in almost half of the cases (47%) no accountability requirements are imposed.[14] In quangos with accountability requirements the average score is 0.63, indicating that 4.5 out of the seven requirements are imposed (standard deviation .27, N=289). Figure 2.8 shows that accountability recently established quangos are less often subject to accountability requirements. However, if accountability requirements are imposed, the number is on average higher.

There is large variation between quangos in accountability requirements they have to meet. Figure 2.9 describes the accountability scale score of quangos with the most frequent tasks and of quangos in policy fields with more than 30 quangos.

It shows that some quangos have to meet many requirements (e.g. quangos charged with registration, and quangos active in the policy fields of education and economics), whereas others face fewer requirements (e.g. quangos charged with quasi-judicature, and quangos in the fields of welfare and justice). Furthermore, quangos based on private law have to meet more requirements (75%) than those based on public law (35%). Perhaps because public law quangos have to meet more regulations already. There are no differences in the accountability of quangos if they are divided into groups based on the motive(s) for their establishment, or the way they are financed.

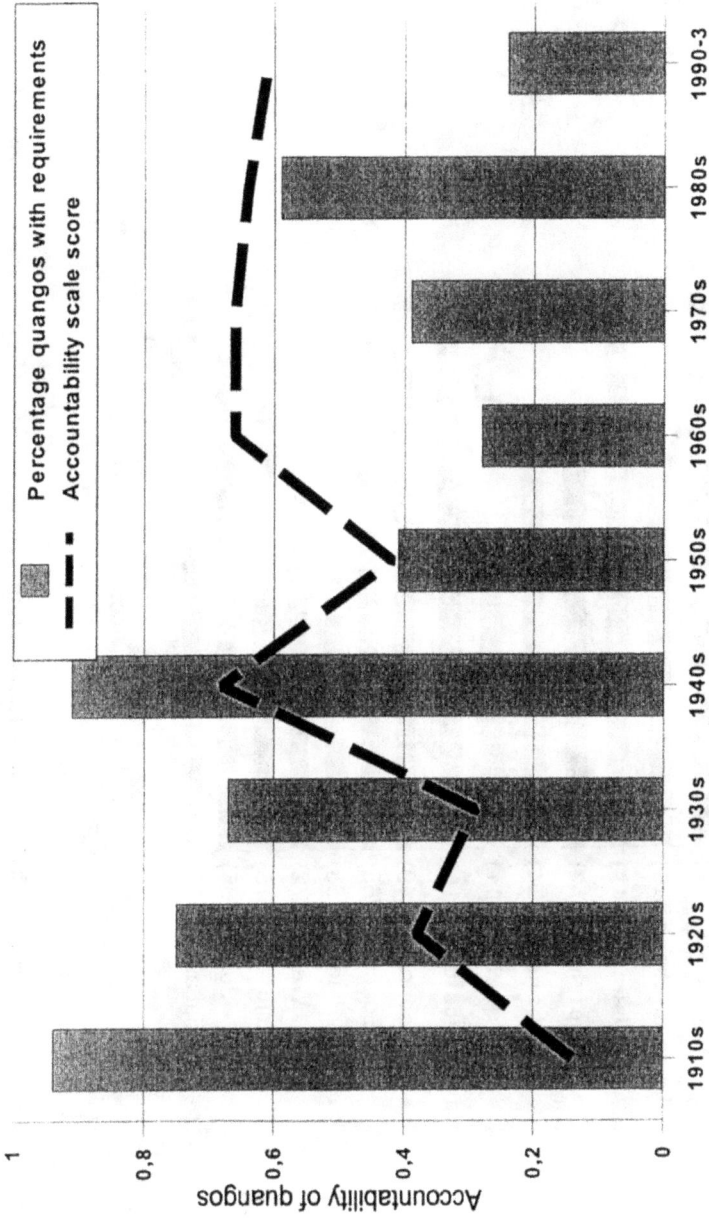

Figure 2.8 Accountability requirements imposed on Dutch quangos, 1900-1993
(*Source:* **Algemene Rekenkamer, 1995 [own calculations]**)

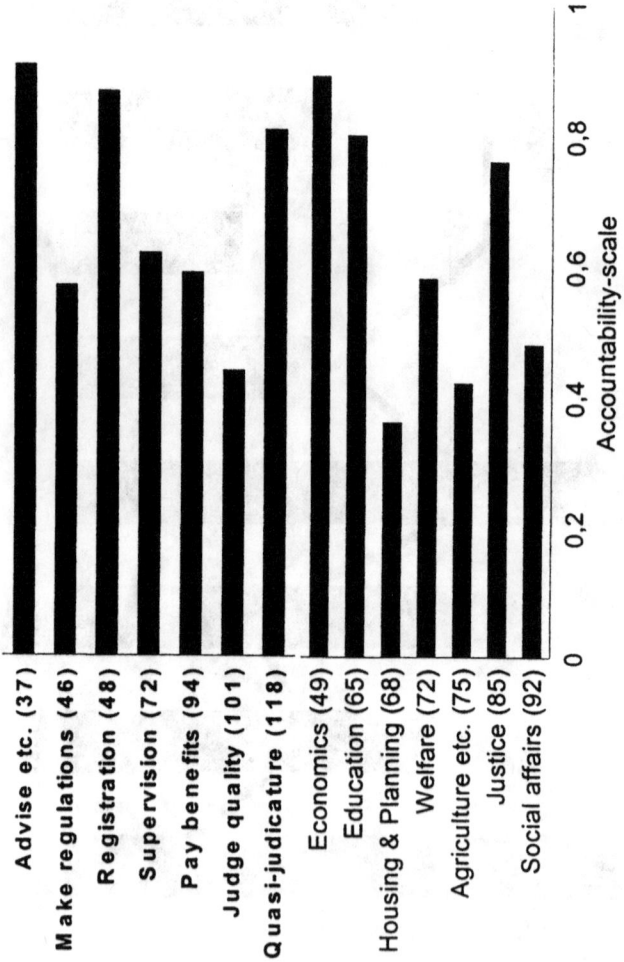

Figure 2.9 **Accountability of Dutch quangos by task and policy sector (*Source:* Algemene Rekenkamer, 1995 [own calculations])**

International comparison of the accountability of quangos The accountability of quangos is debated in most western countries (cf. Greve, 1999; Gray [forthcoming]), yet little empirical research has been done on the subject, except in the UK. Hall and Weir (1996) studied the democratic accountability of British quangos. Their results - displayed in table 2.5 - show that, compared to Dutch quangos, British NDPBs have to meet fewer accountability requirements (cf. table 2.4). Table 2.5 shows, for example, that annual reports and annual accounts are required in respectively 62% and 74% of the cases (Dutch quangos, 72% and 67%). The requirement to hold public meetings is made less often in the United Kingdom (3% of the cases) than in the Netherlands (44%).

Table 2.5 Accountability of executive NDPBs in the United Kingdom, 1994-1996

	1994 (N = 358)	1996 (N = 309)
Subject to scrutiny by Ombudsman	35%	42%
Subject to full public audits	53%	80%
Required to observe Open Government Code of Practice	35%	63%
Required to publish annual reports	56%	62%
Required to publish annual accounts	53%	74%
Required to hold public meetings	0.5%	3%

Source: Hall and Weir (1996:10).

Performance Indicators

Imposing accountability requirements upon quangos does not in itself guarantee that quangos will provide a full and adequate account of their performance (let alone of the quality of their performance). This raises the question to which extent the provided information gives a good insight into quango performance.

In this section I shall try to answer this question by exploring a data base consisting of evaluations of 74 annual reports published by 47 Dutch quangos between 1994 and 1997. These data were provided by the accountancy and consultancy firm Arthur Andersen (1995; 1996; 1997; 1998). Since 1995, this firm has held contests among Dutch public organizations, such as ZBOs, agencies, water boards and local governments, in writing the best annual report of the previous year. Only the data on ZBOs will be used here, which comprise on average 30% of the total number of participants (21 in 1995 [37 participants in total]; 14 in 1996 [47 participants]; 19 in 1997 [89 participants]; and 20 in 1998 [89 participants]).[15] Some examples of participating ZBOs are: the student loan company (winner in 1996), the Social Security Bank (winner in 1997), regional police authorities (one of them was winner in 1998), several public universities, the service for radio and television licence fees, the registry of real property, several chambers of commerce, and some art funds.

A jury evaluated the annual reports on the presence of 139 items in 6 main categories: (1) basic information such as address, board composition, and organizational structure; (2) goals, i.e. objectives, mission, vision, strategy, and long term expectations; (3) management, i.e. personnel, computerization, maintenance, and environmental care; (4) performance indicators of input, output, productivity, effects and quality of production; (5) finances; and (6) user's comfort of the report (e.g., layout). The presence of each of these items was awarded a certain number of points. The organization with the highest number of points was declared winner of the contest. Table 2.6 summarizes some of the results, in particular of the performance indicators. It is important to keep in mind that the evaluation concerns only the *presence* of items and not their content or quality.

The categories basic information and mangerial matters are reported on in all annual reports. Financial arrangements and budgets are given in less than half of the annual reports (separate annual accounts were not evaluated). Most quangos have formulated goals (77%), a mission and/or a strategy. However, there is usually no indication with which means these objectives are going to be achieved (Arthur Andersen, 1998:20-21). Performance indicators are mentioned with respect to input (89%), output (98%), quality (66%) and productivity (60%) in most reports and more often in recent years. Norms are seldom set to determine success or failure (maximum 20% of reports). Nor has information been provided to evaluate performance over time.

**Table 2.6   Evaluation of quangos' annual reports, The Netherlands
1994-1997**

Items	Present in quango's annual reports (in %)				
	All	**1995**	**1996**	**1997**	**1998**
	N=74	**N=20**	**N=14**	**N=19**	**N=20**
Goals	77.0	66.7	92.9	57.9	95.0
Input indicators	89.2	85.7	85.7	94.7	90.0
Input norms	20.3	0.0	14.3	26.3	40.0
Output indicators	98.6	95.2	100.0	94.7	100.0
Output norms	20.3	4.8	28.6	15.8	35.0
Cost prices	28.4	14.3	57.1	26.3	25.0
Productivity indicators	60.5	19.0	28.6	63.2	50.0
Productivity norms	13.5	0.0	0.0	21.1	30.0
Effects of performance	52.7	47.6	64.3	52.6	60.0
Side effects	17.6	19.0	28.6	26.3	0.0
Quality care	66.2	47.6	50.0	84.2	80.0
Quality indicators	29.7	14.3	21.4	52.6	30.0
Quality norms	14.9	0.0	7.1	31.6	10.0
Budget	47.3	28.6	50.0	68.4	45.0

Source: Arthur Andersen (1995; 1996; 1997; 1998 [own calculations])

Table 2.6 shows some progress on a number of items. For example, currently, both 'effects of performance' and 'quality care' are discussed in over half of the reports (52% and 66% respectively). Cost prices are mentioned in 28% of the reports, which is two times as often as in 1995, when the first contest was held. It is not inconceivable that these improvements are partly a result of the contest itself. The evaluation of (consecutive) annual reports provide organizations with guidelines on how to produce a good annual report. However, the average score of organizations is still low. Between 1995 and 1998, the best annual report by a ZBO was rewarded a 7.1, on a scale from 1 to 10. The overall average was 4.5 (standard deviation 1.4). It must be recognized, though, that in general quangos score comparatively high (Poot, Te Loo & Hengeveld, 1999).

To conclude, quangos that report on their performance tend to report mainly on management issues and performance indicators, but hardly ever connect these indicators to objectives and corporate strategy. Also, performance is not compared with pre-set norms. Nor is it evaluated over time, or compared with the performance of other organizations. Some improvement has been made, but there is still much information lacking.

Summary

This chapter described the establishment of quangos in the Netherlands. Three observations were made. First, the number of quangos in the second half of the twentieth century has increased strongly. This trend substantiates the claim made in chapter 1 that a process of quangocratization is taking place. It should be noted, however, that the growth has occured in spurts in the 1950s, the 1970s and the 1980s. Quangos are seldom abolished (3%), although one out of five merges with or transforms into other quangos. Since 1993, a few new quangos have been established, which makes the current total some 600.

In 1993 there were more 'quangocrats' than bureaucrats (i.e. civil servants at national level). According to the NCA survey, quangocrats spent almost one fifth of the total State Budget. So far, however, quangocratization has not led to a significant decrease in the size of government bureaucracy.

Not only has quangocracy increased, there is also an ever greater diversity among quangos with respect to their tasks and legal forms. This second trend is also evident when distinguishing between policy sectors. Quangos are found most often in the fields of social affairs, justice, agriculture, housing, welfare, education, economics and infrastructure. In the fields of defence and foreign affairs only one quango was present.

Differences were also found in the growth and use of quangos. Two patterns were identified. In the policy fields of agriculture, economics, social affairs, welfare and infrastructure, quangos are established in small numbers at regular intervals, albeit for different motives. They are charged with different tasks and given different legal forms. The use of quangos in these sectors does not seem to be limited to specific purposes, as opposed to quangos in the fields of justice, housing and education. Here, quangos are established in spurts. They handle specific tasks and their establishment is generally motivated by the desire to increase efficiency.

Third, this chapter showed that the knowledge of what quangos actually do is limited. Not all quangos (have to) report on their performance. In fact, it was shown that recently established quangos less often have to comply with accountability requirements, but if they have to, with far more requirements. The political debate that was triggered by the publication of the NCA survey led to a number of measures being taken to increase the accountability of quangos (see also chapters 1 and 6).

However, even if quangos have to account for their performance, performance assessment remains problematic. The evaluation of annual reports shows that the reported information is inadequate in several respects - which makes it hard to determine whether performance is adequate. The information in annual reports is restricted to listing input and output indicators. Further analysis is not possible because no norms are set for input, output, productivity and the quality of production (see also table 2.6).

Possible implications of these findings will be discussed in the next chapters. Chapter 3 makes a beginning by offering an explanation for the increase in the number of quangos. Also, the consequences of quangocratization in terms of quango performance will be discussed.

Notes

[1] Parts of this chapter were published before (Leeuw & Van Thiel, 1996; Leeuw, Van Thiel & Flap, 1997; Van Thiel, Leeuw & Flap, 1998; Leeuw & Van Thiel, 1999).

[2] The NCA defines a ZBO as a public law organization, charged with the execution of a public task but without full ministerial accountability, or an organization based on private law but given the legal authority to fulfil a public task (Algemene Rekenkamer, 1995:8-9).

[3] Van Tilborg (in: Coops, 1995) estimates that some 48% of Dutch local governments have considered privatization and/or establishing quangos to provide goods or services.

[4] For quangos in other countries, extensive use was made of the results of the Quango-project of the Political Economy Research Centre (PERC) at the University of Sheffield in 1996 (see Flinders & Smith, 1999). Additional international comparative information was collected during a two-month stay at PERC in 1997, subsidized by the Netherlands Organization for Scientific Research (NWO).

[5] The NCA asked departments to list all quangos present in the policy sector for which they are responsible in 1993. Immediately after publication, some departments discovered quangos that had been overlooked in the NCA survey. It is therefore possible that a small (insignificant) number of quangos has been left out.

[6] In 1954 and 1979 large clusters of quangos were established leading to respectively 77 and 62 quangos being established in one year. As these numbers exceed the scale of figure 2.1 by far, they are not shown to their full extent but rounded off at 30 (the end of the scale). After 1993, 15 decisions were taken to establish new quangos, including 2 clusters (*Staatsalmanak*, 1999). These new bodies are not included in this study.

[7] A decision was operationalized as the passing of the law instigating the establishment of (a cluster of) quangos. In the NCA survey each cluster of quangos is represented by one organization. The date of establishment of a cluster is assumed to be the year in which the law was passed. It is conceivable, however, that some quangos in a cluster were established in another (later) year.

[8] Because the NCA survey does not contain information on the origin of quangos, it cannot be determined how many quangos in the 1980s spurt (see figure 2.1) were newly established or were the results of mergers of existing quangos.

[9] NLG 1 equals 0.45 Euro. 1 Euro equals NLG 2.20.

[10] One British pound equals approximately 0.66 Euro. One Euro equals 1.50 British pounds.

[11] Policy sectors are operationalized as the parent department responsible for a certain field. Note that quangos are not hierarchically related to the parent department. This operationalization is not entirely reliable, because of rearrangements within the departmental structures in the past. Quangos now registered with department A may have been established by department B. The NCA survey is based on the departmental structure of 1993. In 1994, two policy fields (sports and culture) were integrated with other departments.

[12] After the publication of the NCA survey, a political debate was launched on how to restore control of quangos by politicians, which resulted in a series of political measures

and studies to improve accountability (cf. chapter 1). I shall return to this matter in chapter 6.

[13] The sample in the NOM survey (unpublished) is not really representative. 59% of the quangos in the NCA survey was studied in the NOM survey. Quangos more concerned with accountability are overrepresented, as indicated by the high number of organizations that publish annual reports (84% in NOM survey, almost 60% in NCA survey). Moreover, quangos in the policy sectors of justice, home office and finances were under-represented.

[14] The NCA survey includes a variable compliance of quangos with minimal accountability requirements, according to NCA standards (correlation with scale: r=.42, p<.001).

[15] Participants were classified (by me) as a quango when the State Directory listed them as a ZBO. Representativeness of the data is fairly good, although the voluntary participation implies some self-selection. Results are summarized to ensure that they cannot be traced back to individual organizations.

3 Theory

After the descriptive part of this book we now turn to the explanatory part.[1]
In chapter 1 two questions were raised, one about the causes and one about
the consequences of quangocratization:
(i) *under which conditions do politicians choose quangos as executive
agents, rather than government bureaucracy, for the implementation of
policies,* and (ii) *under which conditions will policy implementation by
quangos be more efficient and effective than implementation by government bureaucracy?* This chapter will give a theoretical answer to both
questions. The basic ingredients for these answers were specified before; a
rational actor model, with elements of neo-institutional economics and
public choice theory.[2] The proposed explanation will be further investigated in chapters 4 and 5.

We begin with some important theoretical premises of the model presented in this chapter. The next two sections deal with one research question
each. First the conditions are discussed under which politicians are
expected to prefer quangos to bureaucracy. Second, conditions are specified that are expected to influence the (in-)efficiency of policy implementation by quangos. Finally, some possible extensions are suggested
for the theoretical model. This chapter is summarized by listing all hypotheses.

Premises

Three premises are fundamental to the proposed explanation of quangocratization. The first premise is that macro phenomena can be explained by
using certain assumptions about the behaviour of individuals and the conditions or constraints under which they act (methodological individualism).
In the problem situation at hand, two actors will be distinghuished, who are
both considered key actors: (i) the legislature and (ii) the executive agent.
The behaviour of these *corporate* actors is the aggregated behaviour of
individuals. On the basis of certain assumptions about the behaviour of in-

dividuals, the macro behaviour of the two corporate actors will be predicted or explained (Coleman, 1990:541).[3] Of course, this is a strong
simplification, which does not do justice to the empirical complexity of the
problem. Moreover, in reality other actors, such as interest groups and civil
servants, will play an important role in the process of quangocratization as
well.[4] Therefore, the theoretical model in this chapter is only a first step towards an explanation of quangocratization. On the basis of this study new,
more realistic and more complex elements can be added to the model
(method of decreasing abstraction; Lindenberg, 1992). Some possible
extensions of the model, such as the incorporation of other actors, will
therefore be discussed at the end of this chapter.

The second premise is that the behaviour of individuals is rational, i.e.
they pursue goals. By achieving goals in the most efficient way, actors can
maximize their expected utility. According to the social production function approach - based on work originated by Adam Smith - the two universal goals for all individuals are physical well-being and social approval
(see, for example, Lindenberg & Frey 1993). These universal goals are
reached by way of intermediary, or instrumental, goals. For example,
physical well-being is produced by comfort (i.e. the fulfilment of primary
needs such as hunger and sleep) and stimulation. Social approval is produced by status, affect[5] and behavioural confirmation from significant
others. In its turn, status can be achieved by attaining other sub-goals such
as a job, and so forth. A hierarchy of intermediary goals can be constructed, which are assumed to produce physical well-being and social
approval (cf. Siegers, 1992). Note that only intermediary goals can vary
both over time and between individuals. The two ultimate goals are given
preferences, i.e. they do not change over time, nor differ between individuals. To some extent, however, the two goals can substitute each other.

The achievement of goals is restricted by the amount and type of resources an actor has at his disposal and the constraints he faces. By determining their intermediairy goals and constraints, the behaviour of (corporate)
actors can be modelled and testable hypotheses deducted (constraint-driven
approach).

The third and final premise concerns the relationship between the two
actors specified. It is a principal-agent relationship, i.e. legislature is the
principal who charges an executive agent, such as a quango, with policy
implementation (Coleman, 1990:146-156; Pratt & Zeckhauser, 1991). In
the model below, it is assumed that the choice for an agent precedes the

executive's actions. Therefore, the choice made by legislature is discussed first, followed by a discussion of the (in-)efficiency of quangos. The model does *not* include interactions between the actors. Again, the reason for this restriction is that the model used in this study is just a first step towards an explanation of quangocratization. I shall return to this point.

Problem 1: The Choice of Legislature for an Executive Agent

Politicians

The corporate actor 'legislature' comprises all elected politicians. No distinction is made here between Ministers and Members of Parliament. The decision to charge a quango with the implementation of a particular policy is considered to be their joint decision.[6] Nor will I assume differences between politicians from different political parties. In the adoption process of laws or policies, ideology will, of course, play a major role. However, my interest lies in the decision of politicians to charge a quango with the *implementation* of a particular policy, not in the policy itself, nor in the process of policy adoption. I do not expect ideology to play a decisive role in the choice of politicians for a quango as an executive agent. This expectation is supported by the fact that quangos have existed throughout history in many western countries with very different political traditions (cf. Greve *et al.*, 1999; see also chapter 2), and also by the use of quangos during the global administrative reform of the 1980s by politicians of different political backgrounds (cf. Pollitt, 1999). In the Dutch case, Fernhout (1980:129-131) and Aquina (1988) both have argued that politicians in the Netherlands all favoured quangos, albeit for different reasons (Catholics and Protestants prefer absence of state interference with private life, social democrats fear bureaucratism, and liberals favour market mechanisms over bureaucracy). See also Verhaak (1997:170), who lists the motives for using quangos by consecutive Dutch cabinets of different political constellations since 1981. Therefore, in this study choices for quangos are expected to be influenced by policy and situational characteristics alone, and not by ideologies (see also hypothesis 1.1 below).

As agents acting on behalf of the citizens, politicians will aim their behaviour at fulfilling the goals of voters, who are their principals. However, politicians have their own goals as well. Following public choice theory, I posit that a politician's physical well-being and social approval is dependent on his being re-elected (see e.g., Downs, 1965; Mueller, 1989; Van den Doel & Van Velthoven, 1990; Dunleavy, 1991). If he is not re-elected, a politician cannot continue his job and obtain the benefits that enable him to maximize physical well-being and social approval. Being a politician allows one to: (i) acquire wealth and/or power, associated with being a politician; (ii) propagate and implement ideologies, beliefs or opinions; and (iii) attain (more) electoral support.

Material benefits of the job, such as a salary and other, fringe benefits (office, staff) guarantees physical well-being, because it enables the fulfilment of basic human needs. Moreover, the power and perquisites associated with being a politician contribute to the status one has among other politicians, usually members of the same political party. Besides the voters, other politicians, or party members, are a significant frame of reference, and a major source of social approval. Politicians will therefore act in conformity with the expectations of the colleagues.

Propagation of beliefs or party ideology will strengthen a politician's position in the party, because it affirms his affiliation (behavioural confirmation). I also assume that propagation of beliefs also satisfies a politician's need for discussion and affirmation.[7] And if those beliefs appeal to the voters as well, propagation contributes to electoral support and hence increases the opportunities for re-election.[8]

Finally, but most importantly, the success of politicians is dependent on the amount of electoral support received from the voters. In order to attain the benefits mentioned - approval from fellow politicians, and to increase the opportunities for re-election - politicians will strive to gain and keep electoral support. As the number of voters is limited, politicians have to compete for their support. Such support is acquired by adopting and implementing policies that are favourable to voters. However, individual politicians cannot achieve this by themselves. They have to cooperate with each other, because decisions on policies require a parliamentary majority. Politicians will therefore form alliances with other politicians or parties to adopt policies favourable to voters (or obstruct other politicians' activities to prevent them from increasing their electoral support). So, these *collective* efforts of politicians will be aimed at serving the voters' interests and thus maximize their *individual* electoral support (cf. Coleman, 1990:20-21).

To gain and keep the support of voters necessary for re-election, politicians will adopt policies favourable to the electorate. For the implementation of those policies, they have to choose an executive agent. I submit that politicians can choose between only two types of agents: government bureaucracy or a quango. Their choice will be determined by the extent to which it can contribute to the maximalization of the number of supportive votes. Below I shall explain that the efficiency of policy implementation is decisive in the choice of politicians for a certain executive agent.

Quangos versus Government Bureaucracy

What are the main advantages and disadvantages of the choice of politicians for a quango as an executive agent? Choosing a quango implies the transfer of (some of) the production rights to the agent, one on the main differences between quangos and government bureaucracy. Such a transfer of rights means a reduction of the responsibility of politicians for policy implementation.

Limited responsibility reduces political risks, such as loss of electoral support, because politicians can no longer be held accountable for bad policy implementation. On the other hand, it becomes difficult for politicians to benefit from successful policy implementation, it no longer being ascribed to them directly. However, limited responsibility does not imply no responsibility at all.[9] Some responsibility remains, for example, for the choice for a quango, the budgets given to quangos and the supervision or regulation of quangos. In case of successful policy implementation, politicians can claim to have made the right choice.

Besides limiting responsibility, the transfer of production rights is advantageous to politicians in another way. The fact that a bureaucracy does not own any production rights is inherent to it being designed to be impartial or neutral. Quangos, however, can be used by politicians to enhance the commitment of (new) supportive (groups of) voters. For example, interest groups can be charged with policy implementation and thus become a quango ('hiving in') or they can be appointed members of a quango board (Van Waarden, 1999a:321). This type of patronage is not possible in bureaucracies.[10] By increasing the participation of (groups of) voters in the implementation of policies, their commitment - and hence their electoral support - to politicians will increase (Hood, 1988; Hemerijck, 1994:26).[11]

Based on these suppositions, it would seem logical to expect politicians at all times to prefer quangos as executive agent, as opposed to government bureaucracy. Or, as Gazendam and Homburg (1999) put it, the choice for quangos is the most *politicially efficient* choice. However, politicians have to take the economic aspects of policy implementation (efficiency and effectiveness) into account as well.

Efficient and effective implementation of policies offers politicians the opportunity to either implement more policies from the same budget or reduce taxes. Both options will be appreciated strongly by voters and increase electoral support. However, there does not seem to be an *a priori* reason to assume that either bureaucracy or a quango is always the most economically (in-)efficient executive agent. Both have characteristics that induce and impede efficiency or effectiveness.

The long-standing experience of government *bureaucracy* with policy implementation enhances the chance of efficiency and effectiveness, because knowledge, technology and other resources are already present and can be used for other activities as well. Expressed in the terms of transaction cost theory, such assets can be redeployed (cf. Williamson, 1981; 1989; 1995). Furthermore, because of the experience of bureaucracy with policy implementation, politicians have trust in its performance, which leads to low investments in monitoring (principal agent theory; Pratt & Zeckhauser, 1991). So bureaucracy requires less monitoring costs, which indicate a more efficient policy implementation.[12]

Trust can be abused, however. In this context, Niskanen developed the idea of a 'bilateral monopoly'; politicians have budgets but need bureaucrats to implement policies, while bureaucrats have the expertise and information necessary to implement policies, but need budgets to do so (see Van den Doel & Van Velthoven, 1990:171-178). This mutual dependency can lead to an increase in the costs of production (inefficiency) or overproduction (ineffectiveness) if bureaucrats use their monopoly position for their own benefit, either in a financial manner (budget maximalization) or otherwise (bureau shaping, Dunleavy [1991:ch.6]). Next to this potential source of inefficiency or ineffectiveness in government organizations, there are two other threats related to the more general nature of bureaucratic organizations, namely (i) high costs of internal coordination (Mintzberg, 1997:193,218) and (ii) high costs of implementation of organizational changes (Mintzberg, 1997:221).

The main obstacle to efficiency and effectiveness in *quangos* is that they are usually established to implement just one particular policy. Investments in assets such as knowledge and technology are non-recurrent and task-specific, which hinders their use for other tasks, to the detriment of efficiency. This is particularly the case with newly established quangos, because in quangos established through the hiving off of a departmental unit or the hiving in of longstanding private organizations, the costs for investments may be lower if the necessary assets are already available or seconded.

The main potential efficiency gains of the establishment of quangos lie in the reduction of co-ordination costs. Putting policy implementation at arm's length means that politicians no longer have to deal with all the details of daily operational activities, which may increase the effectiveness of policy implementation. On the other hand, monitoring remains necessary to meet their (limited) political responsibility. Monitoring costs lead to higher costs of policy implementation and hence to lower cost efficiency.

To sum up, choosing a quango as an executive agent can lead to a gain in electoral support due to the benefits of patronage and limited responsibility. If, however, the choice made leads to inefficient and ineffective policy implementation, the resulting loss of votes may exceed the benefits. Politicians will have to weigh the potential gains of their choice against the losses. Also, situational constraints may vary, which leads to different choices. The next section discusses which constraints are decisive to the choices politicians make.

The Choice of Legislature

This section deals with conditions that are decisive to the choice of politicians for quangos as an executive agent. Hypotheses are formulated about the conditions under which politicians are expected to prefer quangos to government bureaucracy as an executive agent. These hypotheses will be tested in chapter 4.

Political ideology Of course, ideology plays a major role in policy design and policy adoption. Its role in decisions on the type of executive agent is assumed to be much less important. The benefits of reduced ministerial responsibility and patronage will appeal to *all* politicians, irrespective of their ideological preferences. Other conditions or situational constraints, such as the type of task and policy sector concerned, are expected to exert much more influence (cf. hypotheses 1.5 and 1.6 below). The following hypothesis is formulated:[13]

[Hypothesis 1.1] Politicians with different politicial ideologies do not differ in their choice for quangos as an executive agent, as opposed to government bureaucracy.

Economic conditions Following the practitioner theory, politicians can be expected to prefer quangos in times of economic down-swing, because the anticipated efficiency gains can relieve fiscal stress. However, the opposite may also be true; in times of economic up-swing one can expect more quangos as well. Economic up-swing can lead to an expansion of government tasks. More policies need to be implemented and the chance that quangos are charged with these tasks increases accordingly.

So, both economic up-swing and down-swing are expected to lead to *more* quangos being established. Furthermore, it could be argued that the way in which quangos are established differs in periods of economic up-wing and down-swing. In periods of economic down-swing, when governments need to cut budgets and decrease the size of government bureaucracy, it is more likely for quangos to be established through the hiving off of departmental units. While in periods of economic up-swing, when the number of public tasks increases, the government sooner hive in formerly private organizations and turn them into quangos, to implement new policies.[14] This leads to two hypotheses:

[Hypothesis 1.2] a: The more severe the economic down-swing, the more often will politicians choose quangos to implement policies by means of the hiving off of departmental units; and b: The stronger the economic up-swing, the more often will politicians choose quangos to implement policies by means of the hiving in of former private organizations.

As it is assumed that both economic up-swing and down-swing lead to a higher number of quangos, economic conditions are in fact not expected to be decisive to the *choice* of politicians for quangos as an executive agent. Politicians will choose quangos as executive agents under *both* conditions.

So, neither political ideology nor economic conditions are - contrary to *common sense* - expected to be decisive with respect to the choice of politicians for quangos. What then are the conditions that do influence this choice? Politicians are expected to choose the executive agent that maxi-mizes the opportunities to increase electoral support. Therefore, the higher the potential increase in electoral support, the more politicians will be inclined to prefer quangos over government bureaucracy. Below two conditions are discussed that can increase electoral support: electoral competition and corporatism.

Electoral competition When the competition for votes is strong among politicians, they need to ensure their electoral support and will search for opportunities to boost the number of supportive voters. Competition is fierce in election years, or when the differences in electoral support for politicians (or parties) are small. In such situations, to increase support and improve one's bargaining power in the co-operative efforts necessary for the adoption of policies and the decisions on policy implementation, politi-cians will use every means to increase electoral support. Quangos do not only offer the opportunity to increase the commitment of (groups of) voters through patronage, they also reduce potential political risks, because the responsibility of politicians for policy implementation becomes limited. Both mechanisms could lead to an increase in electoral support. This brings us to the following hypothesis:

[Hypothesis 1.3] The stronger the electoral competion among politicians, the more often will they choose quangos to government bureaucracy for the implementation of policies.

Corporatism Participation of interest groups is expected to increase elec-toral support (patronage). In situations with many interest groups, the potential gain of votes is larger than in situations where there are only a few interest groups - unless these are large groups, of course. Therefore, I expect more quangos to be established in policy sectors with many interest groups (corporatist sectors) than in fields with fewer interest groups:

[Hypothesis 1.4] In corporatist policy sectors, politicians will more often choose quangos, rather than government bureaucracy as an executive agent, than in non- corporatist policy sectors.

So far I have discussed conditions under which it is beneficial for politi-cians to choose quangos as executive agents, because it induces the opportunity to gain votes. However, there are also cases where the choice for quangos can diminish electoral support. The benefits of patronage and limited responsibility are then reduced strongly, or exceeded by the costs of inefficiency. Below, two such conditions are discussed: collective goods and specific investments.

Collective goods In chapter 1 it was argued that many western governments came into being because markets fail when it comes to the production of collective goods. Individuals transfer part of their rights to elected politicians to ensure the provision of these goods. Therefore, the way in which collective goods are provided is assumed to be an important determinant of the voting behaviour of individuals, which influences the chance that politicians will be re-elected.

Because of the strong interest that voters have, I expect politicians to prefer government bureaucracy to quangos as executive agents when collective goods are concerned. In the case of collective goods, which are highly valued by voters, the potential benefits of limited responsibility for quangos (i.e. lower political risks) are outweighed by the loss of opportunities to claim successful policy implementation concerning goods. Moreover, politicians want to be able to exert direct control and intervene at will, not only to prevent ill performance and reduce political risks, but also to guarantee re-election by demonstrating to the voters how well their interests are being served. The opportunities for direct control and intervention are better in a government bureaucracy. When dealing with quangos, they are limited and often more expensive (because of extra monitoring costs). Therefore, my contention is that the greater the extent to which a good or service that has to be provided bears the characteristics of a collective good - i.e. non-exclusiveness and jointness of supply - the less likely it is that politicians will charge quangos with its provision. The following hypothesis summarizes this argument:

[Hypothesis 1.5] The more policy implementation resembles the provision of collective goods, the less likely it is that politicians will choose quangos as executive agent, rather than government bureaucracy.

Specific investments Policy implementation requires investments in knowledge, equipment, technology and other assets. The more task-specific these investments are, the harder it is to redeploy them to alternative use, without loss of productive value, and the higher the risk of inefficiency becomes (Williamson, 1989:142). The large-scale policy implementation by government bureaucracy necessitates the presence of a large number of assets at all times, which makes redeployment easier and enhances efficiency and effectiveness. Take, for example, the fact that policy implementation often requires legal knowledge. In a ministry, a legal unit can be established that advises all other units (redeployment of knowledge). A quango would have to consult a legal specialist on matters concerning the policy that has to be implemented, but can consult that specialist only on that policy (i.e., it is a non-recurrent investment).[15] Policy implementation by government bureaucracy will therefore be more efficient and effective. Following the ideas of transaction cost analysis (Williamson, 1989:150-151), I would, in case of specific investments being necessary, expect politicians to prefer government bureaucracy (cf. vertical integration) to quangos (cf. market) when it comes to choosing an executive agent.

Specific assets may also create a (semi-)monopoly for agents. Sunk costs make it very expensive for dissatisfied politicians to choose another agent.[16] Politicians might even become dependent on a such an agent, particularly because most agents have a legal monopoly on policy implementation. White (1991) refers to this as *reversal of control*. A dependent principal might be forced to accept a certain level of inefficiency or ineffectiveness. Or, inefficiency or ineffectiveness go unnoticed, because there are no competitors to compare the agent's performance with.

Reversal of control can occur with all agents, either government bureaucracies or quangos. However, as in a bureaucracy specific investments are made less often, because resources or assets are already available and can be more easily re-deployed, the risks of choosing bureaucracy as an executive agent will appear lower to politicians. Moreover, because politicians own all production rights of the bureaucracy, they can exert immediate control over its activities, which is not the case with quangos. In quangos the opportunities for control are limited and the distance between politicians and agent is greater. Hence politicians will prefer government bureaucracy to quangos, when specific investments are involved (cf. Ter Bogt, 1994:215):

[Hypothesis 1.6] The more specific the investments required for policy implementation are, the less likely it is that politicians will choose a quango as the executive agent.

Uncertainty

Until now I have implicitly assumed that politicians are capable of making a well-considered choice or, in other words, that they are fully informed about all the costs and benefits that a particular choice would bring. However, this does not seem a truly realistic assumption. The amount of information actors can assess and comprehend is limited. Simon labelled this 'bounded rationality' (in: Williamson, 1989:138-139; Hendrikse, 1993:91). Here, bounded rationality means that politicians cannot be entirely certain whether, under the circumstances, their choice for a certain executive agent is indeed the best - the most efficient and effective - and will enable them to maximize physical well-being and social approval.

To reduce uncertainty, individuals will seek information (Rogers, 1995: xvii). Politicians can use several strategies when gathering information. The first is imitation, which means that politicians *ex ante* use information on efficient and effective agents. The second strategy is monitoring, which provides *ex post* information on the efficiency and effectiveness of policy implementation. Monitoring can also be used to give voters an account of the efficiency and effectiveness of policy implementation. Both strategies will thus increase the possibilities for politicians to make the 'best' choice, gain electoral support and secure re-election. Gathering information requires investment of time and money, however, and increases the costs of policy implementation. Therefore politicians will try to use cost-saving strategies.

Imitation Imitation is a simple and cheap method of using information, gathered by other people. The information is used to reduce uncertainties, at a minimal cost. Politicians can, for example, copy the choice of other politicians for a certain type of agent. For example, politicians will look for examples of the use of quangos in other countries, regions, levels of government and/or policy sectors. If quangos are perceived to be efficient and effective, politicians will copy the choice for that type of agent,[17] which will result in an increase in the number of (that type of) quangos. To further maximize the benefits of imitation, politicians can copy the choice for a certain type of agent straightforwardly, choosing an agent with similar characteristics, tasks, and operating in similar policy fields. The phenomenon where in different sectors of society, policy sectors, or countries more and more similar organizations are established is called *isomorphism*

(DiMaggio & Powell, 1983:151) or convergence (cf. Unger & Van Waarden, 1995:19-21).

A second type of imitation concerns the acquisition of information by gradually building up experience with particular types of agents, through either experimentation or the repetition of choices. By gradually increasing their experience, politicians will accumulate information that will reduce their uncertainty. When having been evaluated as a successful choice, quangos will be chosen more often as an agent. Moreover, they will be used in an increasingly diversified way. Assuming that the hypotheses formulated previously hold, the idea of imitation could be combined with the aforementioned conditions. For example, one might expect quangos to be first set up in corporatist policy sectors because of patronage benefits. As politicians become more experienced and perceive quangos as efficient, quangos will be set up in non-corporatist sectors as well. Quangos established to implement policies that do not require specific investments will, in a later phase, also be charged with specific tasks. It could even be the case that quangos end up being charged with the provision of purely collective goods.

To conclude the discussion on imitation, the following hypothesis is formulated:

[Hypothesis 1.7] The more information about and experience with quangos politicians acquire, the more often will they choose quangos rather than government bureaucracy as executive agents; quangos will be used for a greater variety of tasks and set up in an increasing number of policy sectors.

So, imitation enables politicians to minimize the political risk of choosing the wrong executive agent, and reduces the potential loss of electoral support. Moreover, the incremental expansion of the number of a certain type of agent creates legitimacy (Tolbert & Zucker, 1982:30). Gradually the choice for that type of agent becomes more common and accepted by voters. In the end, it will become the most legitimate type of executive, and politicians will choose that agent merely to please the voters. Their choices are no longer based on efficiency arguments, but have become symbolic choices (Rowan & Meyer, 1977:361).

Monitoring Monitoring provides politicians *ex post* with information on the performance of agents. They can use this information to evaluate whether their choice of agent was successful and should be repeated (imitation). Moreover, politicians can use the information to show voters in what a good way policies are implemented, and thus secure electoral support. However, there are two problematic aspects to monitoring. First, it requires investments (so-called monitoring costs [Arrow, 1991]), which increase the costs of policy implementation and create possible inefficiencies. To avoid inefficiencies, politicians will try to minimize monitoring costs. Generally, monitoring costs will be lower for the government bureaucracy than for quangos, due to (i) the long-standing relationship between politicians and government bureaucracy, which has induced trust and (ii) the fact that politicians own all production rights and can exert immediate hierarchical control if necessary.

The opportunities to intervene in the activities of quangos are limited. However, politicians can use alternative monitoring devices for quangos that do not require additional investments. For example, the participation by interest groups (i.e. patronage) can be viewed as a way of making quangos more accountable to the demands of citizens. Monitoring is thus replaced by 'accountability to the market', which is expected to ensure efficiency and reduce the need for monitoring by politicians (cf. Waldegrave, 1993; Leeuw, 1995; Stone, 1995).

A second problem is that monitoring devices - such as compulsory publication of annual reports and annual accounts - have to be imposed at the same time that an agent is charged with policy implementation (so, *ex ante*), because accountability requirements have to be laid down in the agent's statutes. The wish to minimize monitoring costs can induce politicians to impose no requirements until these prove necessary (cf. Leeuw, 1995). In other words, politicians decide to trust the executive agent until it is found guilty of inefficiency. In a government bureaucracy, such trust is facilitated by the long-standing relationship between agent and politicians. In the case of quangos, however, it remains difficult for politicians to make an accurate estimate of the need for monitoring, as they often have little experience with that type of agent. For this reason, one would expect that in situations with higher risks of inefficiency or situations where inefficiency and ineffectiveness have a higher damage potential to the chances on re-election, the need for monitoring will be stronger. Because monitoring costs for government bureaucracy are lower than for quangos, politicians will prefer government bureaucracy as an executive agent. This is assumed to be the case when, for example, agents are appropriated with a large budget - because the larger the budget, the higher the damage potential of inefficiency or ineffectiveness; when policy implementation requires specific investments (see also hypothesis 1.6), with the accompanying risk of sunk costs and reversal of control (White, 1991); or when the experience of politicians with quangos is limited.

To sum up, monitoring can be used to gather information on agents and reduce the uncertainty of politicians regarding the effects of their choice. At the same time, politicians want to minimize monitoring costs. This observation leads to the following hypothesis:

[Hypothesis 1.8] When policy implementation requires large investments in monitoring, politicians will less often choose quangos as an executive agent, rather than government bureaucracy.

The reasoning underlying hypothesis 1.8 already touches upon the next topic of this chapter: the efficiency of policy implementation by quangos. As will be argued below, agents have their own interests besides those of the principal, and quangocrats may abuse the trust of politicians and serve their own interests instead. If no monitoring takes place, there is no way of telling whether policy implementation is carried out in an efficient and effective maner. The problem politicians face is that monitoring can be seen as distrustful, and intrude upon the relationship with quangocrats. The effects of such intrusion can range from no to ill performance.

The next section continues the debate on monitoring and the efficiency and effectiveness of executive agents. It sets out to provide an answer to the second main research question: under which conditions will policy implementation by quangos be more efficient and effective than implementation by government bureaucracy?

Problem 2: Quango Performance

Quangocrats

Quangos are corporate actors. As before, I shall make certain assumptions about the behaviour of individual actors to explain the behaviour of corporate actors. People working in quangos will be referred to as quangocrats, analogous to bureaucrats, who are working in a government bureaucracy.

In fact, bureaucrats and quangocrats share several characteristics. They both carry out public tasks, are charged to do so by the same principal (namely, politicians) and are funded with public means.[18] Therefore, I shall use a number of suppositions from public choice models of bureaucrats and apply them to quangocrats (Breton & Wintrobe, 1982; Bendor, 1988; Mueller, 1989:ch.14, 1997; Van den Doel & Van Velthoven, 1990:ch.6; Dunleavy, 1991:ch.6).

Besides similarities, there are also three important differences. These concern (i) the ownership of production rights, (ii) accountability for ill performance and (iii) the potential presence of competitors. Contrary to government bureaucracy, quangos own some production rights, which implies a higher degree of autonomy in the production process, and limits the influence of or control by the principal. At the same time, quangos are also responsible for errors and can be held accountable, whereas in a government bureaucracy the minister is always the one who is accountable. In the worst case this could lead to the closing down of a quango. Bureaucracy, on the other hand, does not face threats of bankruptcy or non-existence (LeGrand, 1991). Also, in some cases quangos face competition, albeit often only of the internal market (i.e. competition with other quangos in the same policy sector, for example, between hospitals or schools). While this does not imply that all quangos have to compete, still it is something that government bureaucracy does not face. The three differences have important consequences for the explanation of the efficiency of policy implementation by quangos.

As the agent of a principal (politicians), the efforts of quangocrats and bureaucrats would be expected to be aimed at the principal's goals, i.e. the implementation of policies in the most efficient and effective manner. However, quangocrats and bureaucrats have goals of their own as well, which can be contradictory to those of politicians. This may result in inefficiencies.

Their function of agents, provides quangocrats and bureaucrats with money and other perquisites such as an office, staff, *et cetera*. Such material benefits allow the fulfilment of basic human needs and produce physical well-being. Moreover, these benefits increase one's status among fellow quangocrats, or bureaucrats, and therefore produce social approval as well.

Social approval can also be obtained by meeting the expectations of two (groups of) significant others: (i) the principal and (ii) fellow quangocrats or bureaucrats.[19] Confirming the expectations of politicians means that the agent's efforts are aimed at efficient and effective policy implementation. The more efficiently and effectively policies are implemented, the more satisfied the principal will be, and the higher the chances are that the agent's existence is continued or even stimulated by new tasks or additional budgets.

Fellow quangocrats or bureaucrats are an important source of social approval. Wilson (1989:45-48) argues that, since public agencies are confronted with multiple, often non-quantifiable and sometimes contradictory policy objectives, they lack a clear mission. Therefore, other factors will determine the performance of public agencies, for instance, peer expectations. These may range from being loyal and committed to the principal's goals to just serving one's own interests, or they may be a combination of these two extremes.

The more the goals of politicians and the executive agent diverge, the higher the chances are that the agent will prefer to serve his own ends, rather than comply with the principal's goals (Hendrikse, 1993:124-132; Douma & Schreuder, 1998:99-121). Niskanen developed a model of the budget maximizing bureaucrat, who uses his expertise and information to increase the bureau's budget beyond limits, thus creating spill-overs. Using a similar line of reasoning, Dunleavy (1991:ch.6) developed the so-called bureau-shaping model, and argued that bureaucrats - since they cannot profit themselves from a higher budget - will strive to maximize fringe benefits or the workload of the bureau, in order to obtain status and social approval. Other academics have argued that loyalty, commitment to policies and professional pride in performance can also be motivations underlying the behaviour of bureaucrats (Bendor, 1988; Van den Doel & Van Velthoven, 1990). All of these approaches share the idea that bureaucrats exert a strong influence on each other's behaviour and performance.

Here, it is assumed that a similar idea can be applied to quangocrats, with one important difference. The fact that quangos can be closed down or dismissed as executive agents, makes it more imperative for quangocrats to *maintain* budgets and safeguard the continuation of their existence, rather than maximize budgets, fringe benefits, or the organization's workload. Although the size of a budget or organization increases status among quangocrats, the pursuit of higher budgets is secondary to the pursuit of continuation of the organization as an executive agent and fighting the threat of being closed down.

Compliance versus Deviance

An agent can use its discretionary authority to serve the purposes of the principal or its own ends. In the first case, the behaviour of the agent is called compliance, in the latter it is called deviance. In reality, compliance and deviance are two extremes of a scale. Most behaviour will be a mix. For modelling purposes, I shall focus on the extreme modes of behaviour, because they have an immediate impact on the efficiency of policy implementation.

In the case of *compliance*, the agent's behaviour is aimed at the goals of the principal (i.e. politicians). Their common goal is efficient and effective policy implementation. The agent receives payment for his efforts, which enhances his physical well-being, and gains social approval from politicians through behavioural confirmation. His existence is therefore safeguarded. Moreover, if fellow quangocrats or bureaucrats highly appreciate efficient policy implementation, loyalty and commitment to the principal, confirmation of peer expectations produces social approval as well.

In this study, *deviance* is used to refer to cases where the agent does not carry out his task in the way intended by the principal. As a result, the efficiency and effectiveness of policy implementation are in danger. Therefore, deviance is considered to be (at least potentially) harmful to the principal's goal. It is important to keep in mind that deviance does not always mean that an agent is inactive. His behaviour or performance is merely not aimed at the principal's goal. Three types of deviant behaviour are distinguished here: adverse selection, moral hazard and deviant policy implementation.

The first type of deviant behaviour is called adverse selection, also known as the problem of hidden information. It concerns the misuse or withholding of information by the agent to increase the (fringe) benefits of his job (Hendrikse, 1993:124). By hiding or manipulating information the agent prevents the principal from choosing the best agent. Ill performing agents are not exposed and therefore not excluded from the pool of possible executive agents (adverse selection).

Hiding information allows the agent to acquire fringe benefits, which increases his well-being. If this type of behaviour is expected and appreciated by peers, it can be a source of social approval as well. Because of the public funding of quangos, most benefits associated with policy implementation are non-pecuniary in nature, apart from salaries (Mueller,

1989:251).[20] Still, additional perquisites do have to be paid for. Consider, for example, increasing the size of the organization through the addition of personnel, or the introduction of new technology without there being an actual need for such investments (cf. bureau-shaping, Dunleavy, 1991:ch.6). The extra costs decrease the efficiency of policy implementation.

Moral hazard, or the problem of hidden action, refers to an agent performing his job with the least possible effort (Douma & Schreuder, 1998:50). Reduction of effort offers the agent more leisure time without a loss of salary, thus improving his physical well-being, but decreasing his productivity, and endangering both the efficiency and effectivity of policy implementation.

Both moral hazard and adverse selection are facilitated by the information asymmetry between principal and agent; the agent has far more knowledge about (the costs of) policy implementation than the principal (Hendrikse, 1993:124-126). Moreover, hidden information can also be used to lead the principal to believe that the agent is acting efficiently, which safeguards the agent's existence. Hiding information is relatively easy for quangocrats, because of the distance between politicians and the quango, and the limited influence of politicians on operational activities who do not own all production rights.

The third type of deviant behaviour was studied by Torenvlied (1996a; 1996b; 2000). He argues that agents can use their discretionary authority to implement policies in a manner that is consistent with their own policy position rather than the intentions of politicians.[21] The larger the gap between intended and realized implementation, the more one could say that the agent is deviant, at least from the principal's point of view. This does not necessarily lead to higher costs, as with adverse selection and moral hazard, but still it is considered undesirable by politicians, because it might affect the effectiveness of policy implementation and reduce their electoral support. Again, agents can make use of the information asymmetry to safeguard their existence, hiding information on deviant policy implementation, or using it to convince politicians of the efficiency of policy implementation.

To sum up, both compliance and deviance enable agents to maximize physical well-being and social approval. Because deviant behaviour requires less effort and/or provides more benefits, it is assumed that agents will prefer it to compliance, *unless* they think they can be caught or sanctioned with, for example, a reduction of the number of tasks, or the size of their budget. In the extreme case, they can be closed down or dismissed as an executive agent. In the next section, I will discuss conditions that influence the choice of agents between compliance and deviance, with special emphasis on the differences between quangocrats and bureaucrats. Hypotheses will be formulated on the conditions under which policy implementation by quangos will be more efficient and effective than implementation by government bureaucracy.

The Choice of Quangocrats

In the previous sections it was shown that quangocrats and bureaucrats have much in common. This section tries to establish in which circumstances their behaviour will diverge, in particular with respect to the efficiency and effectiveness of their performance. As argued before, there are three important differences between quangocrats and bureaucrats: the ownership of production rights, the presence of competitors and the possibility of being held accountable for ill performance. Earlier in this chapter a fourth important difference was mentioned that is now added: the possibility of participation by interest groups in the policy implementation by quangos. This is not possible in (neutral) government bureaucracies.

It is assumed that because of these four differences the efficiency and effectiveness of policy implementation by quangos is higher than that of government bureaucracy. Implicitly, this answers the second research question. Below I shall formulate a number of hypotheses to explain *how* these quango-specific features influence the efficiency and effectiveness of policy implementation by quangos.

The ownership of production rights In section 1.2, the autonomy of quangos was defined as the ownership of production rights. This autonomy provides quangocrats with the freedom to pursue the goals they value most. As quangos own (some of) the production, contrary to government bureaucracy, quangocrats have more discretionary authority than bureaucrats. One might argue that this also means that quangocrats have more opportunities for deviant behaviour, which would imply that policy implementation by quangos is more prone to inefficiency as compared to government bureaucracy. There are more incentives to implement policies in a deviant way (Torenvlied, 1996). Note that this contradicts the practitioner theory underlying quangocratization, which states that politicians expect more autonomy to increase commitment to the principal and enhance the efficiency of policy implementation (see chapter 1).

The claim of politicians that quangocratization will lead to efficiency gains is undermined by the fact that policy implementation is funded with public means. As argued before, all money saved by higher efficiency will have to be transferred back, because politicians will want to implement new policies, or decrease taxes, to please voters. Efficiency gains are therefore not beneficial to the executive agent itself. Not only does this imply that there are no incentives to operate efficiently, but it even increases the incentive to display deviant behaviour. In case of surpluses, politicians will argue that the agent apparently needs less money and they will reduce the budget for next year. The agent will perceive this as an unjust punishment. Even more so, when other, less efficient agents will receive the same budget as before (no punishment), presuming they have not been spotted as being inefficient or ineffective. Moreover, because one agent can apparently profit from the efficiency gains made by another agent - surpluses are spent on the implementation of other policies - individual agents have little incentive to strive for efficiency (a free-rider problem).

In quangos, the incentives to be inefficient can be counteracted by the transfer of production rights, in particular rights that pertain to financial arrangements. The ownership of the right to retain (small) surpluses, or the right to determine the fees[22] charged to customers, make efficiency gains beneficial to the quango itself. Therefore, the more production rights quangos own, the more they will strive to implement policies in an efficient manner:[23]

[Hypothesis 2.1] The more production rights quangos own, the more efficient and effective policy implementation will be, especially when the production rights the quango owns concern financial arrangements.

Competition A monopoly increases the opportunities for agents to display deviant behaviour, without being caught out. Not only is there a lack of information to assess the efficiency of policy implementation as compared to others, but the main information source is the agent itself. The agent can use the information asymmetry to manipulate or hide information, appearing to perform more efficiently than in reality,[24] and thus safeguard continuation of its existence as an executive agent.

The legal monopoly on policy implementation implies that most executive agents are monopolists. This is especially the case when policy implementation requires investments in specific assets, such as knowledge or technology. As argued before, specific investments make it difficult to replace an agent and reduces the chance of being sanctioned for inefficiency.

So, a monopoly or a semi-monopoly as a result of specific investments can induce inefficiency by executive agents. Competition, on the contrary, is expected to lead to more efficiency and effectiveness (cf. Naschold [1996], Boyne [1998]). The possibility of competition was mentioned as one of the differences between quangos and government bureaucracy. Therefore, quangos are expected to be more efficient and effective, if they face competition:

[Hypothesis 2.2] The more competition quangos face, the more efficient and effective their policy implementation will be.

Not all quangos operate in the market. Competition can also be present, though, in clusters of quangos, especially when quangos have to compete for budgets in an internal market. When such a cluster consists of regional monopolists, the effects of competition will be weaker.

Corporatism An important feature of quangos is the possible participation of interest groups in policy implementation through, for example, the appointment as members on the quango board, or hiving in interest groups into the public sector as a quango. Earlier, it was argued that participation of interest groups will increase their commitment to politicians. Stronger commitment implies a higher chance of compliance by the agent to the goal of the principal, namely efficient and effective policy implementation. Furthermore, participation by interest groups can be used to substitute monitoring aimed at ensuring efficiency and effectiveness. Following this line of reasoning, it can be expected that quangos operate more efficiently than government bureaucracy.

However, interest groups have their own goals as well. For example, public choice theory assumes that interest groups pursue maximalization of the provision of goods and services, to serve the interests of their members (cf. Wilson, 1989:76; Mueller, 1989:229-246). If these goals were to become the goals of the quangocrats as well, overproduction and hence inefficient policy implementation may be the result.

A priori no prediction can be made about which of the two effects is stronger. But it does seem likely that the more the objectives of the participating interest groups and the goals of the politicians diverge, the higher at least the *chance* becomes of inefficient and ineffective policy implementation:

[Hypothesis 2.3] The more interest groups that participate in policy implementation by quangos value efficiency and effectiveness, the more efficient and effective policy implementation by those quangos will be.

Accountability While in government bureaucracy the minister is always held accountable,[25] quangocrats can be held accountable *themselves* for their performance. Accountability increases the risk of getting caught at and sanctioned for inefficiency. Therefore, the higher the chances are that quangos will be held accountable, the more quangocrats will prefer compliance to deviance.

Information on the performance of quangos can be obtained through monitoring. Accountability requirements can be imposed on quangos, such as the obligation to draw up an annual report or have the annual account audited by an accountant (see also chapter 2). Such requirements force quangos to provide information on their performance, which makes it more difficult to hide information about inefficient behaviour. Deviance becomes less appealing to quangocrats and the chances of efficient and effective policy implementation increase. Accordingly, the following hypothesis is formulated:

[Hypothesis 2.4] The more accountability requirements are imposed upon quangos, the more efficient and effective policy implementation will be.

Besides accountability requirements, there are other conditions that increase the risk of being caught at performing inefficiently and ineffectively. For example, inefficiencies are more difficult to hide or compensate when quangos are smaller.[26] Budgetary deviations are more difficult to hide; there are no opportunities for hidden information or deviant policy implementation. The idleness of some quangocrats cannot be compensated by others; there are no opportunities for hidden action.

The same holds for quangos that operate in small policy fields, where there are few other quangos to distract attention from their performance.[27] Under such conditions, quangocrats will more often prefer complying with the principal's goals to deviant behaviour, because of the higher risk of getting caught. This leads to the following hypothesis:

[Hypothesis 2.5] The smaller the size of quangos, or the policy sector in which they operate, the more efficient and effective policy implementation will be.

The chances of getting caught at deviant behaviour increase also if the distance between quangocrats and politicians is smaller. Not only will performance become more visible, but closeness also induces commitment. Quangocrats will not want to risk their relationship with politicians by inefficient behaviour.[28] Moreover, efficient policy implementation will provide quangocrats with the social approval of politicians and fellow quangocrats.

Closeness refers to the (formal and informal) ties between quangocrats and politicians. The stronger the ties, the higher the commitment and thus compliance. Strong ties are present in situations where quangocrats are appointed by politicians, when a quango was established by the hiving off of a departmental unit, or when quangocrats are seconded civil servants. The following hypothesis can now be formulated:

[Hypothesis 2.6] The closer quangocrats are to politicians, the more efficient and effective policy implementation will be.

Finally, quangocrats will prefer compliance to deviance if the chance of getting caught and being closed down is expected to be high (cf. Torenvlied, 1996a:50-51 on agent's fear of loss of reputation). The chance of being caught is expected to be perceived as higher in quangos that are hived off rather than hived in. Quangocrats who originate from former departmental units are used to control being strict (hierarchical) and omnipresent, with high chances of being caught at deviant behaviour. Another example could be the way in which quangos are financed. Quangos that have to adhere to the tight rules of the State Budget, have less opportunities to deviate than quangos who charge fees to customers, and will therefore prefer compliance with the principal's goals. This leads to the following hypothesis:

[Hypothesis 2.7] The higher quangocrats perceive the risk of getting caught at deviant behaviour, the more efficient and effective policy implementation will be.

The relationship between accountability of quangocrats and the efficiency and effectiveness of policy implementation seems relatively simple and straightforward. However, monitoring can have *unintended* consequences as well. These are discussed in the next section.

Performance Paradox

So far, it has been assumed that monitoring, or accountability, will provide correct and full information on the efficiency and effectiveness of policy implementation. This need not always be the case. Not only is it not realistic to assume that monitoring will provide *full* information, which can all be evaluated and processed by a principal (cf. bounded rationality), but performance assessment may also have unintended consequences that invalidate the fullness and correctness of information. One such unintended consequence is called the performance paradox (Meyer & O'Shaugnessy, 1993; Meyer & Gupta, 1994). It refers to a weak correlation between performance indicators and performance. This phenomenon is caused by the tendency of performance indicators (PIs) to run down over time. They lose their value as measurements of performance and can no longer discriminate between good and bad performers. As a result, the relationship between actual and reported performance deteriorates.

Such deterioration is caused by four processes (Meyer & Gupta, 1994:330-342). The first process is called positive learning, i.e. as performance improves PIs lose their sensitivity in detecting bad performance. Second, perverse learning may occur, i.e. when, although performance seems to improve, there is no actual improvement and perhaps even a deterioration of performance. The third process, selection, refers to the replacement of poor performers with better performers which reduces differences in performance. And fourth, suppression occurs when differences in performance are ignored. To solve the problem of the running down of performance indicators, Meyer and Gupta suggest that organizations should use various and non-correlated but comparable indicators to assess their performance. They refer to this as the paradoxical model of performance assessment.

It is important to understand that the paradox is *not* about performance itself, but about the *reports* on performance. Contrary to the expectation, PIs do not give an accurate report of performance. This could mean that performance is worse than reported (over-representation), but also that performance is better than reported (under-representation). In the latter case, the performance paradox might be considered harmless. However, when the results of performance assessment are used to evaluate organizations or persons, situations can arise where these are unjustly sanctioned. An example will illustrate this, given by Wiebrens and Essers (1999) who report on the percentage of crimes solved by the Dutch police. The percentage is decreasing, indicating that the police's performance is deteriorating. However, during the time period studied more perpetrators have been arrested, prosecuted, and penalized than before, which would indicate an improvement of performance. Wiebrens and Essers maintain that crime has developed in a way that invalidates the PI 'percentage solved crime'. For one, crime has become more violent, but the PI does not differentiate between, for example, fellonies and misdemeanors (cf. suppression). Moreover, more groups of criminals have been arrested committing a crime together, which reduces the average number of crimes per criminal (cf. reversed perverse learning). Wiebrens and Essers conclude that it is not the police who is performing badly, but the indicator and that the PI should therefore be replaced.

An example of a performance paradox in a case of over-representation is taken from Smith (1995). In the British National Health Service it was agreed that patients should be no longer than two years on a waiting list for an operation. This measure appeared successful, as the average waiting time decreased. However, on further inspection it was found that, the waiting time only beginning after the first hospital consultation, consultation was postponed in order to decrease the waiting time (perverse learning). In fact, the average waiting time did not decrease at all, but was merely shifted in time. The PI did not accurately reflect performance; it reported an improvement where there was none.

Other examples of the performance paradox are found in, for example, the educational field (see SCA [School Curriculum and Assessment authority], 1997; Weiss & Piderit, 1999). In the next section other situations in which the performance paradox can occur will be discussed.

As with deviant behaviour, it might be argued that the occurence of the performance paradox is facilitated by the information asymmetry between principal and agent. The unequal distribution of information can cause efficiency and effectiveness gains to be underestimated. Inefficiency and ineffectiveness can also remain undetected, because of manipulation of information by the agent. A performance paradox can thus be an unintended or the deliberate result of behaviour of agents and principals.

Unintended performance paradoxes An unintended performance paradox can, for example, be the result of minimization of monitoring costs. A one-shot introduction of (a minimal amount of) accountability requirements may reduce monitoring costs in the short run, but, as noted earlier, performance indicators have a tendency to run down and need to be changed over time (Meyer & Gupta, 1994). If they are not, indicators do no longer provide an accurate picture of performance (cf. the police example before). This need not imply that an executive agent is performing inefficiently, as it could well be that indicators became obsolete through positive learning. In that case, a compliant quango is not recognized as such. On the other hand, minimal monitoring could also lead to other, more perverse effects as will be discussed below.

Another cause of an unintended performance paradox is the elusiveness of the objectives of public policies (Wilson, 1989:32-33). Because politicians want to please as many voters as possible, policies often have many, and sometimes contradictory, goals. This complicates the evaluation of the efficiency and effectiveness of policy implementation, for it is difficult to determine which objectives are most important and to whom (cf. suppression). Moreover, policy goals are often non-quantifiable and hard to measure. The risk of not choosing the best indicator(s) increases under such conditions, invalidating performance assessment. Again, this does not necessarily imply inefficient policy implementation; there is just no proper way to assess (in-)efficiency. This situation becomes even more complicated when the agent is a monopolist. The lack of comparative information or benchmarks makes evaluation and asessment of performance difficult, also for the agent.

Furthermore, the chance of a performance paradox occurring is enhanced by a strong emphasis on monitoring and efficiency within the organization. The extensive use of PIs can create a situation in which agents learn what aspects of their work are important to the principal. Smith (1995) labels this 'measure fixation'. By increasing the efficiency and effectiveness of those aspects, agents are assured from the principal's approval (gaming, *ibid.*). Such learning effects and anticipatory behaviour of agents could, in the end, lead to ossification, i.e. organizational paralysis due to an excessively rigid system of performance evaluation (*ibid.*). Agents will aim all their efforts at meeting the principal's monitoring demands. It is then no longer relevant whether policy implementation is taking place in the most efficient manner (cf. suppression). As long as performance appears to be efficient, both principal and agent will be satisfied. Their goals are attained and there is no need to change their behaviour.

Deliberate performance paradoxes Agents can also use the information asymmetry to *deliberately* evoke a performance paradox. For example, agents can 'sabotage' monitoring when they consider monitoring an act of distrust by the principal (cf., among others, Barkema, 1994; Ghoshal & Moran, 1996). Sabotage, such as delay or non-cooperative behaviour (Breton & Wintrobe, 1982), does not necessarily impair efficient and effective policy implementation, but contaminates the relation between reported and actual performance (cf. adverse selection).

On the other hand, deviant agents can use the information asymmetry to hide inefficient and ineffective policy implementation from the principal (perverse learning). By misrepresenting or misinterpreting PIs (Smith, 1995) agents increase the opportunities to behave in a deviant manner without being caught (cf. moral hazard). Moreover, the continuation of their existence as an executive agent is safeguarded, because the principal is convinced that policy implementation is done efficiently and effectively. In fact, one could argue that a deliberate performance paradox is a type of deviant behaviour.

Smith (1995) mentions several ways in which agents can escape being caught at deviant behaviour, and create a performance paradox. For example, they can emphasize easily quantifiable aspects of performance (tunnel vision), and leave out reports on aspects of policy implementation that are difficult to measure. Also, they can confine themselves to reporting on the performance of parts of the organization, preferably those parts that are most efficient (suboptimization), or on short term objectives (myopia). In this context, LeGrand & Bartlett (1993:31-34) refer to cream skimming.

Cream skimming, or cherry picking, is the tendency of executive agents to discriminate against inefficient aspects of the policies to be implemented, by providing services or goods only to those citizens who make the least or least expensive use of them (e.g. in health care, chronically ill patients are excluded). Cream skimming not only allows agents to reduce their efforts, it also reduces expenditures and makes agents appear efficient.

The less monitoring agents face, the stronger the information asymmetry, and the more leeway agents have to deliberately create a performance paradox and hide their deviant behaviour. In the case of monopolist agents, besides a lack of information to evaluate performance, there are no substitute agents. This can force the principal to allow some inefficiency, ineffectiveness or deviant behaviour by the agent (cf. 'reversal of control'; White, 1991).

In sum, the performance paradox can occur as an unintended or a deliberate result of the behaviour of principals and agents. Because both actors lack the incentives to change the situation a paradox in progress will continue to reinforce itself. Principals will want to avoid additional (monitoring) costs and agents can use a performance paradox to appear to be performing well, thus safeguarding their existence. Only a compliant agent whose performance is under-reported, can be expected to want to eliminate the paradox. However, a compliant agent is *also* inclined to comply with the principal's wish to minimalize monitoring costs, which will reduce the desire to alter performance assessment.

A performance paradox can obscure the assessment of the efficiency and effectiveness of policy implementation, and interfere with the expected effects of conditions on efficiency and effectiveness of quangos. Below, I shall discuss circumstances under which a performance paradox might occur, either unintended or deliberately.

Unintended and deliberate performance paradoxes are the results of different circumstances. However, a deliberate paradox can occur *only if* the conditions for an unintended paradox are present as well, particularly an information asymmetry.

As noted before, there is a strong relationship between deviant behaviour and a deliberate performance paradox. In fact, the performance paradox can be seen as a type of deviant behaviour, because it prevents the principal from detecting inefficient or ineffective behaviour by the agent. Conditions that induce deviant behaviour will also increase the chance that other perverse effects occur, such as a performance paradox. The same conditions as discussed before on deviance will therefore be examined below on their effect on the occurence of a performance paradox. The same numbering is used, added with a 'P' to indicate that they relate to the performance paradox. Some new hypotheses will be added also.

Ownership of production rights Earlier, it was argued that the more production rights quangocrats own, the less they behave in a deviant manner (cf. hypothesis 2.1). In that case, there is no need to manipulate information to hide inefficiencies either (so, no hidden information nor perverse learning). A performance paradox is less likely to occur.

Moreover, if quangocrats have more production rights, they stand to benefit more from efficiency gains, such as surpluses.[29] Also, they can use their ownership of rights to counteract inefficiencies, for example by firing bad performers. In order to do so, quangos require good insight into their performance, unobscured by a performance paradox. The following hypothesis can be formulated:

[Hypothesis 2.1P] The more production rights quangos own, the smaller the chance that a performance paradox will occur.

Competition A monopolist quango is expected to have more opportunities to hide information on the efficiency of policy implementation, because usually it is the sole supplier of information on its performance. However, the lack of competitors reduces the threat of dismissal and decreases the necessity of hiding inefficiencies. Therefore, while a monopolist situation is expected to induce more inefficiency (cf. hypothesis 2.2), it is not necessarily expected to lead to a deliberate performance paradox as well. An *unintended* performance paradox can occur, though, because of the lack of comparative information (e.g. under-representation).

As stated earlier, competition is expected to improve efficiency (cf. hypothesis 2.2). Because competition makes it imperative that quangos appear as efficient as possible, it can also lead to a deliberate performance paradox (e.g. manipulation of information). The following hypothesis is formulated:

[Hypothesis 2.2P] If quangos are monopolists, the chance that an unintended performance paradox occurs increases; whereas if quangos face competition, the chance increases that a deliberate performance paradox occurs.

A (semi-)monopoly can be the result of a lack of competition but can also be caused by high specific investments.

Corporatism Hypothesis 2.3 predicted that the participation of interest groups could improve quango performance, provided that interest groups value the same goals as politicians, namely efficiency and effectiveness. If the goals of interest groups diverge from those of politicians, inefficiency and ineffectiveness can be the result. In both cases, a performance paradox can be expected to occur. In the first case, quangocrats want to appear as efficient and effective as possible and might try to manipulate information. Also, the commitment to efficiency and effectiveness can lead to over-estimation of certain aspects of performance, although this need not necessarily be done deliberately. In the second case, quangocrats want to hide their inefficiencies by manipulating information deliberately.

Politicians can use the participation of interest groups as a substitute for formal, and perhaps more expensive, monitoring devices. However, in that case politicians place themselves outside the monitoring process, which reduces the transparency of performance assessment for them. Politicians no longer can be sure about the adequacy of performance evaluations. Furthermore, the distance between politicians - who decide on the fate of quangos - and monitoring gives room for manipulation of information, particularly when interest groups have other intentions than politicians.

It would seem therefore that the participation of interest groups does not prevent an unintended performance paradox, and even may cause a deliberate paradox when the goals of interest groups diverge from those of politicians:

[Hypothesis 2.3P] The more the goals of interest groups participating in quangos diverge from the goals of politicians, the higher the chance that a performance paradox occurs.

Accountability Hypothesis 2.4 stated that accountability requirements stimulate efficiency. However, the effect of monitoring by means of accountability requirements and performance indicators is not that simple and straightforward.[30] Here the difference between an unintended and deliberate performance paradox becomes important.

An *unintended* performance paradox is the result of a discrepancy between PIs and the objectives of policy implementation (Smith, 1995). This discrepancy can arise if performance has improved beyond the measurement capacity of the indicators (cf. positive learning; Meyer & Gupta, 1994:331), or if the objectives of performance are difficult to translate into appropriate indicators. In quangos with only a few performance indicators, fixed indicators, indicators that cannot be compared over time, or that are focussed only on easily quantifiable aspects of performance, an (unintentional) performance paradox is more likely to occur. In that case, reports on performance do not give a full and fair representation of actual performance, whether that performance is efficient or not. This leads to a new hypothesis:

[Hypothesis 2.8P] The more diverse the system of performance measurement (number, range, variation and comparability of indicators), the smaller the chance that a performance paradox will occur.

Because the elusiveness of policy objectives contributes strongly to the occurence of a performance paradox - making it more difficult to determine PIs and performance - it is expected that the clearer these objectives are formulated, the smaller the chances are that an (unintended) performance paradox will occur. Accordingly, the following (new) hypothesis is formulated:

[Hypothesis 2.9P] The more policy objectives are formulated in clear and specific terms, the smaller the chance that a performance paradox will occur.

Moreover, as Wilson (1989:109) stresses, clear goals will induce a sense of mission among employees of public agencies. However, if that mission emphasizes the use of PIs to achieve efficiency and effectiveness of policy implementation, it can create a situation in which the behaviour of quangocrats becomes more and more focussed on indicators. Such 'measure fixation' or suboptimization (Smith, 1995) and perverse learning (Meyer & Gupta, 1994) can invalidate the relationship between performance and indicators.[31] A performance paradox will be the result. This leads to the following hypothesis:

[Hypothesis 2.10P] The more efficiency, effectiveness and the use of performance indicators are stressed in a quango, the higher the chance that a performance paradox will occur.

Hypotheses 2.8P-2.10P discussed three new conditions relating to accountability that increase the chance of an unintended performance paradox. Only if these conditions are present, can a deliberate performance paradox occur also. Little diversity in the system of performance assessment and unclear policy objectives are prerequisites for hiding or manipulating information.

Conditions that influence the chances of getting caught at being inefficient will determine whether or not quangocrats try to display deviant behaviour. Three such conditions were mentioned before that influence whether quangocrats will prefer deviance or compliance: size, closeness and risk perception. Below these are discussed again and one more new condition is added: supervision.

Size Small quangos in terms of, for example, number of personnel and budget, were expected to be more efficient and effective because ill performance is difficult to hide or undo (cf. hypothesis 2.5). Small quangos therefore have stronger incentives to perform efficiently. This could evoke manipulation of information and thus a performance paradox.

However, small quangos are expected to have less means to manipulate information. Also, quangos operating in small policy sectors were expected to perform more efficiently, because their performance is more visible. The chance of getting caught at deviant behaviour or evoking a deliberate performance paradox decreases with the size of the policy sector (and the number of other quangos present in that sector). This leads to the hypothesis:

[Hypothesis 2.5P] The smaller quangos are, or the smaller the policy sector in which they operate, the smaller the chance that a performance paradox will occur.

Closeness Closeness was expected to enhance commitment to the principal and stimulate compliance (cf. hypothesis 2.6). Therefore, it does not seem likely that quangocrats who are close and committed to politicians will try to hide or manipulate information on their performance.[32] Moreover, if quangocrats are close to their principal, the chance of getting caught at deviant behaviour or creating a deliberate performance paradox increases. The following hypothesis is formulated:

[Hypothesis 2.6P] The closer quangocrats are to politicians, the smaller the chance that a performance paradox will occur.

Perception of risks Only quangocrats who prefer deviance to compliance will try to manipulate information to hide their inefficiencies and safeguard their existence as an executive agent - in particular when they perceive the risk of getting caught as low. Risks were expected to be perceived as higher in quangos that are, for example, hived off rather than hived in, or financed from the state budget rather than through fees or levies (cf. hypothesis 2.7). The following hypothesis is formulated:

[Hypothesis 2.7P] The higher quangocrats perceive the risk of being caught at deviant behaviour, the smaller the chance that a performance paradox will occur.

Supervision Through the appointment of a supervisor or regulator, performance is more thoroughly monitored, which increases the risk that quangocrats will be caught at deviant behaviour. The presence of a supervisor makes it more difficult to hide or manipulate information, but at the same time increases the interest of quangocrats to appear as efficient and effective as possible. Quangocrats will therefore create a performance paradox only if they think that the supervisor will not be able to detect it, because, for example, it operates at a distance.[33] Also, when the supervisor has no comparative information - as is the case with monopolist quangos - chances decrease of getting caught at deviant behaviour and creating a performance paradox. The more opportunities a supervisor has to monitor a quango's performance, the less likely it becomes that it will create a performance paradox. The following new hypothesis is formulated:

[Hypothesis 2.11P] The more opportunities a supervisor has to assess the performance of quangos, the smaller the chance becomes that a performance paradox will occur.

Extensions of the Model

In the construction of the theoretical model, I have made a number of simplifying assumptions. Moreover, the model was limited to only two corporate actors between whom no interaction was allowed. This makes the model rather static and abstract. To improve the model, one could add new elements (cf. method of decreasing abstraction; Lindenberg, 1992), in particular other actors and possible interactions between actors. Below, I shall discuss these possible extensions (see also chapter 6).

Other actors   In the model, it was assumed that legislature comprises all elected politicians: ministers and Members of Parliament (MPs). In view of the fact that legislation is their mutual responsibility, this seemed logical. However, in reality ministers and MPs have different roles and authorities. Also, between MPs there are many differences, in particular as to whether they belong to governing parties or not. (As stated before, I do not expect political ideology to play a decisive role in quangocratization.) It would therefore be worthwhile to make a distinction between these different types of (still corporate) actors. The interests of ministers and MPs when it comes to the choice of an executive agent might be contradictory. Ministers want to reduce political risks, whereas MPs can be expected to prefer to hold ministers accountable.

   Within the corporate actor 'quango', a distinction can be made between the board, management and operators (cf. Wilson, 1989). Assumptions can be made about the different and potentially conflicting interests of these (corporate) actors. For example, while operators benefit from deviance, managers are held accountable for inefficiencies and will strive for compliance. Another interesting point in this respect relates to Torenvlied's (1996a,b) work on deviant policy implementation. Executive agents use their discretionary authority to implement policies according to their own policy position. In some cases, politicians allow executive agents such discretion, because the agents are more familiar with the policy field, and customers, ('street-level quangocrats').

Although government bureaucrats were discussed during the development of the model (in light of their similarities and differences with quangocrats), no attention was paid to their interest in quangocratization. However, as Dunleavy (1991:ch.6) has pointed out, bureaucrats may have a high interest in the hiving off of their departmental unit, since that will provide them with more autonomy and hence more status.[34] Particularly in a system where bureaucrats play an important role in the decision making process (cf. Van Waarden, 1999b), they can use their influence to, for example, facilitate the hiving off of their own unit and turn it into a quango (Christensen, 1999).

Finally, interest groups played no (active) role in the model, whereas in reality they are important actors in policy making and implementation. Not only do they provide an opportunity to establish patronage (i.e. by letting them participate in quangos as board members), they can 'capture' an agent and strongly influence its behaviour. Future incorporation of interest groups into the model could focus on different aspects, such as their interest in patronage, whether patronage can substitute monitoring, and how participation of interest groups will affect legislature's choice of an executive agent, or quango performance.

Interaction No interaction between legislature and executive agent was included in the model. In reality, these actors will no doubt try to influence each other (see, for example, the performance paradox). The efficiency of policy implementation by a particular agent will have consequences for the next choice politicians make. Therefore, a feedback loop could be added to a more elaborate model.

Another possibility to include interaction relates to the assumption that politicians will co-operate to pass legislation. Allowing for conflict between politicians would create a more dynamic representation of reality (see e.g. models on decision-making in policy networks, Stokman 1994; Stokman & Zeggelink, 1996). Moreover, it would immediately raise the (now neglected) issue of a free-rider problem: why would one (group of) politician(s) make a choice that other politicians benefit from as well (i.e. by an increase in their electoral support)? The same holds for monitoring. Monitoring was assumed to increase efficiency gains. However, as all politicians benefit from efficiency gains - surpluses can be used to implement new policies or reduce taxes - one single politician has no incentive to increase his efforts of imposing accountability requirements. This would imply that monitoring would not take place at all, even if imposing monitoring increases the status of politicians.

Finally, the model's complexity could be increased by allowing for politicians to have a choice between more than two executive agents (cf. table 1.1). See, for example, Van Leerdam (1999), who has developed a model to predict the choice of legislature between contract agencies or ZBOs. Politicians could use competition between different types of executive agents and/or quangos as a means to increase the chance that policy implementation will be done efficiently and effectively.

Summary

This chapter set out to provide an explanation of quangocratization by answering two questions: (i) under which conditions do politicians choose quangos as executive agents, rather than government bureaucracy, for the implementation of policies, and (ii) under which conditions will policy implementation by quangos be more efficient and effective than implementation by government bureaucracy? Both questions were dealt with consecutively. The theoretical model used the assumptions of rational choice theory: actors pursue goals given the constraints of the situation in which they find themselves. Goals and constraints are used to predict or explain behaviour.

After describing the factors that determine the choice of an executive agent (in this case a quango) by politicians, several conditions were discussed that are expected to influence this choice. Table 3.1 provides an overview of the hypotheses that were formulated and which will be tested in chapter 4.

Next, attention was paid to the efficiency and effectiveness of policy implementation by quangos. After establishing the determinants of the behaviour of quangocrats, conditions were discerned that are expected to stimulate quango performance. Table 3.2 summarizes the hypothesized effects.

Table 3.1 Expected effects on choice of politicians for quangos as an executive agent

No.	Hypothesis	Expected effect
1.1	Political ideology	0
1.2	Economic conditions	+[*]
1.3	Electoral competition	+
1.4	Corporatism	+
1.5	Collective goods	-
1.6	Specific investments	-
1.7	Imitation	+
1.8	Monitoring	-

0 = no decisive effect; - = a negative effect; + = a positive effect
* In fact, a curvilinear effect is expected.

The issue of the effect of monitoring was raised several times (cf. hypotheses 1.8 and 2.4). Politicians were expected to use monitoring to collect information on the efficiency of policy implementation. However, it was revealed that the relationship between monitoring and the correctness of information is not simple and straightforward. This was labelled the performance paradox. Conditions were discussed that could elicit such a paradox. Table 3.2 also includes the hypotheses that predict under which conditions a performance paradox will occur. All hypotheses in table 3.2 will be further investigated in the two case studies in chapter 5.

The theoretical model constructed in this chapter is but a first step towards an explanation of quangocratization. In order to better represent reality, it needs to include more actors and allow for more dynamics and complexity. Some suggestions were made to that end. The results of the empirical testing of the hypotheses, discussed in chapters 4 and 5, will perhaps provide some more suggestions for possible extensions or alterations of the model (see chapter 6).

Table 3.2 Expected effects on the efficiency and effectiveness of policy implementation by quangos and on the occurrence of a performance paradox

No.	Hypothesis	Effect on Quango Performance	Occurrence of Performance Paradox
2.1(P)	Ownership production rights	+	-
2.2(P)	Competition	+	+
2.3(P)	Corporatism	+	+/-
2.4(P)	Accountability require-ments	+	?
2.5(P)	Size	-	+
2.6(P)	Closeness to politicians	+	-
2.7(P)	Risk perception	+	-
2.8P	Diversity Pis		-
2.9P	Clear policy objectives		-
2.10P	Emphasis on efficiency, Pis		+
2.11P	Supervision		+/-

- = negative effect; + = positive effect; +/- = mixed prediction;
? = no prediction

Notes

[1] Parts of this chapter were published earlier in Van Thiel, Leeuw, Siegers & Flap (1999).

[2] 'Actor' can refer to individuals, groups of individuals or organizations. In this study, individual actors will be referred to as 'he'.

[3] This approach is supported by Scharpf, who - concerning the application of methodological individualism to political processes - said that "[i]n the political process [...] the most relevant actors are typically acting in the interest, and from the perspective, of larger units, rather than for themselves. This allows us to simplify analysis by treating a limited number of large units as composite (i.e., aggregate, collective, or corporate) actors with relatively cohesive action orientations ..." (1997:12).

[4] Current academic literature focusses on the role of *policy networks* between political actors in the decision making process. There are severval models on how these actors try to influence each other and the final decision through, for example, exchange or conflict (Bueno de Mesquita & Stokman, 1994; Stokman, 1994; Stokman & Van Oosten, 1994; Stokman & Zeggelink, 1996). Chapter 6 will return to this point.

[5] Affect as a source of social approval will be left out of the model used in this chapter. Affect is usually given by family members or friends. As my interest in politicians' behaviour is limited to a professional setting, affect from family and friends is not considered relevant here.

[6] All legislation is the mutual responsibility of the parliament and the cabinet. In practice, parliaments often grant a minister the right to take decisions on policy implementation on his own. However, this does not preclude parliaments' formal responsibility, nor their right to hold a minister accountable for his decisions.

[7] Of course, propagation of beliefs can also lead to disagreement and frictions. That does not, however, contradict the fact that politics is essentially about debate and propagation of beliefs. The self-expression is regarded as more prestigious than refraining from discussion; it stimulates the career as a politician.

[8] Here, it is not considered important whether electoral support is given to a single politician or a political party. If votes are given to an individual politician, he will be re-elected straightforwardly. If votes are given to a party, it is assumed that the party will reward the politician that brought about the increase in supportive votes, in the form of re-election.

[9] Often politicians remain responsible 'by reputation'. Even though policy implementation has been hived off and formally is no longer the responsibility of politicians, a failing quango is still considered a public affair, both by voters and the media. This has already led to some 'scandals', where politicians were held accountable or even forced to resign because of the poor performance of a quango (e.g. the prison service [a Next Steps agency] in the UK and the regulator of social security [Ctsv] in the Netherlands [*De Volkskrant*, 1996]).

[10] Interest groups can, however, influence government bureaucracy. See also hypothesis 2.3.

[11] Patronage (cf. Flap, 1990) bears some resemblance to what is known in public choice theory as the rewarding of *rent-seeking* behaviour by interest groups (Mueller,

1989:229-246; Tollison, 1997). Interest groups pursue benefits (rents) for themselves and their supporters, in exchange for electoral support. However, interest groups seek monopolist rents, at the exclusion of other groups. Politicians, on the other hand, will want to maximize their support by rewarding as many groups as possible and therefore will not grant one group monopoly rents. Instead, they will divide (or promise to divide) patronage favours between different competing interest groups. See also hypothesis 2.3.

[12] This implies a trade-off between trust and monitoring. Although trust has never kept politicians from monitoring policy implementation by government bureaucracy, for example, by the national audit offices, it does reduce the need for (extensive) monitoring and hence monitoring costs.

[13] All hypotheses on the choice of politicians for a quango as an executive agent refer to the first research question and are therefore numbered with a 1.

[14] This hypothesis does not concern the establishment of quangos by means of creating entirely new organizations. Following the same line of reasoning, new quangos may be established both in periods of economic decline and welfare.

[15] Of course, quangos could share specific assets. However, the costs of negotiating the investment and use of assets would still lead to higher average costs than investments made by a government bureaucracy.

[16] It can also be argued that expensive specific investments and/or low usage frequency of assets could be a reason for politicians to hive them off or privatize policy implemenation. However, such high and very specific transaction costs raise the problem of finding investors (or shareholders) willing to invest (cf. Hazeu, 2000:77-79).

[17] By implication, if the choice for a quango as an executive agent is not perceived as successful, politicians will not repeat that choice. This need not always be the case, however. As was argued before, the political responsibility for policy implementation by quangos is limited. Therefore, politicians can repeat their choice for a quango even if its performance is not regarded successful, because it is not the politicians who are held accountable for ill performance, but the quango.

[18] Moreover, quangocrats can actually be bureaucrats if they are seconded civil servants, or have the same legal position as civil servants. This would particularly be the case in quangos established through the hiving off of departmental units.

[19] In the literature on bureaucrats often a third important group of significant others is distinguished: interest groups. For example, Wilson (1989:76) discusses 'client politics' by agencies; Van Gunsteren (in Leeuw [1995:58]) refers to the 'capture' of agencies by interest groups; and public choice theorists use the concept of 'rent seeking' (Mueller, 1989:229-246; Tollison, 1997). See also the section on extensions of the theoretical model.

[20] Policy implementation is funded with public means (tax revenues, premiums, levying). Efficiency gains should therefore either be paid back to the citizens, used for the implementation of other policies, or used to reduce the state deficit. Most organizations implementing public policies are therefore not allowed to keep (large) surpluses, nor to make profits, although recently ever more quangos have been looking for opportunities to do so (see e.g. In 't Veld, 1995; Commissie Cohen, 1997).

[21] It should be noted that politicians sometimes *purposively* allow executive agents a high degree of discretionary authority in acknowledgement of their expertise, or to grant 'street level bureaucrats' (Lipsky, 1979) professional autonomy in applying general policies to individual situations. Torenvlied (1996a:36,60-61) refers to this as the tolerance level of politicians for policy deviations.

[22] It should be noted, however, that the determination of fees can also lead to inefficiency, especially in the case of a (semi-)monopolist quango. Comparable information on fees is absent, which creates opportunities for quangocrats to maximize fees.

[23] All hypotheses on quango performance refer to the second research question and are therefore numbered with a 2.

[24] In case of a monopoly, not only the principal but also the agent has difficulties establishing whether the agent is performing well, because of the absence of comparative information.

[25] Recently, Dutch politicians and civil servants have started a debate on whether it should be possible to hold (senior) civil servants accountable for failures in policy development and implementation (*De Volkskrant*, 1999a). For example, civil servants could be questioned by parliamentary committees.

[26] Small quangos may also profit from their size; they are less visible to politicians. While this reduces the chance of getting caught at being inefficient or ineffective, it may also threaten the continuation of their existence. If quangos are not noticed, it becomes more difficult for compliant quangos to obtain social approval, while deviant quangos lose the opportunity to obtain (larger) budgets, more tasks and fringe benefits.

[27] This hypothesis may seem contradictory to hypothesis 2.2 which stated that monopolist quangos are less efficient and effective. However, the absence of competitors that could perform the same task (a monopoly) is different from the absence of other organizations in the same policy field (a visible quango). A monopolist quango in a small policy area is expected to have more opportunities to display deviant behaviour, but at the same time it is more visible and therefore not inclined to deviate. Beforehand, it cannot be predicted which of the two aspects will be most decisive.

[28] Following Granovetter's (1973) seminal article on "the strength of the weak ties", a debate started on the effects of the cohesion of networks. In general, it is assumed that strong ties induce compliance. However, Flache and Macy (1996) argue that high cohesion in groups can also lead to deviance. "[P]eer pressure" they conclude (p.23) "can be an effective instrument for blocking compliance, especially in groups in which the cost of compliance is high relative to the value of approval". So, if the exchange of social approval between peers is more important to quangocrats than acquiring the principal's approval through compliance, they may prefer deviance over compliance even if they are close to the principal.

[29] Obtaining (large) surpluses may not always be in the best interest of quangos. The principal may perceive surpluses as a sign that a quango apparently can do the same job with less money, and decide to cut the budget for next year. Therefore, most quangos that obtain surpluses will be inclined to 'retain' them by, for example, making capital reservations for the next years or making extra investments in new personnel or equipment.

Surpluses are then not reported in the *nett* result of performance. This could be seen as a way of hiding information i.e. a performance paradox. However, it is not so much the *right* of the quango to retain surpluses that leads to the hiding of information, but the way in which the *principal* deals with reported surpluses. Therefore, this line of reasoning is not contradictory with hypothesis 2.1P below.

[30] The performance paradox can be seen as an unintended consequence of monitoring (cf. Leeuw, 1996). The need for monitoring after the establishment of a quango has led to other unintended consequences. For example, Ghoshal and Moran (1996) discuss the increased amount of rules imposed upon quangos after being established, and the establishment of regulators, charged with supervision of quangos. Both developments restrict the autonomy of quangos, while quangos were meant to have *more* autonomy than government bureaucracy. Kickert *et al.* (1998:161) have referred to this phenomenon as the 'myth of autonomization'.

[31] Moreover, as more attention (time and money) is given to PIs, the costs of policy implementation by the quango will increase, leading to possible new inefficiencies.

[32] As stated before, closeness does not necessarily always have to lead to more compliance (cf. Flache & Macy, 1996). If quangos are closer to each other than to the principal, their interest in the exchange of social approval among peers may exceed their desire to comply to the principal's wishes. The chance that a performance paradox will occur increases. This could be assumed to be the case when, for example, quangos are held accountable for ill performance and threatened with dismissal. By combining forces, quangos will fight that threat from the principal.

[33] On the other hand, the smaller the distance between the regulator and a quango is, the more opportunities the quango has to 'capture' the regulator (cf. Van Waarden, 1995). Such capture allows the quango to manipulate information without being caught, because the regulator will not report it.

[34] Being the head of a quango also renders a higher salary (cf. Algemene Rekenkamer, 1995: 51-52).

4 Causes

This chapter deals with the first research question posed in chapter 1: under which conditions do politicians choose quangos as executive agents, rather than government bureaucracy, for the implementation of policies? In chapter 3 eight hypotheses were formulated. This chapter sets out to test these hypotheses.[1] However, not all data required for such a test are available. Most important, there is no information on the choice of politicians for government bureaucracy as an executive agent, only information on the number of decisions to establish quangos, from the NCA survey (Algemene Rekenkamer, 1995).[2] Therefore, it is assumed that within the population of choices of an executive agent, choosing government bureaucracy is the same as not choosing a quango. This implies that conclusions based on this study relate to conditions that induce quangocratization and not to conditions that discourage the choice of government bureaucracy as an executive agent.

Another problem with the data is that the NCA survey does not provide all necessary information to test the hypotheses. In some cases additional information could be collected from other sources. Below the additional information sources that were used and the decisions that were made to enable testing of the hypotheses are described, as well as the type of analysis that was used. Next, the results are discussed. I will start with some descriptive statistics and then proceed to the results of the testing of the hypotheses. Two additional analyses have been performed on (i) the establishment of clusters of quangos and (ii) the amount of accountability requirements imposed upon quangos. The results of these additional analyses are used to improve the interpretation of the results of the testing of the hypotheses. Finally, all findings are summarized and the implications of the results are discussed for the theoretical model as developed in chapter 3 and for future research on the causes of quangocratization.

Operationalizations and Data Collection

Choice of Politicians for Quangos

The choice of politicians for quangos as an executive agent is measured as the number of decisions to establish a (cluster of) quango(s) per year. A decision is reflected by the passing of a law, which constitutes the legal basis of the quango or cluster at hand (also referred to as the statutes of a quango). Per year, the number of laws on the establishment of quangos is counted as the number of decisions. Because decisions can lead to the establishment of more than one quango at the same time, the analysis will be repeated using the actual number of established quangos per year as dependent variable.

The primary data source is the survey of the Netherlands Court of Audit (NCA) on Dutch quangos, in particular ZBOs of the category 'public bodies' in table 1.1 (Algemene Rekenkamer, 1995).[3] Chapter 2 already gave a detailed description of the information on quangos in this database, which is why I shall not go into much detail here.

It is important to note that the unit of analysis is the number of decisions or quangos *per year*, which means that the number of observations N equals the number of years (and not the number of decisions or the number of quangos). The lack of information on the choice of the legislature for government bureaucracy as an executive agent made it necessary to use this type of dependent variable. Because no comparison could be made between the choice for alternative types of agents, individual decisions on executive agents cannot be analysed. Instead, I shall investigate which conditions lead to large numbers of quangos in a certain year. These conditions are regarded as the causes of quangocratization.

The number of years is restricted to the period 1950-1993 (N=44) to facilitate data collection on the explanatory variables (see below). The exclusion of earlier years is also meant to eliminate some methodological problems, such as the collection of data on wartime periods and on periods of which no records exist. The majority of quangos in the NCA survey is still included in the analysis, though. Between 1950 and 1993, 124 decisions were taken to establish a quango, resulting in 392 quangos (77% and 71% respectively of the total number of decisions [162] and the total number of quangos [545] in the NCA survey). Figure 2.1 in chapter 2 already displayed the number of decisions and the number of established quangos. Below some more descriptive statistics will be offered.

Explanatory Variables

Based on the theoretical model developed in chapter 3, three models are distinguished - and tested - to explain the choice of politicians for quangos as an executive agent. First, the *base model* consists of three control variables only: time, size of government and size of policy sector. This model is used to make sure that the analyzed increase in the number of quangos is more than just an autonomous trend. Second, the *rational actor model* that, besides the control variables, also includes the conditions specified in hypotheses 1.1 to 1.6. This model is called the rational actor model because it assumes politicians to be rational actors. This assumption is released in the third model, the *bounded rationality model*. Imitation and monitoring are added as explanatory variables to the rational actor model. Politicians were expected to use imitation and monitoring to reduce the uncertainty on the effect of their decision - which is the result of their bounded rationality.

Information on the explanatory variables was collected from the NCA survey and other secondary sources (see also Appendix A). The limited number of observations (N=44) necessitates economical use of the explanatory variables. If more than one operationalization of a variable was present, the best one was selected, preferably on theoretical grounds. All operationalizations and selections are explained below.

As the unit of analysis is the number of decisions per year, most explanatory variables are time-related. However, it does not seem realistic to expect that a particular variable in year t can induce a decision (i.e. a law) on the establishment of a quango in the same year. The procedures to develop, pass and implement laws are usually a lengthy process. That is why time-lags are included in the analyses, of one year and four years respectively.

Control variables Three control variables together form the base model: time, size of national government and size of policy sectors. These variables are included to ascertain whether quangocratization is not merely an autonomous trend. For example, it could seem logical to expect that when a government takes on more tasks, the chance that quangos are charged with these tasks increases, at least in a statistical sense. Therefore, the size of the national government and the size of policy sectors are included in the analyses.

The size of the government is measured as the total number of civil servants at national level (taken from: Van der Meer & Roborgh, 1993). The number of civil servants is measured only once every decade between 1950 and 1993. Therefore, it is assumed that the number of civil servants within one decade is fixed. The larger the size of the government, the more quangos are expected to be established (+).[4]

The size of a policy sector is measured as the number of divisions within the parent department (taken from Carasso *et al.*, 1994). The number of departmental divisions in 1992 is used as a proxy (time-constant variable). There are two reasons for this choice. First, the classification of departments has changed over time and is not always consistent with the classification as used in the NCA survey. A quango that was established in policy sector A in 1950 could well be classified under policy sector B in 1993. Because 1993 is the year of measurement in the NCA survey, the size of the policy sectors in 1992 - as measured by Carasso *et al.* - was used as a proxy. There are no differences in the classification of departments between 1992 and 1993.

The second reason for using the proxy is that it is measured per quango (or actually policy sector), instead of per year. To create a measure for size of policy sector per year, a weighting formula is used. Each decision is weighted by the (log of the) size of the policy sector in which the quango operates. To ascertain the effect of size of policy sector on the decisions in a year, all decisions are aggregated per year and divided by the total number of decisions in that year. More quangos are expected to be established in larger policy sectors (+).[5] This type of weighting formula is used for other variables as well, see below.

Political ideology Hypothesis 1.1 stated that politicians with different political ideologies do not differ in their choice of quangos as executive agents. Political ideology is measured as the composition of the cabinet in office one or four years previous to the decision to establish a quango. Data on the composition of cabinets were taken from annual reports on parliamentary affairs (Kiezer en Parlement, 1950-1993) and the Central Bureau of Statistics (CBS, 1998c).

The Dutch political system has a strong tradition of having coalitions of Christian democrats with either Social Democrats or Liberals. Between 1950-1993 there are only four years in which other coalitions existed. Therefore, a dummy variable is used, indicating the presence of the social democratic party ('left wing coalition'), or not. The expected effect of this variable should be (close to) zero, and not statistically significant.

Economic conditions In chapter 3, it was argued that both economic up-swing and down-swing will lead to more quangos. A distinction was made, though, between quangos established through hiving off and hiving in. The NCA survey does not contain information on the origin of quangos, which means that it cannot be determined whether quangos are established by hiving in or hiving off. Therefore, the testing of hypothesis 1.2 will be limited to testing the effect of economic conditions in previous years on the number of decisions to establish quangos.[6] Both economic up-swing and down-swing were expected to lead to a higher number of decisions to establish quangos.

Two well established indicators of economic conditions have been found. First, the percentage of economic growth, calculated as the percentage increase in gross market prices of national income (taken from: CBS, 1994, 1998d). An increase in the percentage of economic growth equals an increase in the economic up-swing and a decrease of economic down-swing. The second indicator is the percentage unemployed people of the total work force (CBS, 1998e). Increasing unemployment indicates less economic up-swing and more economic down-swing.

Because the data on the percentage unemployed are only partially available for the period 1950-1970, only the first indicator is used in the analyses. A time-lag is applied.

Electoral competition Hypothesis 1.3 predicted that competition for votes among politicians will increase the number of decisions to establish quangos. Two operationalizations for electoral competition were found: elections, and the size of the parliamentary majority of a cabinet in office (source: Kiezer en Parlement, 1950-1993).

Elections are expected to increase the competition between politicians, and hence the number of decisions to establish quangos (+). A dummy variable is used that indicates whether in previous years (one and four years ago) elections were held or not.[7]

The second possible indicator is parliamentary majority, measured as the percentage of the total number of seats in the Second House of Dutch parliament, occupied by the political parties of the governing coalition. The larger the majority, the less electoral competition there is and hence the fewer decisions to establish quangos are taken (-). However, this opera-

tionalization is considered inappropriate, because it presupposes differences between politicians with different roles (ministers or MPs) or from
different political parties. Because such differences were assumed not to
exist in the theoretical model, the indicator 'elections' was preferred over
'parliamentary majority'.

Corporatism To test whether quangos are indeed established more often in
corporatist policy sectors, as predicted in hypothesis 1.4, the degree of
corporatism of each sector had to be assessed. Policy sectors are defined as
coinciding with the department responsible for policies in that sector (e.g.,
the policy field of education is headed by the Ministry of Education), in
other words, the parent department of a quango. The degree of corporatism
is measured as the number of external advisory boards per department.
These boards are officially acknowledged by the government and consulted
in the policy making process. Information on the number of boards was
collected from the State Directory that lists all officially acknowledged
external advisory boards, more than half of the members of which are
professional experts, not civil servants of the department at hand.

However, the Dutch State Directory has listed these boards only since
1993. Before that, it listed committees, councils, tribunals, boards and
quangos, in categories that repeatedly changed over time. The classification of departments changes as well, which complicates counting the
advisory boards per department. That is why the listing as given in 1993 is
taken as a proxy for corporatism (time-constant variable). Advantageous to
this approach is that 1993 was also the year of measurement in the NCA
survey, which means that the same classification of parent departments for
quangos is used. At face value, the number of advisory boards in 1993
seems to reflect the degree of corporatism per department over time, i.e.
policy sectors with the most or least numbers of advisory boards in 1950
have high or low numbers of boards in 1993 as well (*Staatsalmanak*, 1950-
1993).

The inclusion of corporatism in the analysis is problematic because of
its measurement per department and thus per decision, instead of per year.
Decisions to establish quangos in policy sectors with different degrees of
corporatism need to be aggregated in some way to establish the influence
of corporatism on the total number of decisions in a particular year. To
solve this problem, a weighting formula is used. The total number of
decisions per year is weighted with the amount of corporatism per decision. For example: in year *t* three decisions are taken, one to establish a

quango in a moderately corporatist sector and two in highly corporatist sectors. Each decision in that year is multiplied by its weight (the log of the number of advisory boards in the sector in question). All decisions are aggregated and divided again by the total number of decisions.[8] The outcome of this formula shows the degree of corporatism of the total number of decisions in year *t*. In this manner, corporatism is calculated for each year. Contrary to other variables, no time-lag is applied because the corporatism variable is based on decisions in the year *t* itself.

Corporatism is expected to lead to more decisions to establish quangos (+). Because of the way corporatism was operationalized, the analyses can only show the establishment of large numbers of quangos (or none at all) in corporatist policy sectors in certain years. If such a result is indeed found, it will be - implicitly - concluded that corporatism causes quangocratization.

Collective goods   Hypothesis 1.5 stated that quangos wil not often be charged with the provision of collective goods. In other words, the decision to establish a quango will almost always concern non-collective goods.

Using the NCA survey, collective goods can be operationalized in two ways: the task with which quangos are charged or the policy sector in which they operate (cf. Van den Doel & Van Velthoven, 1990:48-51). To determine the degree of 'collectiveness' of tasks and policy sectors, the two characteristics of collective goods are used: non-exclusiveness and jointness of supply. For example, non-exclusiveness means that individual citizens cannot be excluded from the use of a good or, reversibly, citizens cannot escape policy implementation. Tasks of a supervisory nature (registration, certification, licensing, supervision) resemble collective goods more than tasks such as the granting of benefits on request, research, and advice. However, specific investments are also operationalized on the basis of the tasks of quangos (see below). To avoid the risks of multicollinearity, only the second operationalization - the collectiveness of policy areas - is therefore used in the analyses.

Policy sectors are categorized according to their degree of collectiveness, using the second characteristic of collective goods: jointness of supply, i.e. the costs of production do not rise with an additional consumer. In chapter 1, the example of national defence was used to illustrate this property. A division is made between three categories of policy sectors, i.e. parent departments. Departments that perform core government functions, such as Defence, Finances, Justice, Foreign Affairs and the Home Office, are considered to provide collective goods. Departments that were established during the building and expansion of the modern western welfare state (e.g. education, welfare and social affairs) are attributed a moderate degree of collectiveness. In these policy sectors, goods are provided that can be classified as publicly provided private goods. The lowest degree of collectiveness is assigned to departments charged with tasks of an 'entrepreneurial' nature; services are rendered to particular groups of people of organizations (e.g., housing, traffic, economics and agriculture). These categories are used as weights (3, 2 and 1 respectively)[9] in a similar weighting formula as with the operationalization of corporatism. No time-lag is applied, for the same reason as before. The analyses will show whether, as expected, large numbers of quangos are established in policy sectors where non-collective goods are provided (-).

Specific investments Hypothesis 1.6 stated that the more specific investments implementation of a policy requires, the less likely it is that a quango will be charged with this task. Therefore, only small numbers of quangos are expected to be charged with tasks that require specific investments.

To measure the amount of specificity, the tasks of quangos as listed in the NCA survey are re-coded. Some tasks require production means (knowledge, equipment) that can be used for other principals as well and are not that task-specific. For example, advice can be given or research can be done for all kinds of principals (non-specific). Tasks such as the large-scale granting of financial benefits, licensing, registration and the collection of fees are considered moderately specific; although administrative activities can be undertaken by many organisations and on behalf of many principals, they often require special software or knowledge of policies (moderately specific). Policy implementation that has immediate (legal) consequences for citizens is assigned the highest degree of specificity, because this task is the prerogative of the government. Tasks such as supervision, certification, self-regulation, quasi-judicature, and the development and implementation of regulations can be carried out only on behalf of the government.

Again, a weighting formula is used to ascertain the influence of the degree of specifity on the total number of decisions or quangos in a particular year (weights of 1, 2 and 3 respectively).[10] No time-lag is added. Decisions to charge quangos with policy implementation are expected to concern mostly tasks that require less specific investments (-).

Imitation Hypothesis 1.7 introduced imitation as an explanation of politicians' choice of quangos as an executive agent. It was argued that politicians - to reduce uncertainty and gain information about the effects of their decisions - try to acquire experience with quangos. Repetition of decisions will result in an increase in the number of quangos. Therefore, the number of previous decisions is included in the analyses with a time-lag of one and four years respectively. In case of imitation one would expect a high number of previous decisions to lead to more decisions in year t (+).

Imitation was also expected to lead to an increase in the diversity of quangos, with respect to the tasks with which they are charged and the policy fields in which they operate. To measure this increase in diversity, three interaction terms are included in the analyses. These are: time with (i) corporatism, (ii) collective goods, and (iii) specific investments. No time-lags are applied, as before with these variables. The expected effects of the interaction terms are:

1. after establishment of quangos in corporatist policy sectors first, they are also established in non-corporatist policy sectors (-);
2. after being first charged with non-specific tasks, quangos are also charged with specific tasks (+); and
3. after being first charged with the provision of non-collective goods, quangos are also charged with the provision of collective goods (+).

Monitoring Hypothesis 1.8 stated that politicians will not prefer quangos as an executive agent if a large number of accountability requirements is necessary. Therefore, it is expected that politicians will choose quangos as an executive agent most often if only a few accountability requirements need to be made (-).

To measure the accountability requirements of a quango the accountability scale as developed in chapter 2 is used. The scale is based on seven accountability requirements laid down in the law underlying the establishment of quangos. All information was taken from the NCA survey. Because the information is only available per decision and not per year, again a weighting procedure was necessary. To ascertain the influence of accountability requirements on the total number of decisions for each year, decisions were weighted according to the scale score (range 0-1), aggregated per year and divided by the total number of decisions. No time-lag is applied, because accountability requirements are imposed in the same year as the decision is taken.

Table 4.1 lists all operationalizations and the expected effects of the explanatory variables.

Method of Analysis

Linear regression is considered an appropriate method of analysis. However, inspection of the data shows that two basic assumptions of linear regression are violated, namely (i) independency of the observations and (ii) a normal distribution of the dependent variable (cf. Long, 1997:12; Berry & Feldman, 1985:10-11).

Table 4.1   **Operationalizations of the conditions expected to influence the choice of politicians for quangos as an executive agent**

No.	Hypothesis (effect)	Operationalization (expected effect)
1.1	political ideology (0)	left-wing cabinet (0, n.s.)
1.2	economic success (+)	percentage economic growth (+)
1.3	electoral competition (+)	election year (+)
1.4	corporatism (+)	number of acknowledged advisory boards (+)
1.5	collective goods (-)	collectiveness of policy sectors (-)
1.6	specific investments (-)	specificity of tasks (-)
1.7	imitation (+)	1. number of choices previous year (+)
		2. time * corporatism (-)
		3. time * collective goods (+)
		4. time * specific investments (+)
1.8	monitoring (-)	accountability scale score (-)

0 = no effect, + = positive effect, - = negative effect, +/- = mixed prediction, n.s. = not statistically significant

Independency of the observations means that the number of decisions to establish quangos in year t is not influenced by the number of decisions in year $t-1$. If decisions are not independent, there is auto-correlation between the observations (see e.g. Nooij, 1995:100; Barry & Feldman, 1985:76). There are several ways to deal with auto-correlation.[11] Most preferable is the introduction of additional time-related explanatory variables in the regression analysis - based on theoretical grounds, of course. Such variables were already introduced. Time was one of the control variables, and the lagged value of the dependent variable $X=Y_{t-1}$ was used above as operationalization of imitation. Together these variables are expected to eliminate the effect of auto-correlation.[12]

The second violation of the assumptions of regression analysis concerns the distribution of the dependent variable: the number of decisions to establish quangos per year. This is a count variable. As counts are always positive integers and have a high variance, their distribution is not normal and the application of (ordinary) linear regression inappropriate.[13] Instead, a method of analysis should be used which is based on a Poisson distribution, for example Poisson regression analysis (Long, 1997: ch.8; Agresti, 1996:80-93; Land, McCall & Nagin, 1996:394-402; Gardner, Mulvey & Shaw, 1995:396; Barron, 1992:179-190).

Poisson regression analysis often leads to over-estimation of statistical significance, due to over-dispersion, which means that the variance of the dependent variable exceeds its mean (cf. Agresti, 1996:92; Land *et al.*, 1996:388). There are several remedies for the problem of over-dispersion, the most popular of which is the use of Negative Binominal Regression Analysis (cf. Long, 1997:230-249). NBRA is a more "skeptical" method than Poisson regression (Gardner *et al.*, 1995:399-402), and gives a better fit because it is more flexible (see Land *et al.*, 1996:392-394). NBRA tests for the presence of over-dispersion, indicated by alpha.

In the analysis of the number of decisions to establish quangos no over-dispersion was found (alpha=.07, n.s.). Therefore, a Poisson regression analysis was used. The results are given below, after some descriptive statistics.

Descriptive Statistics

Chapter 2 already provided an extensive description of the data collected by the Netherlands Court of Audit, the primary data source for this analysis. Therefore, I shall confine myself here to the descriptive statistics of the variables constructed and used in the analysis. Table 4.2 contains some general descriptive statistics.

The number of cases equals the number of years. The table shows that the number of decisions to establish quangos (i.e. dependent variable) ranges from 0 to 10. Below I will show that the number of quangos resulting from one decision has a broader range. Figure 4.1 shows the distribution of the number of decisions and the number of established quangos.

Table 4.2 also shows the descriptive statistics of the explanatory and control variables. Inspection of the data shows that the three interaction terms that measure imitation and diversity are correlated (on average r = .33, n.s.).

Table 4.2   Descriptive statistics of variables in the analysis to explain the number of decisions to establish quangos in the Netherlands, 1950-1993 (N=44)

Variable	Mean	S.d.	Min	Max
Dependent variable:				
Number of decisions per year	2.82	2.40	0	10
Explanatory variables:				
Left wing cabinet	.34	48	0	1
Economic growth	8.46	4.32	0.6	20.3
Elections	.27	.45	0	1
Corporatism	2.46	.33	1.9	3.2
Collectiveness of policy sectors	1.70	.42	1	2.5
Specificity of tasks	2.17	.42	1	3
Monitoring	.28	.27	0	.86
Control variables:				
Size government	4.72	.20	4.47	4.99
Size policy sector	1.69	.03	1.63	1.76

Sources (own calculations): Kiezer en Parlement (1950-1993); Staatsalmanak (1993); Carasso *et al.* (1994); Van der Meer & Roborgh (1994); Algemene Rekenkamer (1995); CBS (1994; 1998c, d, e)

Two other features of the data are important to keep in mind when interpreting the results of the analyses. First, the size of the government has increased strongly over time (r=.92, p<.001). Second, quangos in small policy sectors are often charged with the provision of non-collective goods (r=.50, p<.001). Now we turn to the results of the analysis.

The Choice of the Legislature for Quangos

Tables 4.3 and 4.4 show the results of the Poisson regression analysis of the number of decisions to establish quangos, with a time-lag of one and four years respectively. Below the results are discussed.

Base Model

Quangocratization is partly an autonomous trend. The increase in the number of quangos is related to the increase in the government size, particularly when considering a time-lag of four years (see table 4.4). When the government expands, the number of policies to be implemented increases also. The chance of quangos being charged with the implementation of policies increases, which results in more decisions to establish quangos. This finding corroborates an observation made earlier in chapter 2. Bureaucratization and quangocratization go hand in hand.

Rational Actor Model

In this model six more explanatory variables are tested. The results are discussed per variable below.

Political ideology The composition of cabinets in office has no statistically significant influence on the number of decisions to establish quangos one or four years later (see tables 4.3 and 4.4). Apparently, political ideology does not play a major role in the choice of legislature for quangos as executive agents (see below for more discussion). Hypothesis 1.1 is confirmed.

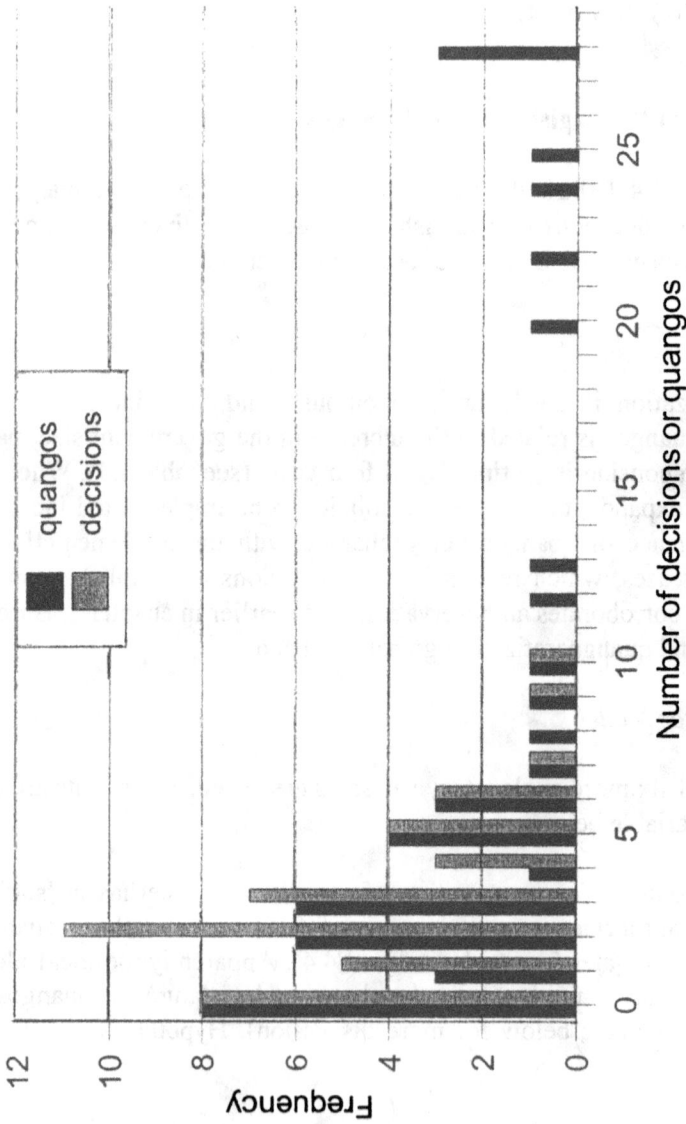

Figure 4.1 The number of decisions to establish quangos and established quangos, per year, the Netherlands, 1950-1993 (*Source*: Algemene Rekenkamer, 1995 [own calculations])

Economic conditions Besides the analyses reported in tables 4.3 and 4.4, two other analyses were carried out. First, an analysis was carried out to establish the expected curvilinear effect of economic conditions.[14] No statistically significant results were found, however. In tables 4.3 and 4.4 only the results of the testing of the linear effect are reported (n.s.). Second, an analysis was performed with the other indicator for economic conditions: the percentage unemployed of the total work force. These analyses also show no statistically significant influence on the number of decisions to establish quangos.

Table 4.3 Results of Poisson regression analysis of the number of decisions per year to establish quangos, the Netherlands, 1950-1993 (N=43, time-lag 1 year)

Explanatory variables	Base Model		Rational Actor Model		Bounded Rationality Model	
			Coefficients (z-value)			
Time	-.03	(1.25)	-.06*	(-2.05)	-.03	(-.89)
Size government	4.41**	(2.59)	5.76**	(2.94)	2.95	(1.31)
Size Policy Sector	-6.32	(-1.77)	-7.08	(-1.89)	-7.06	(-1.83)
Left-wing cabinet			.36	(1.73)	.31	(1.40)
Economic growth			-.03	(-1.14)	-.04	(1.08)
Elections			-.77**	(-2.94)	-1.24***	(-3.98)
Corporatism			-.07	(-.22)	.02	(.06)
Collectiveness			.16	(.63)	.08	(.30)
Specific investments			-.14	(-.46)	-.02	(-.06)
Previous decisions					.14**	(2.70)
Time * corporatism					.03	(1.04)
Time * collectiveness					-.02	(-.82)
Time * specificity					-.02	(.48)
Monitoring					1.16*	(2.44)
Constant	-9.21	(-.93)	-13.75	(-1.29)	-1.58	(-.13)
Log-likelihood	-84.08		-77.07		-67.95	
Pseudo R^2	.15		.22		.31	

* p < .05 ** p <.01 *** p <.001

Sources: Kiezer en Parlement (1950-1993); Staatsalmanak (1993); Carasso *et al.* (1994); Van der Meer & Roborgh (1994); Algemene Rekenkamer (1995); CBS (1994; 1998c, d, e)

It looks like economic conditions have no decisive influence on the decision of politicians to charge quangos with policy implementation. Such a conclusion would confirm the line of reasoning underlying hypothesis 1.2. However, there are too many reservations to be made because of the limited nature of the testing of the hypothesis to draw such a conclusion. For more discussion, see the last section of this chapter.

Table 4.4 Results of Poisson regression analysis on the number of decisions per year to establish quangos, the Netherlands, 1950-1993 (N=40, time-lag 4 years)

Explana-tory variables	Coefficients (z-value)					
	Base Model		**Rational Actor Model**		**Bounded Rationality Model**	
Time	-.02	(-.77)	-.04	(-1.24)	-.06	(-1.60)
Size government	4.15*	(2.40)	4.72*	(2.42)	5.69**	(2.65)
Size Policy Sector	2.10	(.58)	3.08	(.79)	1.33	(.33)
Left-wing cabinet			-.29	(-1.15)	-.37	(-.97)
Economic growth			-.01	(-.47)	.02	(.66)
Elections			.44*	(2.01)	.31	(1.27)
Corporatism			.49	(1.44)	.18	(.39)
Collectiveness			.10	(.36)	.08	(.26)
Specific investments			.14	(.49)	.29	(.92)
Previous decisions					.07	(1.07)
Time * corporatism					.05	(1.20)
Time * collectiveness					.01	(1.7)
Time * specificity					-.02	(-.46)
Monitoring					.76	(1.28)
Constant	-22.09*	(-2.05)	-28.07*	(-2.28)	-29.81*	(-2.31)
Log-likelihood	-84.08		-77.07		-67.95	
Pseudo R^2	.18		.22		.25	

* $p < .05$ ** $p < .01$ *** $p < .001$

Sources: Kiezer en Parlement (1950-1993); Staatsalmanak (1993); Carasso *et al.* (1994); Van der Meer & Roborgh (1994); Algemene Rekenkamer (1995); CBS (1994; 1998c, d, e)

Electoral competition Contrary to the expectation formulated in hypothesis 1.3, competition for votes between politicians leads to *fewer* decisions to establish quangos.[15] Hypothesis 1.3 is therefore rejected.

Table 4.3 shows that elections lead to fewer decisions to establish quangos one year later. Perhaps politicians are less interested in policy implementation during elections, giving priority to the development of new ideas and policies, to please voters. Politicians consider the choice of an executive agent as less salient to voters. See below for further discussion.

Corporatism There is no statistically significant relationship between the degree of corporatism in a policy sector and the number of quangos established in it. Therefore, no conclusions can be drawn with respect to hypothesis 1.4.

Collective goods There is no evidence to support the expectation that quangos are less often established in policy sectors which provide collective goods. No conclusions can be drawn with respect to hypothesis 1.5.

Specific investments Quangos are not charged more often with non-specific tasks, as was expected. Hypothesis 1.6 is not confirmed (but see the results of the additional analysis below).

In sum, the rational actor model does not provide much more explanation for quangocratization than the base model did. The increase in the number of quangos cannot be attributed to particular political parties, nor to economic conditions. The tasks of quangos did not appear important either, nor were characteristics of policy sectors such as corporatism. Electoral competition was even found to lead to *fewer* quangos instead of the expected increase in their number.

Bounded Rationality Model

Releasing the assumption that politicians are rational actors, two more hypotheses were formulated in chapter 3 to explain the choice of politicians for quangos as executive agents. The results of the testing of these hypotheses are discussed below.

Imitation Politicians are inclined to repeat their decision to establish quangos; if more decisions in favour of quangos were taken in the previous year, politicians are more likely to decide to charge a quango with policy implementation in the present year. The repetition of decisions confirms hypothesis 1.8.

The imitation effect is no longer present after four years, though. The analyses do not confirm the expected increase in the diversity of tasks and policy sectors (but see the results of the additional analyses below).

Monitoring It was expected that if policy implementation requires monitoring, quangos will be less often chosen as the executive agent. So, a negative relationship was expected between the number of decisions to establish quangos and the number of accountability requirements. The results in table 4.3 contradict this expectation. Table 4.3 shows that an increase in the number of decisions to establish quangos is met with an increase in the degree of monitoring. Apparently, politicians do not refrain from establishing quangos if monitoring costs will have to be made. Hypothesis 1.8 has to be rejected. Below I will investigate under which conditions politicians will impose accountability requirements on quangos.

Comparison of the Three Models

The bounded rationality model with a time-lag of one year gives the best fit of all models tested (see the improvement in the log-likelihood ratios and R^2 when comparing tables 4.3 and 4.4). Quangocratization is caused by an increase in the size of the government and the repetition by politicians of their choice for a quango as an executive agent. The explanatory power of this model still leaves room for improvement, though (pseudo R^2 does not exceed .31). In the last section of this chapter I will elaborate more on these conclusions, see also chapter 6.

Two More Analyses

To improve the interpretation of the above results, two more analyses were carried out. First, to find out whether decisions on single quangos differ from decisions on clusters of quangos, the same analysis as before is repeated, but now with the total number of established quangos as the dependent variable. Second, attention is also paid to the conditions that determine the degree of monitoring politicians impose. The results of these and the former analyses are discussed in the last section of this chapter.

The Establishment of Clusters of Quangos

To ascertain the differences between decisions to establish a single quango and decisions to establish clusters of quangos, a separate analysis is performed of the number of established quangos per year.[16] The same hypotheses are tested as before, and the same three models are used: base model, rational actor model, and bounded rationality model. Tables 4.5 and 4.6 present the results.

Operationalizations and method of analysis The number of established quangos per year is measured by weighting the number of decisions per year with the number of quangos resulting from those decisions. For example, if in a given year three decisions were taken, resulting in one, one and twelve quangos respectively, fourteen quangos are assumed to have been established in that year. Between 1950 and 1993, 124 decisions were taken, resulting in 392 quangos. Of those 124 decisions, 13.7% involved the establishment of a cluster of quangos (on average 23 quangos resulted from one decision to establish a cluster).

Inspection of the data shows two extreme outliers of 62 and 77 quangos established in one year. These outliers were re-coded to facilitate model fit. Values were set at the next highest maximum, which reduced the range of the number of established quangos per year to 0 to 28. Figure 4.1 already displayed the distribution of the number of established quangos per year.

Furthermore, there is over-dispersion. For this reason, instead of Poisson regression analysis a Negative Binominal Regression Analysis (NBRA) was carried out, using a time-lag of one and four years respectively. Tables 4.5 and 4.6 confirm the presence of over-dispersion in all analyzed models (alpha differs statistically significant from zero).

Comparison of analyses The analysis of the number of quangos gives a worse fit than the analysis of the number of decisions did (pseudo R^2 is maximum .12 against .31 in table 4.3).[17] The hypotheses of chapter 3 provide a better prediction of the *decisions* of politicians to charge a quango with policy implementation than the *number* of quangos established as a result of those decisions.

Again, the bounded rationality model gives the best explanation for quangocratization. However, not all explanatory variables have the same effect as before. Below, the differences between the analyses are discussed.

Time Clusters of quangos are established less often these days (see the effect of time in table 4.6). This corroborates the observations made in chapter 2 where figure 2.1 showed that clusters were mainly established in the 1950s and 1970s. The increase in the number of quangos in the 1980s is due to an increase in the number of decisions to establish (single) quangos.

Specific investments Hypothesis 1.6 predicted that politicians will charge quangos less often with the implementation of a policy if specific investments will have to be made. The analysis in section 4.4 did neither confirm nor refute this hypothesis. Tables 4.5 and 4.6, on the contrary, show that clusters of quangos are charged more often with tasks that require specific investments than with non-specific tasks. Apparently, politicians do not *decide* to charge quangos with tasks that require specific investments more often, but *if* they do the executive agent is usually a cluster of quangos. Most quangos (74.5%) belong to a cluster, although only 13.7% of the decisions results in the establishment of a cluster. The conclusion is that quangos are charged *more* often with specific tasks. Hypothesis 1.6 is rejected.

Imitation and diversity The decisions of politicians to establish quangos are repeated year after year. The establishment of clusters of quangos is, however, not;[18] large numbers of quangos are established in intervals of a number of years (four in the analysis). Although the imitiation interval is longer, hypothesis 1.7 still stands. However, table 4.6 shows that clusters of quangos are established increasingly less often in policy sectors with a high degree of collectiveness. While this finding suggest an increase in diversity (from quangos operating in policy sectors with a high degree of collectiveness to quangos operating in sectors with a low degree of collectiveness), the diversity-trend is contrary to the one expected. Apparently, clusters of quangos are charged more often with the provision of collective goods. Because clusters of quangos are established less often these days, the number of quangos in policy sectors with a high degree of collectiveness has decreased. The diversity of quangos has therefore increased, albeit in the opposite direction of the one predicted.

To sum up, the analysis of the number of established quangos adds one cause to the explanation of quangocratization, namely that politicians tend to choose quangos most frequently for the implementation of policies that require specific investments. Hypothesis 1.6 is rejected.

Monitoring and Accountability

The analyses just discussed show that politicians choose (single or clusters of) quangos as executive agents even if a high degree of monitoring is necessary. Not only does this finding contradict the expectation formulated in hypothesis 1.8, it also seems awkward when one remembers the low accountability demands imposed on quangos, demonstrated in chapter 2. In order to better understand this result, an additional analysis was performed of the conditions that determine the decision of politicians to impose accountability requirements on quangos. The analysis below is *not* meant to test any hypotheses, but is of an exploratory nature. The aim is to ascertain whether conditions that influence the choice of politicians for a quango also influence their decision to impose accountability requirements on that quango. (Most of) the same variables are used as before.

Operationalizations and method of analysis Accountability requirements are laid down in the law by means of which a quango is established (cf. the definition of a decision to establish a quango). Because a cluster of quangos is established by one and the same decision, the same requirements are imposed upon all quangos in that cluster. Accountability will therefore be measured per decision, and not per quango or year. Between 1950 and 1993, 124 decisions to establish (clusters of) quangos were taken.

In chapter 2, an accountability scale was developed on the basis of seven requirements. That scale was also used in the previous analyses (the variable 'monitoring'). For the problem at hand, only the presence or absence of requirements is of interest, so whether accountability requirements are imposed (1) or not (0). Out of the 124 cases, 49 quangos face no requirements at all.

Most of the same conditions and variables are used as before. Two variables have been slightly altered: instead of economic growth, the percentage unemployment is used to measure economic conditions, and instead of the collectiveness of policy areas, the collectiveness of tasks is used. No time-lag is applied.

Table 4.5 Results of Negative Binominal Regression Analysis on the number of established quangos, per year, the Netherlands, 1950-1993 (N=43, time-lag 1 year)

Explanatory variables	Coefficients (z-value)					
	Base Model		Rational Actor Model		Bounded Rationality Model	
Time	-.05	(-.74)	-.01	(.22)	.06	(1.01)
Size government	3.40	(.71)	.38	(.10)	-2.83	(-.77)
Size government sector	13.88	(1.90)	6.74	(.96)	4.24	(.63)
Left-wing cabinet			.31	(.76)	.37	(.96)
Economic growth			.05	(.74)	-.01	(-.18)
Elections			-.19	(-.33)	-.48	(-.87)
Corporatism			-.55	(-.90)	-.24	(-.43)
Collectiveness			-.56	(1.09)	.37	(.79)
Specific investments			1.25*	(2.18)	1.47**	(2.58)
Previous decisions	-.03	(-1.26)				
Time * corporatism					.02	(-.44)
Time * collectiveness					-.08	(-1.68)
Time * specificity					-.02	(.42)
Monitoring					1.83*	(1.98)
Constant	-37.03	(-1.24)	-14.02	(-.61)	4.33	(.20)
Log Likelihood	-133.69		-127.59		-123.56	
Pseudo R^2	.02		.06		.09	
Alpha	1.67***		1.18***		.94***	

* p < .05 ** p <.01 *** p <.001

Sources: Kiezer en Parlement (1950-1993); Staatsalmanak (1993); Carasso *et al.* (1994); Van der Meer & Roborgh (1994); Algemene Rekenkamer (1995); CBS (1994; 1998c, d, e)

Table 4.6 Results of Negative Binominal Regression Analysis on the number of established quangos, per year, the Netherlands, 1950-1993 (N=40, time-lag 4 years)

Explana-tory variables	Base Model		Rational Actor Model		Bounded Rationality Model	
Time	-.13*	(-2.20)	-.11	(-1.68)	-.13*	(-2.06)
Size government	9.58*	(2.50)	7.77	(1.88)	10.04*	(2.52)
Size govern-ment sector	-1.96	(-.24)	2.28	(.29)	-1.46	(-.19)
Left-wing cabinet			-.57	(-1.11)	-1.11	(-1.62)
Economic growth			.07	(1.29)	.10	(1.91)
Elections			.83*	(1.69)	.43	(1.02)
Corporatism			-.44	(-.70)	-.40	(-.66)
Collectiveness			.39	(.74)	.35	(.72)
Specific investments			1.55***	(3.30)	1.76***	(3.75)
Previous decisions	.06**	(2.51)				
Time * corporatism					.04	(.68)
Time * collectiveness					-.10*	(-2.18)
Time * specificity					-.07	-.1.07
Monitoring					.32	(.29)
Constant	-39.90	(1.80)	-41.93	(-1.71)	-46.93	(-1.92)
Log Likelihood	-119.04		-115.93		-110.77	
Pseudo R²	.05		.08		.12	
Alpha	1.38***		1.13***		.80***	

Coefficients (z-value)

* p < .05   ** p <.01   *** p <.001

Sources: Kiezer en Parlement (1950-1993); Staatsalmanak (1993); Carasso *et al.* (1994); Van der Meer & Roborgh (1994); Algemene Rekenkamer (1995); CBS (1994; 1998c, d, e)

Four new explanatory variables are added. First, 'previous require-ments' is measured as the average accountability scale score in the year prior to a decision. Following the idea of imitation, it can, for example, be expected that politicians learn from earlier experience and impose fewer requirements after a while. Next, two new variables are introduced that both relate to the size of a quango: expenditures (in NLG millions) and the number of employees (x 1000). Information on these variables was taken from the NCA survey.[19] In chapter 3, it was assumed that the larger the size of a quango, the greater the damage potential of ill performance, and the greater the need for monitoring will be. The fourth new variable is a dummy variable that shows whether a decision to impose accountability requirements concerns a cluster of quangos, or a single organization. Here, the focus lies on differences in the number of accountability demands they face.

Given the type of dependent variable, logistic regression is considered the appropriate method of analysis (see e.g. Menard, 1995). Table 4.7 gives the results.

The results in table 4.7 show that whether (or not) accountability requirements are imposed depends mostly on the type of task with which a quango is charged and the degree of corporatism of the policy sector in which it operates.

Quangos charged with tasks that require many specific investments face accountability requirements more often than quangos with less specific tasks. Previous analyses showed that clusters of quangos are charged more often with specific tasks. However, politicians do not impose accountability requirements more frequently on clusters, as one would expect (see table 4.7). Perhaps this is because politicians impose requirements less often when tasks are involved that require specific investments *and* resemble the provision of collective goods. Table 4.6 showed that clusters are established less often than they used to, and are increasingly less often charged with collective tasks. This could account for the finding that clusters do not face accountability requirements more often than single quangos.

In corporatist policy sectors, accountability requirements are imposed upon quangos less often. Perhaps, in corporatistic policy sectors politicians use their (in)formal contacts with interest groups as a substitute for more formal monitoring devices like accountability requirements (cf. patronage).

All other conditions seem to be of less importance. Political ideology, economic conditions and electoral competition have no (statistically significant) effect on whether or not accountability requirements are imposed. Also, the size of a quango itself has no influence.

Finally, there are two trends discernible. First, politicians impose accountability requirements less often (see 'time' in table 4.7). This trend confirms the development already shown in figure 2.8; requirements are imposed less often. But if imposed, however, the number of requirements is higher. Following the idea of imitation, it can be argued that politicians learn from their earlier decisions to impose accountability demands, that is, they know in which cases monitoring is necessary and when it is not. There is no direct evidence, though, to support this idea. There is no statistically significant relationship between the decision to impose monitoring in year t and the decision to do so in the year $t+1$.

The second trend is that accountability requirements are imposed more often when the government increases in size. Perhaps, government expansion has led to more monitoring of *all* executive agents - government bureaucracy and quangos. In the next section, I shall go deeper into this and explore some alternative explanations for other findings in the above sections.

Conclusions and Discussion

Table 4.8 summarizes the results of the testing of the hypotheses on the causes of quangocratization. In general, it can be concluded that the *bounded rationality actor model gave the best predictions*. So, politicians use imitation and monitoring to reduce the uncertainty they face regarding the effects of their choice of an executive agent. Chapter 6 will go into this conclusion more extensively when confronting the results of this study with the practitioner theory underlying the establishment of quangos.

Below, the conclusions per hypothesis are discussed (see table 4.8). The results from the two additional analyses will be included as well. If hypotheses were rejected, implications for the theoretical model developed in chapter 3 will be discussed. Attention will also be paid to some methodological aspects of the analyses. Finally, some recommendations will be made for future research. In general, it needs to be emphasized that the testing of hypotheses in this chapter is hindered by the lack of data on the choice of politicians for government bureaucracy as executive agent. The conclusions should therefore be regarded with some reservations. For future research, it is recommended that data is also gathered on the choice for government bureaucracy (or perhaps even other types of executive agents).

Table 4.7 Results of logistic regression analysis of the accountability of quangos, the Netherlands, 1950-1993 (N=12)

Explanatory variables	Estimate	Z-value
Time	-.28**	(-3.23)
Size government	18.41**	(2.72)
Size policy sector	6.06	(.85)
Expenditures quango	11.53	(1.05)
Personnel of quango	-.20	(-.66)
Left-wing cabinet	-.84	(-1.44)
Unemployment	-.16	(-.93)
Elections	.92	(-1.76)
Corporatism	-1.23**	(-2.71)
Collectiveness task	4.12	(1.53)
Specific investments	4.95*	(2.46)
Collective * specific tasks	-2.79*	(-2.27)
Cluster	-1.05	(-1.35)
Previous requirements	.94	(.97)
Constant	-99.49**	(-2.82)
Log likelihood	-58.72	
Pseudo R^2	.29	

* p < .05 ** p <.01 *** p <.001

Sources: Kiezer en Parlement (1950-1993); Staatsalmanak (1993); Carasso *et al.* (1994); Van der Meer & Roborgh (1994); Algemene Rekenkamer (1995); CBS (1994; 1998c, d, e)

Political ideology As expected (hypothesis 1.1), political ideology does not play a decisive role in the decision of politicians to charge a quango with policy implementation. Politicians of all political parties have used quangos as executive agents. The data and analyses also give no indications as to whether politicians of different political parties differ in their preference for (i) quangos as executive agents in case of particular tasks or policy sectors are concerned, or (ii) clusters or single quangos, and (iii) establishment of quangos through hiving in or hiving off.

A replication of this study with quangos established after 1993 is to be recommended. In 1994 and 1998 new cabinets came into office consisting of Liberals, Democrats and Social Democrats. These new coalitions ended 50 years of dominance of the Christian Democrats in Dutch government.

The Christian Democrats participated in all coalitions between 1950 and 1993, which makes it almost impossible to test the effect of political ideology on quangocratization. It might even be argued that the fact that ideology does not affect politicians' preference for quangos can be attributed to the continuous presence of the Christian Democrats in Dutch cabinets. Supposing the Christian Democrats have a strong preference for quangos, it is logical that both the left-wing and right-wing coalitions that have been in office between 1950 and 1993 have used quangos for policy implementation. The absence of Christian Democrats in the cabinets of the 1990s offers the opportunity to test the real effect of political ideology on quangocratization.

At face value, no simple trend can be detected in the period after 1993 (source: *Staatsalmanak*, 1993-1999). Although several quangos have been established (cf. chapter 2), the publication of the NCA survey in 1995 has triggered hot debate and led to initiatives to curb the establishment of quangos (see also chapters 1 and 6).

Economic conditions Because information on the origin of quangos was not present in the NCA survey, it could not be ascertained whether quangos had been established by means of hiving in or hiving off. Hypothesis 1.2 could therefore not be fully tested. Future research should include study on the origin of quangos.

No statistically significant effects were found of the influence of economic conditions on the decision of politicians to establish a quango. This *might* be interpreted as supportive to the line of reasoning underlying hypothesis 1.2, which entailed that both in times of economic up-swing and down-swing quangos were expected to be established in large numbers. However, the results of the analyses do not corroborate these expectations. More research is therefore necessary, before hard conclusions can be drawn on hypothesis 1.2.

Table 4.8 Results of the analysis of the number of decisions to establish quangos and the analysis of the number of established quangos

No.	Hypothesis (operationalization)	Predicted effect	Observed effect	Conclusion
1.1	Ideology (left-wing cabinet)	0	n.s.	Confirmed
1.2	Economic conditions (economic growth)	+	n.s.	No conclusion
1.3	Electoral competition (elections)	+	-	Rejected
1.4	Corporatism (number of advisory boards)	+	n.s.	No conclusion
1.5	Collective goods (policy sectors)	-	n.s.	No conclusion
1.6	Specific investments (task-specificity)	-	+	Rejected
1.7	Imitation (previous decisions)	+	+	Confirmed
1.8	Monitoring	-	+	Rejected

0 = no effect, + = positive effect, - = negative effect, n.s. = not statistically significant

If both economic up-swing and down-swing would lead to quango-cratization, the question rises what the effect is of quangocratization on economic conditions. The practitioner theory claims that policy implementation is carried out more efficiently and effectively by quangos than by government bureaucracy (see chapter 1). If this were the case, one would expect less economic down-swing, or at least a decrease in government expenditures, following the establishment of quangos. However, a decrease in government expenditures can also be achieved by imposing budget cuts on quangos at the time of their establishment. In that case, politicians anticipate efficiency gains from charging a quango with policy implementation. I shall return to this point in chapter 5, where the effects of the establishment of quangos on the efficiency and effectiveness of policy implementation are investigated.

Electoral competition Electoral competition was expected to induce politicians to choose quangos as an executive agent more often; it offers them the opportunity to decrease political risks and increase the commitment of voters. The results of the analyses show the opposite to be true: in times of fierce political competition, *fewer* quangos are established. Hypothesis 1.3 is therefore rejected.

Before discarding the theoretical model developed in chapter 3, alternative explanations for these results need to be studied. For example, it was suggested that in election periods politicians might prefer to pay attention to the development of new policies (i.e. make promises to the voters) and be less interested in how and by whom those policies will be implemented (for not all promises are kept). Politicians may think policy implementation is less salient to voters than policy development. This would mean that in election periods fewer decisions are taken about executive agents. Four to seven years after elections, an increase in the number of decisions on executive agents will follow, four to seven years being the average amount of time needed to develop, pass and implement policies (Algemene Rekenkamer, 1994:6). However, as stated earlier, data are only available on decisions to establish quangos and this alternative explanation cannot be tested.

Another explanation for the findings on electoral competition can be sought in the assumption that "[l]osses weigh heavier than gains of the same amount" (Lindenberg, 1993:15 based on Kahneman & Tversky). If electoral competition is fierce, politicians can expect to win more votes when they can claim successful policy implementation by government bureaucracy. If implementation has been put at arm's length, they cannot claim successes nor intervene easily when ill performance occurs. The benefits of keeping policy implementation within range (i.e. charge government bureaucracy with it) outweigh the benefits of putting it at arm's length. This leads to a new hypothesis: the stronger the electoral competion among politicians, the *less* often will they choose quangos for the implementation of policies.

A third alternative explanation concerns the effects of patronage. In chapter 3, it was argued that by appointing members of interest groups to a quango board, politicians can enhance the commitment of those interest groups and increase their electoral support. However, in a political system based on co-operation and division of power like, such as the Dutch coalition system, patronage benefits cannot be assigned exclusively to one party. In a political system where one party holds all the power like, for instance, the UK system, patronage benefits are much higher (cf. Hall & Weir [1996] on the 'new magistracy'). Following this argument, it can be hypothesized that only in situations where parties hold large parliamentary majorities - and, consequently, electoral competition is low - will politicians use quangos to benefit from patronage. To test this prediction, more information is needed on the composition of the quango boards. This information is not available in the NCA survey.

Corporatism The measurement of the degree of corporatism of policy sectors was not without problems. Besides the problems of re-classifications of departments and the lack of comparative information on the number of advisory boards over time, there have also been reductions in the number and types of advisory boards after 1993. Solving these problems falls outside the scope of this study.

Quangos are not established more often in corporatist policy sectors, as was expected (hypothesis 1.4). It was assumed that politicians would do this to increase the commitment (and votes) of interest groups. Perhaps politicians, in corporatist sectors, have other means to secure commitment. For example, politicians can offer interest groups a seat in one of the many advisory boards found in corporatist sectors (cf. the operationalization of corporatism). In that case, quangos are expected to be established less often in corporatist policy sectors. The analyses do no corroborate this expectation, however. More research on the possible substitutive effect of corporatism is needed.

Quangos in corporatist policy sectors face fewer accountability requirements. Again, it can be argued that in corporatist policy sectors politicians have alternative means at their disposal to ensure accountability (see also below). The general idea is that the stronger the involvement of interest groups - for example through membership of advisory boards - the higher the frequency of contacts will be between interest groups, quangos and politicians. The relationships between these actors are intensified. Imposing accountability requirements could then be perceived as a sign of distrust and is therefore not advisable. To state things differently, formal instruments of evaluation and accountability are replaced with informal ones, such as trust, socially exerted control and social networks (see, e.g. Bulder, Leeuw & Flap, 1996).

Collective goods Hypothesis 1.5 predicted that quangos are charged less often with the provision of collective goods. No evidence was found to confirm this hypothesis. In fact, the analysis of the number of established quangos showed that clusters are established increasingly less often in collective policy sectors, which suggests that they were established more often in such fields in the past. Such a finding would refute hypothesis 1.5. Decisions to establish clusters of quangos should therefore be analyzed further.

The way in which the variable 'collective goods' is measured needs improvement. The re-coding of policy sectors or tasks could be more refined by, for example, introducing more, or other types of, categories.[20] The available data and the level of analysis (per year) did not allow for a more detailed operationalization. I recommend that more attention be paid to what exactly constitutes a collective good - and use expert opinions, for example - before further investigating the relationship between the collectiveness of tasks or policy sectors and quangos. The same holds for the operationalization of specific tasks (see below).

Specific investments   Most quangos are charged with tasks that require specific investments. Hypothesis 1.6 is therefore rejected. Although politicians do not *decide* more often to charge quangos with tasks that require specific investments, if they do make such a decision, it usually concerns clusters of quangos. Clusters make up for the majority of quangos (74.5%).

The underlying argument for hypothesis 1.6 was that politicians do not tend to choose quangos as executive agents if specific investments are needed, as it increases the costs of policy implementation. Investments have to be made in non-recurrent assets (e.g. knowledge, equipment), assets which in a government bureaucracy are often already available. Moreover, charging a quango with very specific tasks could create a (semi)-monopoly (cf. White's (1991) reversal of control). Politicians were expected to try to prevent such a situation. This expectation was refuted by the results.

An explanation for the rejection of hypothesis 1.6 can perhaps be found in the typical nature of specific assets. Although it is probably true that in a large government bureaucracy assets can be more easily re-deployed, there are disadvantages associated with keeping specific tasks within a government bureaucracy. For example, specific tasks can be seen as a deviation from standard operating procedures (Wilson, 1989:133), or a disturbance of bureaucratic routines. Managing such tasks could take up much time or require skills and expertise that are not available. Charging a quango with policy implementation would solve these problems; a quango is not part of the core government bureaucracy, which allows for the involvement of external experts, in particular members of interest groups or voluntary organizations, to ensure efficiency of policy implementation. As argued in chapter 3, the interest of private organizations in these tasks will probably be low, therefore a *quasi*-autonomous organization is charged with them.

An additional benefit of putting specific tasks at arm's length is a reduction of the political risk of being held accountable for ill performance. If bureaucracy is indeed less well equipped to carry out a certain task, the risk of ill performance increases, and also the risk that politicians will be held accountable. Charging a quango with the task reduces that risk. It might even be argued that politicians deliberately put the implementation of highly specific policies at arm's length when these policies are considered controversial (cf. Torenvlied, 1996a:61). In case of ill performance, the *quango* will be held accountable.

To test this alternative explanation, more attention needs to be paid to which tasks require more, or less, specific investments. Here, the original categorization of tasks in the NCA survey was re-coded. This categorization could be more refined (e.g. how to classify quangos with more than one task). It would also be necessary to ascertain whether there are any tasks with which quangos are *never* charged.

Imitation The analyses suggest that imitation indeed takes place, albeit not always in the direction that was predicted. Hypothesis 1.8 is therefore confirmed, with the annotation that the direction of imitation is not as expected.

Decisions to establish quangos are repeated year after year. Decisions to establish clusters of quangos are repeated after a longer interval (four years). This repetition of decisions has led to an increase in the number of quangos over time.

A change in the diversity of quangos has been demonstrated only for clusters of quangos, whose establishment in policy sectors with a high degree of collectiveness has decreased. This trend is mainly the result of the decrease in the number of decisions to establish clusters of quangos. Figure 2.1 shows that most clusters were established in the 1950s and 1970s. No overall decrease is found with respect to the establishment of quangos in policy sectors with a high degree of collectiveness; hypothesis 1.5 was not rejected. Nevertheless, the results of the analyses suggest that, in the past, clusters of quangos were charged in particular with the provision of collective goods. To test this, further analysis of the decisions on clusters is necessary.

Monitoring Hypothesis 1.8 stated that politicians are disinclined to charge quangos with tasks that require intensive monitoring. This hypothesis was rejected. It should be noted, though, that only decisions to establish quangos were analyzed. There is no knowledge of charging tasks that require monitoring to government bureaucracy. My analyses only show that politicians do not hesitate to also charge quangos with tasks that require monitoring. The accountability of quangos on average being weak (see chapter 2), a separate analysis was performed in order to gain more insight into the findings on monitoring.

Politicians impose requirements on quangos more often if the task in question is charged more frequently to quangos. Earlier, it was assumed that politicians will want to minimize monitoring costs. By imposing (the same) requirements in the same instances, the average monitoring costs will decrease. For example, requirements are imposed more often on quangos with specific tasks (unless these tasks resemble the provision of collective goods). An extra argument to explain the presence of high monitoring demands in the case of specific tasks could be that politicians fear the possible consequences of the information asymmetry. Because the expertise and knowledge about a policy and its implementation is concentrated in a quango (sunk costs), politicians depend on that quango for information on its performance. This could lead to a so-called reversal of control (White, 1991). To prevent dependency, politicians oblige quangos to provide information on their performance and allow inspection by others, such as the Ombudsman or (departmental) accountants.

The absence of accountability requirements in corporatist policy sectors can also be explained by the desire of politicians to minimize monitoring costs. In corporatist sectors, it was argued, contacts between politicians, interest groups and quangos are expected to be more frequent and intense, which replaces the need for formal monitoring devices, such as accountability requirements.

Finally, the exploratory analysis confirms the trend described in chapter 2. Accountability requirements are imposed less and less often. However, figure 2.8 showed that *if* accountability requirements are made, several requirements are imposed in one go. A possible explanation for this could be that politicians have learned from experience when monitoring is - or is not - necessary. Such an explanation corresponds with the ideas on imitation set out in chapter 3. Imitation and monitoring are two ways for politicians to deal with the uncertainty on the results of their decision about a certain type of executive agent.

Chapter 4 dealt with the first research question about the causes of quangocratization, chapter 5 will deal with the consequences, in particular quango performance. The results of chapters 4 and 5 will be summarized and integrated in chapter 6.

Notes

[1] Earlier drafts of parts of this chapter were published before (Van Thiel, Leeuw, Siegers & Flap, 1999).

[2] See chapter 2 for the definition of a quango in the NCA survey.

[3] The database contains only quangos that existed in 1993; quangos that were abolished before 1993 are excluded. As demonstrated in chapter 2, only 3% of the quangos was abolished. The number of missing data is therefore limited and will not pose a problem to the analysis.

[4] On the other hand, it might also be argued that the more quangos are established - particularly through hiving off - the smaller the core government will become. See chapter 6.

[5] To allow for time-variation in this calculation, one needs to trace, per decision or quango, in which policy sector a quango is established and whether in 1993 it is listed in the same sector or in another, because of reclassification. However, the NCA survey does not contain information on the original policy sector - only the classification of 1993 has been used. The listings in the State Directory before 1993 are inconclusive on this matter. Therefore, it was decided not to include time-variation and use a time-constant variable as a proxy.

[6] If the practitioner theory is correct and the establishment of quangos leads to more efficient and effective policy implementation (but see the criticism in chapter 1), one could also argue that the choice for quangos as an executive agent reduces government expenditures, decreasing economic decline or increasing the chances of economic growth. See also chapter 6.

[7] It could also be argued that the *prospect* of elections increase electoral competition. Therefore, a separate analysis will be performed on the effect of elections in the year after the decision to establish a quango.

[8] Corporatism in year t = sum of (decision in year t * degree of corporatism per decision) / number of decisions in year t. Degree of corporatism is measured as the natural log of the number of advisory boards per department.

[9] Other weights were also tried, but did not lead to other results than those reported here.

[10] Other weights were also tried, but did not lead to other results than those reported here.

[11] A method to solve the problem of auto-correlation is to use difference scores, and thus correct for the influence of auto-correlation on the dependent variable: $Y'_t = Y_t - Y_{t-1}$. However, this method requires some *a priori* notion of the type of dependency between the observations. Chapter 3 provides (too) little guidance on this matter. Another method to counteract the effects of auto-correlation could be the use of a Cochrane Orcutt regression analysis (Johnston, 1984:304-330). Both methods require a normal distribution of the dependent variable, however, which is not the case here (see the second violation).

[12] A regression analysis confirmed the presence of auto-correlation (Durbin Watson coefficient DW=1.40). The introduction of the additional explanatory variables t and Y_{t-1} solved this problem (DW=1.98; DW=2 means no auto-correlation).

[13] Because there is no information on decisions *not* to charge a quango with policy implementation, logistic regression could not be applied.

[14] The percentage economic growth raised to the square was added to the regression

equation to determine the expected curvlinear effect.

[15] A separate analysis shows that the *prospect* of elections in the next year does not lead to more decisions to establish quangos (n.s.).

[16] The correlation between the number of decisions and the number of established quangos is moderate (r=.49, p<.01).

[17] Convergence problems forced me to drop the imitation variable from the rational actor model and the bounded rationality model. Instead, it was included in the base model.

[18] Barron (1992:187-193) hints at the possibility that over-dispersion and auto-correlation are related to each other. He calls this the "contagion" effect: the increase in a dependent variable is not caused by interdependency of the observations, but an artefact of the data caused by over-dispersion. Although in this analysis over-dispersion was found (see alpha in table 4.5), no autocorrelation was present. Therefore it does not seem likely that there is a contagion effect at work.

[19] A cluster of quangos is represented in the NCA survey by one quango of that cluster. The number of employees and expenditures of that representative quango is used in the present analysis. Chapter 2 already mentioned that the data are incomplete for both variables. Expenditures are only listed if they come from the State Budget (in approximately 60% of the cases). Employees are not included if they are seconded civil servants (in approximately 30% of the cases).

[20] See, for example, Van Waarden (1992, based on work by Musgrave) who proposes to categorize policy sectors by their functions of allocating goods and subsidies in the market, distributing goods fairly, and ensuring the stability of the society.

5 Consequences

This chapter sets out to find an answer to the second research question raised in chapter 1: *Under which conditions will policy implementation by quangos be more efficient and effective than implementation by government bureaucracy?* Chapter 3 identified four conditions that make quangos more efficient and effective executive agents than government bureaucracy. Seven hypotheses were formulated about the efficiency and effectiveness of policy implementation by quangos. To test these hypotheses, information on the efficiency and effectiveness of policy implementation by a large number of quangos would be necessary. Such a large amount of information could not be collected, however, which is why I need to use another research strategy.

A meta-analysis of existing (case) studies on quangos would not be a valuable strategy, because in those studies the focus is mostly on the history and characteristics of quangos, and not on their performance (cf. review in chapter 1). Typically, organizations such as the Netherlands Court of Audit, the Scientific Council for Government Policy, the Home Office and the Ministry of Finance, which can all conduct surveys among quangos, do not examine the performance of quangos but rather concentrate on other matters (WRR, 1983; Algemene Rekenkamer, 1995; *Rapportage Doorlichting Zelfstandige Bestuursorganen*, 1997; Ministerie van Financiën, 1998). It has to be admitted that a survey of the performance of quangos would be a very difficult task. The diversity in tasks, policy sectors, and budgets (see chapter 2) means that the performance of quangos varies strongly, both in terms of what kind of services are provided and the measurability of those services. For example, it would be very difficult, if not impossible, to compare the performance of the Chambers of Commerce with that of the National Bank, or the Child Welfare Councils with public universities. Moreover, chapter 2 showed that the accounts quangos give of their performance are often incomplete.

Because information on the performance of all quangos is not available, and because it is not feasible to collect such data on a large scale, the remaining research option is to select a limited number of quangos and study their performance; that is, take a case study approach. For this study, it was decided to select a small number of quangos, whose performance is examined over time and compared with the performance of their predecessors, which were not quangos (intra-quango comparison).[1] For practical purposes only two quangos were selected.

The selected quangos do not belong to the same cluster. Although the performance of quangos in the same cluster is comparable, there is little if no variation in the conditions under which they operate; they have similar tasks, a similar legal structure, similar means of financing, and have to meet similar accountability requirements (see for an example the study of Bulder, Van de Wal, Leeuw & Flap [1997] on legal aid in the Netherlands). Because of these similarities, it would not be possible to test for the influence of conditions on performance, which is, after all, the aim of my study.

The theoretical framework in chapter 3 will form the basis of the case study research. Changes in efficiency and effectiveness of policy implemenation after the establishment of the quangos will be explained by means of the seven hypotheses formulated in chapter 3. A comparison of the results of the two case studies - but not of the performance of the cases which cannot be compared - will be used to test the hypotheses. Of course, a real statistical test is not possible due to the limited number of cases, but some conclusions can be drawn about the validity of the theoretical expectations set out in chapter 3 (*analytical generalization*; Yin, 1994:30).

An argument in favour of a case study approach that has not been mentioned yet, is that there is only little (empirical) knowledge about the performance paradox (Meyer & Gupta, 1994). To gain more knowledge on this phenomenon an exploratory research strategy is recommended (Yin, 1994; Swanborn, 1996). Chapter 3 described the performance paradox and its disturbing influence on the assessment of efficiency and effectiveness of policy implementation. The aforementioned seven hypotheses were reassessed and four more hypotheses formulated to predict whether or not a performance paradox will occur. These hypotheses will be evaluated as well.

First, I will discuss the research design and the methods that were used. The two cases to be studied are described next.[2] The chapter will conclude with a summary of the results, confronting them with the theoretical expectations of chapter 3.

Research Design

The main focus in the case studies is on the performance of the selected quangos, i.e. the efficiency and effectiveness of their policy implementation, compared to prior implementation by a non-quango. The hypotheses derived in chapter 3 on (i) the efficiency and effectiveness of policy implementation by quangos and (ii) the potential presence of a performance paradox will be investigated. The two focal questions in the case studies are therefore:

[Question 1] Has the establishment of a quango led to a more efficient and effective policy implementation and can changes in efficiency and effectiveness be explained by the conditions discerned in hypotheses 2.1-2.7?
[Question 2] Is there a performance paradox present in the selected cases, and if so, can this be explained by the conditions mentioned in hypotheses 2.1P-2.11P?

Efficiency and Effectiveness of Policy Implementation

Efficiency is measured as the ratio of costs to output. The type of task with which an organisation is charged determines output. For example, if an organization is charged with the payment of benefits, output indicators can be the number of benefits paid to clients, the number of clients and the total amount of paid benefits. Costs can refer to costs of a policy such as the total of benefits or subsidies paid to clients (programme costs), or to the costs of the production process (running costs), such as salaries, office space and equipment.

Efficiency is considered to have improved when output increases while costs remain equal or decrease, or if costs decrease while output remains stable or increases. It is important to note that an increase or decrease in programme costs can also be caused by changes in the policy implemented. For example, if the average level of a benefit is raised, programme costs will increase (with the same number of benefits). However, this should not be seen as a sign of inefficiency, because the change in the ratio of costs to output is not caused by a change in the performance of the quango. On the other hand, a decrease in the size of programme costs as a result of efforts made by the quango (e.g. through fighting fraud or reducing errors) will be seen as an efficiency improvement. Therefore, the origin of changes in the programme costs needs to be traced before conclusions can be drawn whether it reflects a change in the efficiency of policy implementation.

Besides output and costs, the *quality* of output is important. Effectiveness is defined as the degree to which a quango manages to implement a policy successfully, without errors, in time, and to the satisfaction of its clients. Effectiveness is considered to have improved when the number of wrong decisions about the (non)-payment of benefits decreases, the time required to process information is reduced, or the number of complaints by clients drops.

In the case studies, attention is paid to all three aspects of performance, i.e. costs, output and quality. Information on performance is obtained through analysis of documents, such as annual reports and accounts, and interviews. To determine whether the establishment of a quango has led to more efficient and effective policy implementation, performance has to be studied over a period of time, both before and after the quango was established. To that end, the policy implemented by the quango has to be studied, and the goods or services it provides. The policy objectives will determine the output that has to be produced. An overview of output, costs, the ratio of costs to output, and quality of output will show whether policy implementation has become more efficient and effective (or not).

Presence of a Performance Paradox

The performance paradox refers to a weak correlation between reported and actual performance (see chapter 3 for a more detailed explanation). Sometimes performance indicators (PIs) report on limited aspects of performance only, giving information about easily quantifiable aspects of performance, but leaving out less tangible aspects. In that case, reports underestimate actual performance. PIs can also be manipulated to make performance appear better than it really is, or to hide ill performance. In that case, reported performance provides an overestimation. It is important to keep in mind that a performance paradox has to do more with the *reports* on performance than actual performance. If present, a performance paradox invalidates the conclusions about the performance of the selected cases.

To uncover a performance paradox, reports of performance need to be studied and compared to actual performance. However, because *all* reports of performance can be subject to the performance paradox, it is nearly impossible to assess actual performance. We are faced with a conundrum.

Other solutions to overcome the problem of gathering information on the actual performance of quangos are to (i) collect information from other sources than the quango itself (e.g. competitive quangos[3] or other organizations, clients, regulators, or the Ombudsman) and compare that with the reported performance, or (ii) develop new PIs that are not already being used by the quango itself, and use these to reassess performance.[4] A lack of information from other sources increases the chance of a performance paradox occurring. If new indicators lead to different assessments, one might conclude that there is a performance paradox.

If other information sources are absent or new PIs cannot be developed, a third solution can be applied. Meyer and Gupta (1994) argue that certain characteristics of the performance assessment system increase the chance of a performance paradox arising (cf. chapter 3). For example, when only a limited number of PIs are used for a long time, positive learning can lead to a loss of the discriminating value of those indicators. Meyer and Gupta recommend the use of many, non-correlated indicators, and to vary those over time. Moreover, for *each* policy objective indicators should be developed; if, for example, PIs only stress quantifiable objectives, reports will underestimate non-quantifiable aspects of policy implementation. To investigate whether such a situation exists, an analysis of the performance assessment system is necessary. Aspects that need to be studied are: the translation of policy objectives into PIs, by whom the translation has been made and how; the amount and type of PIs used in annual reports and other reports on performance; and changes in the use of PIs over time. Furthermore, it is important to establish how much and what type of information on the performance of a quango is required and to which extent the quango complies with accountability demands. Finally, if information on performance is present but not reported, the cause for this lack needs to be determined, especially when reporting the missing information would lead to different conclusions on the efficiency and effectiveness of policy implementation. An analysis of the quality of the performance assessment model can be assisted by expert opinions (cf. Arthur Andersen, 1995; 1996; 1997; 1998).

Hypotheses 2.1P-2.11P will be used to try to explain a performance paradox, if present. Caution is warranted, however, for two reasons. First, the performance paradox is a complex phenomenon. It can be an unintended result of the behaviour of principals and agents, as well as a deliberate attempt to hide or manipulate information (cf. chapter 3). Second, the presence of conditions that may evoke a performance paradox, is no proof that a performance paradox is indeed present. Chapter 6 will return to this point.

Conditions

Table 3.2 in chapter 3 summarized all conditions that were expected to be of influence on the efficiency and effectiveness of policy implementation and the occurrence of a performance paradox. Here, the hypotheses 2.1(P) to 2.11P formulated in chapter 3 are re-grouped into four categories, to structure the case descriptions. Below, each category is described, including the hypotheses belonging to it, and the way in which conditions are measured. Table 5.1 will give an overview of hypotheses, operationalizations, descriptive categories and methods.

Production rights Hypothesis 2.1 stated that the more production rights a quango owns, the more efficient and effective policy implementation will be, and the less likely it is that a performance paradox will occur. Especially production rights regarding financial arrangements were expected to exert an influence. In the case studies, attention will be paid to the following financial arrangements: whether the quango budget is determined by fees, levies and tariffs or by the State Budget of the parent department; if the quango has the right to retain surpluses; if the quango has to compete for budgets and with whom. Another production right that will be studied is the right to hire and fire employees. The legal position of quangocrats is also expected to influence the closeness of agent and principal (hypothesis 2.6; see category 'perceptions'). Finally, it is important to examine which production rights have *not* been given to the quango, but have remained the prerogative of the principal, who is usually the minister in charge of the parent department. The main data source for production rights, financial arrangements and the legal position of quangocrats will be the statutes underlying the establishment of the selected quangos.

Organizational characteristics A number of hypotheses concerned organizational characteristics. For example, hypothesis 2.2(P) predicted that competition would increase efficiency and effectiveness, but might also create a performance paradox. In the case studies, the market position of the selected quangos will be investigated, for example, whether the quango is a monopolist or a member of a cluster, and also how specific its tasks are - because specific investments can create a semi-monopoly. Whether a quango is allowed to undertake commercial activities for other principals will be studied as well.

The size of a quango was also expected to influence the efficiency and effectiveness of policy implementation and whether or not a performance paradox will arise (hypothesis 2.5[P]). Smaller quangos are expected to be more efficient and effective, and less prone to performance paradoxes. Size is measured by means of the budget of a quango and the number of employees. The size of the policy sector in which the quango operates will have to be taken into account as well, measured as the number of divisions in the parent department, the number of civil servants it employs and the departmental budget.

Finally, hypothesis 2.6(P) predicted that the origin of a quango was of importance; the closer a quango is to the parent department, the more efficient and effective policy implementation is expected to be, and the less likely it is that a performance paradox will occur. Quangos established through hiving off were assumed to be closer to the parent department. The way in which a quango was established will therefore be taken into account. Attention will also be paid to the composition of the quango board, in particular to the presence of members of interest groups. Hypothesis 2.3 predicted that participation of interest groups in policy implementation will increase the efficiency and effectiveness. A mixed prediction was made with regard to the effect of corporatism on the occurrence of a performance paradox (cf. hypothesis 2.3P).

Documents such as statutes, annual reports and other studies will be used to gather information on the forementioned organizational characteristics. Additional information will be obtained from interviews.

Accountability requirements Hypothesis 2.4 predicted that the more accountability requirements are imposed on a quango, the more efficient and effective policy implementation will be. In the case studies, attention will be paid to the accountability demands the selected quangos have to meet, such as the obligatory publication of annual reports, an audited account, *et cetera*. Also, the presence of an appointed supervisor or regulator will be examined. Hypothesis 2.11P offered a mixed prediction on the effects of the presence of a supervisor.

However, as discussed extensively in chapter 3, the relationship between accountability demands and the efficiency and effectiveness of policy implementation can be disturbed by the performance paradox. Reported performance can provide an over- or underestimation of actual performance. Therefore attention will be paid as well to the likely occurrence of such a paradox. For example, it was argued that if the discrepancy between policy objectives and PIs grows larger, it becomes more likely that a performance paradox will occur (hypothesis 2.9P). The divergence between policy objectives and the mission quangos themselves have formulated will be studied. Other hypotheses were also formulated, in particular about the performance assessment system quangos use. The amount of accountability requirements was expected to influence this, although no prediction was made how. Diversity of PIs - in terms of variation and comparability over time - was expected to reduce the chances of a performance paradox occurring (hypothesis 2.8P) and will therefore be studied as well.

All accountability requirements are laid down in the statutes. PIs are found in annual reports and accounts. Also, interviews and statements can provide information on how quangocrats use and value PIs.

Perceptions Two hypotheses concerned perceptions of quangocrats: risk perception and the focus on efficiency and PIs. Both will be measured using interviews and statements given to respondents.

Hypothesis 2.7(P) stated that as quangocrats perceive the risk of getting caught at deviant behaviour, the more efficient and effective policy implementation will be, and the less likely it is that a performance paradox will arise. Risk perception is operationalized as aversion or reluctance to take or accept responsibility for errors, the presence of sanctions, and the way in which quangocrats deal with change (e.g. do they take initiatives to change or not).

Hypothesis 2.10P predicted that a strong emphasis on efficiency, effectiveness and the use of PIs increases the chance of a performance paradox occurring. The importance attached to indicators will be investigated, as well as the consequences of non-compliance with indicators, and the number of indicators - assuming that the more emphasis is placed on indicators, the more indicators there will be. Attention is also paid to how important efficiency is to the quango, for example, whether efficiency and effectiveness are organizational goals and what sanctions are imposed upon the quango when inefficiency or ineffectiveness are discovered.

Selection of Cases

Cases have to meet four criteria to qualify for selection. First, they have to fall within the definition of a quango as used in this study (see chapter 1): they are charged with policy implementation by politicians, funded with public means, but operate at a distance from the government. Second, it is necessary that prior to the quango's establishment another organization already existed - not being a quango - which carried out the task in question. Otherwise a comparison of performance before and after the establishment of a quango is not possible. So, quangos that are newly established to implement new policies are excluded. Third, organizations should provide accounts of their performance. With a view to the ease of data collection it is preferable if the date of establishment is relatively recent. Cases set up in the 1980s or 1990s with relatively high accountability requirements are therefore most suitable. The fourth criterion is rather pragmatic and involves the accessibility and co-operation of organizations.

Based on these criteria two organizations were selected from the same policy sector: education.[5] Quangos in this policy sector often have to meet a lot of accountability requirements (cf. figure 2.9 in chapter 2), which heightens the chance of finding information on performance. Both cases thus meet the third criterion.

From the quangos in the educational field, two recently established quangos were selected. The first quango is IB-Groep, a former departmental unit which was hived off in 1994 and is charged with, amongst others, the payment of student loans and grants. This case meets the first criterion; IB-Groep is a quango of the public body type (cf. table 1.1 in chapter 1). Its predecessor is the *Informatiseringsbank*, an organization that was very similar to a contract agency. IB-Groep has been studied to some extent already.

The second quango is a regional training centre for vocational and adult education (ROC). In a short period of time almost all schools for vocational and adult education have merged into 46 ROCs. Little attention has been paid so far to this major change in the educational policy field. By forming a ROC, the schools are given more autonomy to execute their public task; to prepare adults for society and the labour market. All schools and ROCs have to send annual reports and annual accounts to the parent department, to account for the way in which they spent their budget. Information on ROC performance is therefore expected to be present. The selected ROC - which will remain anonymous - was established in 1996 through a merger of five formerly independent schools (the quango's predecessors). Below a more detailed description is given of the cases and their history.

Methods and Procedures

Case study research is defined as the study of contemporary phenomena in their natural appearance and environment over a certain period of time (Yin, 1994:13; Swanborn, 1996:22). Here, to identify the effects of quangocratization the efficiency and effectiveness of policy implementation are studied during a number of years before and after a quango was charged with the implementation. Moreover, it will be verified if there is a performance paradox because, if present, it can exert a distorting influence on the assessment of efficiency and effectiveness. Although the sample of two case studies is much too small to draw valid general conclusions, they will be used to explore the hypotheses 2.1(P)-2.11P(cf. Yin, 1994:30).

Often, the uniqueness of cases impedes generalization of results beyond that case. To compensate for low external validity, three measures are taken. First, multiple sources of information and different methods are used (triangulation; Yin, 1994:91-93). In the cases below, data are obtained from two types of sources (documents and respondents) and by means of three different methods (content analysis, interviews, statements; see also table 5.1). Triangulation of data sources and research methods increases the amount of information, and enables researchers to check the consistency of findings (Yin, 1994:32-37; Swanborn, 1996:104-105).

Documents such as annual reports, accounts and available evaluation reports of several years are analysed. Interviews were held with informants within and outside the organization. The outside informants will be referred to as experts. There are two types of experts: from the parent department, in this case the Ministry of Education, and accountability experts. Results from these interviews have been anonymized. Only when all informants have given the same answers are responses used for the analysis.

Informants from the selected quangos have been asked to respond to a short list of statements as well. Some conditions cannot be measured directly from documents or asked in interviews. To measure these conditions, statements were developed. Informants were asked to indicate to which degree they believe the statement to be true for their organization. Again, answers are used only if all informants gave the same answer.

A second way to increase the validity of results is enlarging the number of observations through, for example, increasing the number of variables or dividing cases into sub-units (King, Keohane & Verba, 1994:208; Swanborn, 1996:95-108). In both case studies below, the number of observations ranges from a few years before to a few years after the establishment of the quango.

Sub-units of organizations can be analyzed separately. For example, IB-Groep consists of a number of divisions with different tasks, while the ROC provides different types of education. Sub-units were indeed analyzed, but the results are not reported here (see the separate case study reports).

Third, the selection of cases is important. If possible, multiple case designs - also known as comparative designs - are preferred to single case designs (Yin, 1994:45-50). Cases can be chosen because they differ with respect to the values of the independent variables, and thus represent contrasting conditions, or because they are replications of earlier case studies (Swanborn, 1996:55-66). In the present study, cases are selected that do not belong to the same cluster, this to ensure that policy implementation takes place under different conditions.

Although case studies are usually perceived as qualitative research, the use of quantitative statistical methods is not precluded, neither in the analysis (Yin, 1994:ch. 5) nor in the presentation of results (Miles & Huberman, 1994; King *et al.*, 1994). Most of the data obtained on the cases in this study are quantitative, displayed in tables or graphs. For each case, a log was kept with a detailed description of the data sources (informants and documents) and procedural steps or decisions taken during the gathering and processing of information (not included here; see the separate case study reports).

Table 5.1 Hypotheses, operationalizations, and methods used in the case studies

No.	*Hypothesis* and operationalization	Category in case report[1]	Method of analysis[2]
2.1(P)	*Ownership production rights* - right to retain surpluses - financial arrangements - fire/hire quangocrats	R	D, Q
2.2(P)	*Competition* - market position - member of cluster - specific investments - commercial activities	O	D, Q
2.3(P)	*Corporatism* - composition board	O	D
2.4(P)	*Accountability requirments* - amount of demands	A	D
2.5(P)	*Size* - number of personnel - budget - size of policy sector	O	D
2.6(P)	*Closeness to politicians* - origin of quango - number of contacts - legal position quangocrats	 O P R	 D Q, S D, Q
2.7(P)	*Risk perception* - willingness to take responsibility - use of sanctions in quango - initiative to changs	P	Q, S
2.8P	*Diversity Pis* - range of indicators - variation over time - comparability over time	A	D, Q, S
2.9P	*Clear policy objectives* - mission of quango - policy objectives	A	D
2.10P	*Emphasis on efficiency, PIs* - emphasis on efficiency - emphasis on Pis	P	Q, S
2.11P	*Supervision* - presence of a regulator	A	D, Q

[1] Categories: A= accountability requirements, P = perceptions, R = production rights, O = organisational characteristics

[2] Methods: D = analysis of documents, Q = interview, S = statements

Case Study 1: Informatie Beheer Groep (IB-Groep)

IB-Groep was established in 1994.[6] This former departmental division is charged with the implementation of several educational policies. The case study was done in 1998,[7] and compares the performance four years before and four years after establishment.

First I will give a case description along the lines of the categories that were discerned before. Next, the performance of IB-Groep is evaluated over time (1990-1997) to ascertain the consequences of quangocratization. Finally, evidence pertaining to the presence and workings of a performance paradox will be discussed. In the last section of this chapter the results of the case study will be confronted with the theoretical expectations.

Case Description

Origin The establishment of IB-Groep as a quango in 1994 was the end-result of a process of increasing autonomy of the organization. This process started with the movement of three divisions of the Ministry of Education from The Hague to Groningen between 1969 and 1985. These divisions were charged with the implementation of a number of educational policies, among which the payment of student grants. Although operating at a physical distance, the divisions were still part of the Ministry, and the management of, for example, finances and personnel remained the prerogative of the ministry (Kuiper, Van Vliet, Boxum, Schreuder, De Ridder & Scheltema, 1992).

In 1986, a new law on student grants came into force. The implementation of this law by the division in Groningen created many problems - structural financial deficits and much negative publicity - due to the complicated and sometimes incomplete legislation (Noordegraaf & Kickert, 1993).[8] These problems were an important reason for the Department to initiate a structural re-organization in 1988, in which the three divisions were integrated into one organization: the Information Bank (in Dutch: *Informatiseringsbank*). The autonomy of the Information Bank was enhanced by the incorporation of some managerial divisions of the central Ministry, such as personnel and finances (Ter Bogt, 1997).

The Information Bank was an autonomous part of the Ministry of Education, located at a distance from the parent department, and with relative freedom in managerial matters. It was agreed that the Information Bank would be responsible for the implementation of policies, while the Ministry remained responsible for the development of new policies or adjustments of existing legislation. Negotiations would lead to annual management contracts stating the tasks, performance and budget of the Information Bank. New policies developed by the Ministry would be examined ex ante by the Information Bank on the feasibility of their implementation. Despite the semi-autonomous position of the Information Bank, the Minister of Education remained formally responsible for all operational activities. In 1991, it became clear that the Information Bank wanted more autonomy and preparations were made to turn it into a quango.

In January 1994, the Information Bank was hived off and transformed into a quango under a new name: Group for Information Management (in Dutch: *Informatie Beheer Groep*, henceforth IB-Groep).[9] IB-Groep has a legal personality based on public law, and its statutes are laid down in a law (*Wet Verzelfstandiging Informatiseringsbank*, 1993). Contrary to the (radical) re-organization in 1988, the establishment of the quango was an incremental process consented by both parties involved (i.e. the Ministry and IB-Groep). It meant legal ratification of the semi-autonomous position of the former Information Bank, but no significant change of tasks. However, ministerial responsibility no longer included all operational activities and became restricted to policy development and supervising IB-Groep. Interesting enough, informants of IB-Groep *and* the parent department acknowledge that the change into a quango had more impact on the parent department than on IB-Groep, the latter seemed better prepared for the change. The Ministry of Education had difficulties adjusting to the limitation of their influence. At first, this led to an increased need for information, contrary to the intentions lying behind the establishment of the quango. This urge has receded, though, and nowadays the relationship between IB-Groep and the ministry is characterized by both parties as good, intensive and professional, although some tension has remained, especially about the desire of IB-groep to increase its activities for other principals (see also below).

Different factors contributed to the choice for a quango.[10] First, the hiving off of departmental divisions fitted the trend of the 1980s of emphasizing public sector efficiency and reducing the size of central government (so-called Great Efficiency Operations). Second and perhaps more important, the problems with the implementation of the 1986 law on student loans became a political threat to the Minister of Education, who was held responsible (Ter Bogt, 1997). This is reflected in the statutes where limiting ministerial responsibility is mentioned as the primary aim of the establishment of the quango. Third, it was expected that an autonomous organization would be able to operate more efficiently, as is demonstrated by the following quote from the statutes:

> Establishment of the quango is expected to increase the efficiency and decisive-ness of policy implementation and is meant to ensure impartial and high quality implementation of highly regulated decisions. (Source: Rapportage Doorlichting Zelfstandige Bestuursorganen, 1997, part II:75 [my translation, SvT])

The transformation of a departmental division into a quango was expected to relieve the organization of the strict rules of the Budget and Accounts Act. IB-Groep does indeed use a different accounting system (accrual accounting) than the Information Bank did (cash accounting). Below, we will see that this slightly hinders the evaluation of performance over time.

Tasks Most people only associate IB-Groep with the payment of student grants, because of all the publicity this task has generated. However, IB-Groep has other tasks as well, such as: (i) paying indemnifications for the study costs of children of parents with low incomes; (ii) collection of tuition fees; (iii) registration and allocation of (prospective) students in higher education; (iv) recognition and evaluation of foreign certificates; (v) registra-tion of education programmes in higher education; and (vi) logistic coordi-nation of state examinations in secondary education. All policies are devel-oped at the parent department. In total, the statutes list over forty policies (based on seven laws) that IB-Groep has to implement. The payment of benefits to unemployed or disabled teachers used to be a responsibility as well, but that task - and the according division - was hived off into another quango, called USZO, in January 1996.[11]

Policy objectives The statutes do not explicitly mention a goal of IB-Groep other than the (efficient and effective) implementation of the policies men-tioned. IB-Groep has re-formulated this goal as: supplying high quality services to clients, who include students, pupils, parents, teachers, the parent department, schools, polytechnics and universities (cf. the mission statement in the annual report of 1997). Cost-efficiency is very important but, accord-ing to informants from IB-Groep and the parent department, not as important as improvement of the quality of services.[12] Inefficiencies are therefore accepted, provided that quality has improved significantly. I shall return to this issue during the discussion on the performance of IB-Groep.

Market position IB-Groep is a monopolist quango, i.e. it is not part of a cluster of quangos,[13] nor does it face any competition with regard to the policies it has to implement. There is no organization that could take over IB-Groep's job at short notice because the necessary expertise and equipment (including software) are too specialized and expensive to be replaced. A transfer of existing tasks would therefore not be profitable to the parent department, if only because it would require a change of law.

With regard to *new* tasks the situation is different, however. The parent department is free to charge any organization with new tasks and there are, in fact, some organizations capable of executing tasks comparable to those of IB-Groep. The large scale processing of administrative information, for example, could be done by the Social Security Bank, the privatized general pension fund for civil servants, the Tax Bureau, insurance companies, and the contract agency of the Ministry of Education charged with all financial transactions with schools. Informants of the parent department state, however, that the department is satisfied with the performance of IB-Groep. This is evident from, for example, the fact that several new tasks have been given to IB-Groep. Moreover, the parent department has an interest in keeping IB-Groep busy with policy-related tasks because this ensures IB-Groep's dedication to the parent department.

IB-Groep is allowed to undertake 'commercial' activities for other principals, but only when the minister has approved of those activities.[14] Approval is given if the activities meet four conditions listed in the statutes: (i) they are strongly related to the official tasks; (ii) they require the use of the same production means; (iii) only cost-effective prices are charged and; (iv) they do not lead to unfair competition against private providers of similar services. Commercial activities are sensitive to competition because IB-Groep has to compete with other organizations for new tasks. So far, IB-Groep has concentrated mainly on the educational policy sector when looking for new activities.

Commercial activities are a subject of dispute between the quango and the parent department, and the primary source of tension in an - as described by informants from IB-Groep and the parent department - otherwise good relationship. The parent department argues that it is not in the department's interest for IB-Groep to spend time on the acquisition and execution of activities for other principals. Moreover, the Cohen Committee recently cautioned against commercial activities by public organizations, because these organizations would have advantages over private ones, such as their monopoly and publicly financed starting capital, which would lead to unfair competition (Commissie Cohen, 1997). IB-Groep, however, wants to expand. Here lies a fundamental difference of opinion. By increasing the number of tasks, IB-Groep can ensure its survival in case the amount of policy-related tasks decreases. The parent department, however, generally wants public organizations to be as small as possible, to minimize budgets. According to the ministry, if the number of tasks reduce, the organization should decrease in size as well. Recently, a new guideline was published on market activities for public organizations (*Aanwijzingen*, 1998), which limit the expansion of IB-Groep into the private market.[15] Effects of this new guideline and the outcome of the discussion between the quango and the parent department cannot be determined yet.

Legal position of employees All employees of IB-Groep are civil servants. Within the existing legal framework, IB-Groep has the right to formulate its own policies on personnel matters, but the regulation of salaries is subject to the same rules as the ones that apply to civil servants at the parent department.

In 1994, IB-Groep 'took over' all equipment and employees of the former Information Bank, including the employees of the regional bureaus. For the large-scale production and registration of information, extensive use is made of specialized software and large numbers of temporary staff charged with the electronic input of data (cf. Ter Bogt, 1997).

Organizational structure and composition of board With regard to the organizational structure, the statutes only prescribe a Board of Supervisors consisting of five independent experts appointed by the minister,[16] and a chief executive board (CEB) of three directors charged with all daily operations. The Board of Supervisors is the highest ranking body, and chief executives account to it for all activities. Most financial and personnel matters have to be approved by the Board before they can be implemented. See below for more information on the size of IB-Groep (e.g. number of personnel, and its budget).

In 1995, IB-Groep re-organized. The current organizational structure is shown in figure 5.1. The CEB consists of three people: the CEO, an executive charged with production affairs, and an executive charged with finances. They receive clerical support from two units: Concern Control charged with finances, and Strategic and Managerial Support. Policy implementation is concentrated in three production divisions and one supportive division: Educational Services, Student Loans and Grants; Tuition Fees and Indemnifications and Facilities. The 16 regional bureaus of IB-Groep are incorporated into the Facilities division.

In 1997, a new re-organization was initiated, which has to be completed before 2001. It encompasses a radical change from a product-oriented organization to a process-oriented organization, which is why it is preferably referred to as a business process redesign. Self-regulating teams will become responsible for a number of clients instead of a particular line of products. As responsibilities will be decentralized to the teams, a large number of managers will lose their job. In total, 230 full-time equivalents will be eliminated (almost 14% of total personnel). The re-design is meant to improve the client orientation and the quality of the services of IB-Groep. The parent department has shown its support for the redesign by lending money.

Financial arrangements An important distinction has to be made between programme and running costs. Programme costs refer to the sum of grants and benefits paid by IB-Groep to groups of clients (students, parents, teachers). Programme revenues consist of collected fees, debts and interest on debts. Running costs refer to operational costs such as salaries, investments in and maintenance of computers and software, office space, *et cetera*. Programme costs and revenues are borne fully by the parent department. Running costs were borne by the parent department until 1994 and are now borne by IB-Groep. As a quango, IB-Groep has the right to retain surpluses of running costs, but it is also responsible for deficits.

The financing of IB-Groep is negotiated annually, and based on expected output and costs agreed upon in the management contract. Since 1994 there has been some effort to calculate cost-prices, but these are not published, nor used as a management tool (cf. also Ter Bogt, 1997). The parent department relies on IB-Groep to provide the information necessary to determine programme costs and revenues from IB-Groep.

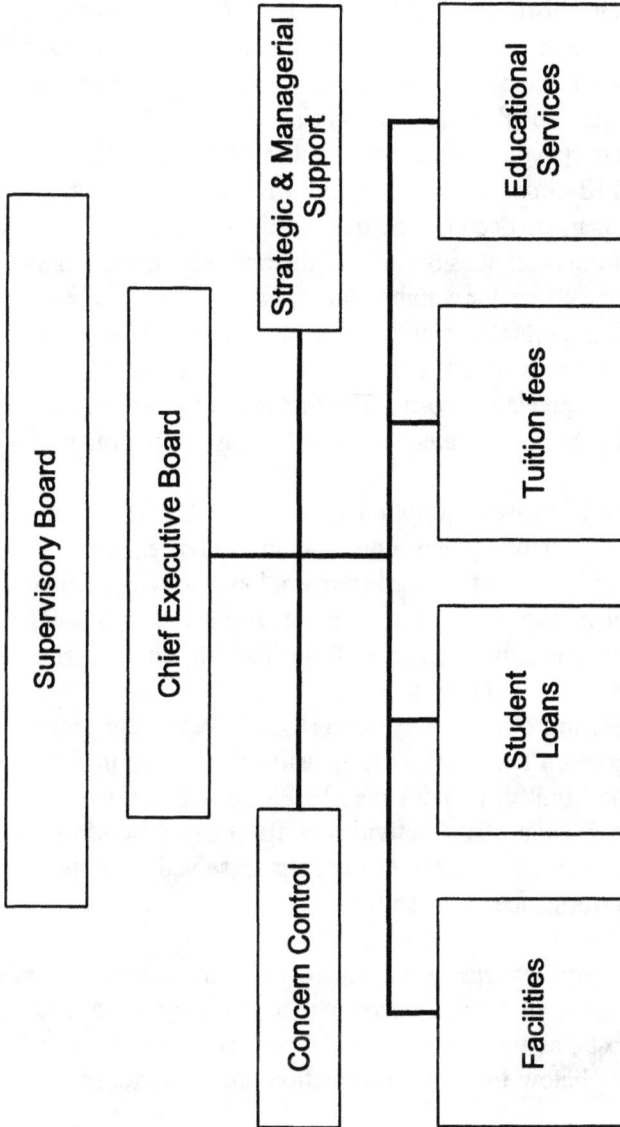

Figure 5.1 Organizational structure of IB-Groep (*Source*: Jaarverslag Informatie Beheer Groep, 1997)

The required amount and type of information supplied by IB-Groep is laid down in the annual management contracts. Programme costs, programme revenues, and running costs are all accounted for in the State Budget of the Ministry of Education. So, eventually the Minister can be held responsible in parliament for IB-Groep's running costs also.

Two remarks remain to be made about the financial status of IB-Groep. First, although IB-Groep is a legal entity, it is not allowed to borrow money in the capital market. Second, the quango does not have to pay VAT (in Dutch: *BTW*) for its activities because of their public nature. It only has to do so when charging others for commercial activities.

Finally, it is important to note that one of the explicitly stated goals of IB-Groep is to have only small nett surpluses (i.e. after deduction of capital reserves and/or depreciation costs). The fact that the quango is not after high 'profits' needs to be kept in mind when evaluating its performance.

Property rights The case description shows that when IB-Groep was hived off into a quango, it was given more autonomy. For example, it is free to decide on expenditures with regard to operational activities (running costs). Furthermore, it now has the right to retain surpluses. It is autonomous in hiring new employees, but limited in firing them by the regular constraints set by the legal position of civil servants.

IB-Groep has full discretionary authority with respect to production matters and equipment. The CEB is responsible for errors in the production process, but the Minister remains responsible for legislative errors and failures in the supervision of the activities of IB-Groep. Therefore, ministerial responsibility is limited. Still, the Minister has reserved the right to intervene in case of ill performance (see also below).

Accountability requirements With regard to accountability, the statutes of IB-Groep prescribe an audited account of programme costs and revenues, and running costs, as well as an annual report of its activities to the parent department. See below for more information on the performance indicators IB-Groep uses.

The Minister of Education has reserved the right to intervene in IB-Groep's affairs or give additional instructions in case of ill performance. Supervision is charged to the board of supervisors and the departmental accountant. Additional investigations and audits can be initiated if the Minister wants to.

To meet ministerial responsibility communication takes place between the quango and the parent department at regular intervals and at different levels (cf. Kickert *et al.*, 1998:124). Part of this communication is formalized, for example, between the Minister and the Board of Supervisors (two times a year), and between the CEB of IB-Groep and the departmental chief executives (four times a year). There are also many non-formalized operational meetings on the development and feasibility of new policies with which IB-Groep could be charged. In general, all communication between quangos and the Ministry of Education is co-ordinated through an especially established departmental division called RZO.

In case of ill performance, individual clients can file a complaint. This should not be confused with the right clients have to appeal against decisions on the payment of benefits or grants. Appeals concern the contents of decisions, whereas complaints concern the operative procedures of IB-Groep, for example, the way in which clients are treated at the regional offices. In 1998, IB-Groep published a Quality Charter that lists the rights of clients (see also below).

Perceptions As a former departmental unit, IB-Groep still has strong ties with the parent department. The frequent meetings and negotiations strengthen the bond, as does the fact that the Ministry of Education is the main principal of the quango (over 90% of all activities). Responses to the statements used to gather information show a relatively strong sense of loyalty to the parent department. Nevertheless, IB-Groep is searching for ways to expand its clientele, which fits with it quest for autonomy. IB-Groep cannot be characterized as an organization that is afraid to take risks or responsibilities. Not only was it actively involved in the process of becoming a quango, it also anticipated this change better than the parent department did (according to informants from IB-Groep and the parent department). Over time, IB-Groep has shown to be willing to take on more tasks and responsibilities, also on behalf of new principals.[17] There still exists, however, a strong association of the quango with the parent department, especially in the media, which hinders the acquisition of new tasks. Potential principals do not yet see IB-Groep as an organization that could fulfil tasks for them. Perhaps this explains why the quango pays so much attention to the improvement of the quality of customer service (or responsiveness to clients) and the development of performance indicators of the quality of services. By building up a good client-oriented reputation, IB-Groep hopes to attract new principals.[18]

The mission statement even explicitly mentions quality of services as a primary goal.

IB-Groep has an advanced system of performance assessment. Performance indicators (PIs) play an important role in the organization. There is a strong commitment to performance assessment, even of those elements of performance that seem difficult to quantify. The current PIs have been developed by the quango itself and have been in use for many years. At first sight, it seems there is a very large number of performance indicators listed in the management contracts. On closer look, it turns out that a comparable set of indicators has been developed for all individual tasks (see below for more discussion).

The focus of IB-Groep seems to be more on quality than on (cost)-efficiency. This is evident in, for example, the recently published Quality Charter (*Kwaliteitshandvest*, 1998). Informants from IB-Groep state that cost-inefficiencies would not close down the quango. Informants from the parent department share this opinion; quality of services is at least as important as cost-efficiency.

Efficiency and Performance from 1990 to 1997

Total performance As mentioned before, IB-Groep is charged with the implementation of a large number of policies. This makes it an important quango in the educational policy sector. Between 1990 and 1997, approximately 17.8% of the budget of the parent department was spent by IB-Groep. Table 5.2 shows some indicators of its total performance, in terms of programme costs (table A) and running costs (table B).

Table 5.2A shows that programme costs were relatively stable until 1992, but have decreased ever since. The strong decrease in 1996 is mainly caused by the hiving off of the division charged with paying teacher benefits. The introduction of a conditional grant in mid 1995, which made students' right to a grant or loan dependent on their achievements, led to a decrease in programme costs.

Programme revenues rose strongly in 1990 and 1994, due to improvements in collection procedures and special collection projects that made early payment of debts more profitable to students.

Running costs were highest in the period before 1994 (table 5.2B). Anticipating the change into a quango, many investments were made in computers, software, telecommunications, the training of personnel, hiring experts and moving into a new office. Moreover, a number of re-organizations took place, such as the decentralization of budget management in 1991, the centralization of purchasing agents in 1992, and the merger of some divisions in 1993. Although in 1994 there was a decrease in running costs, IB-Groep still had a small deficit. Since 1995, running costs have been relatively stable, resulting in small (nett) surpluses.

The change to a new accounting system in 1994 makes it difficult to compare certain running costs over time, such as the cost of salaries. Between 1990 and 1997, the number of employees increased by 63.8% (see table 5.2A). However, the extensive use of temporary staff and hired external (computer) experts hinders the assessment of costs, because as the categories of personnel do not always fall into the same category of costs. Therefore, caution is warranted when interpreting the numbers in table 5.2B. It is apparent, however, that the percentage of running costs of salaries has increased, from 39% in 1990 to 51.4% in 1997.[19] Despite several attempts, the percentage absenteeism among employees is still higher than the national average of civil servants (CBS, 1998g).

Because more running costs come from salaries, the share of other running costs has decreased. Table 5.2B suggests, however, that some running costs have increased. Due to re-categorizations of running costs, simple conclusions cannot be drawn here. Take, for example, the costs of automatization: after 1994, these include the hiring of experts, which formerly fell under the heading of salaries. Communication costs seem to have decreased but part of these, namely the costs of the regional bureaus, are now included in managerial overhead, which has increased as a result. Depreciation costs first appeared in 1994, when the new accounting system was introduced, and have been rising ever since.

Table 5.2A shows that IB-Groep is increasingly undertaking commercial activities for other principals (in 1997 almost 15% of the company's turnover).[20] The Ministry of Education remains the main principal, though. Typically, commercial activities take place within the educational field, probably because of the legal limitations imposed on these activities. The activities resulting from the take-over of the company charged with the distribution of the public transport passes for students in higher education form also part of these activities.

Table 5.2A Costs, revenues, personnel and mail IB-Groep, 1990-1997. All costs and revenues are in NLG million, indexed for 1990

	1990	1991	1992	1993	1994	1995	1996	1997
Programme costs	5328.9	5397.4	5572.2	4789.5	4761.8	4485.8	3661.5[a]	3709.8
Programme revenues	1472.0	1130.8	1132.6	1282.3	1437.6	1136.8	1083.2	1281.2
Commercial activities	n.a.	n.a.	1.9	1.4	9.6[b]	17.2	23.6	23.9
Running costs	170.3	177.2	170.8	166.1	155.5	161.2	158.8	160.3
(% of total costs)	(3.1)	(3.2)	(3.0)	(3.4)	(3.2)	(3.5)	(4.2)	(4.1)
Surplus running costs	-10.3	-0.4	-12.5	-6.4	-1.3	0.2	0.3	0.3
Personnel in fte[c]	1072.4	1126.0	1154.0	1223.0	1415.0[b,d]	1492.0	1396.0[a]	1679.0
(% absenteeism)	-	(7.4)	(6.4)	(6.9)	(6.3)	(6.6)	(6.9)	(6.4)
(average % absent.)[e]	-	-	(6.7)	(6.7)	(6.0)	(6.2)	(5.9)	-
Incoming calls[f]	-	-	-	-	3043.9	3368.0	4359.0	4260.6
(% response)	-	-	-	-	(33.8)	(47.0)	(51.9)	(54.4)
Incoming mail[f]	-	4.9	4.6	4.7	4.5	3.6	2.9[a]	3.4
Outgoing mail[f]	-	15.0[g]	15.0	14.7	13.5	10.1	13.7	13.4

- No (reliable) information available
n.a. Not applicable
[a] Decrease caused by hiving off of a division
[b] Increase due to take-over OV-Studentenkaart BV
[c] Full-time equivalents, permanent and temporary tenure
[d] Increase caused by take-over employees of regional bureaus
[e] Average in national government
[f] x 1000
[g] Estimate by IB-Groep

Sources: Jaarverslag Informatiseringsbank (1990-1993); Jaarverslag Informatie Beheer Groep (1994-1997)

Table 5.2B Running costs of IB-Groep, 1990-1997. All amounts are in NLG million, indexed for 1990

	1990	1991	1992	1993	1994	1995	1996	1997
Running costs total	170.3	177.2	170.8	166.1	155.5	161.2	158.8	160.3
Salaries[a]	66.5	56.1	59.7	58.9	74.8[b]	81.8	73.9[c]	82.4
(% of running costs)	(39.0)	(31.7)	(35.0)	(35.4)	(48.1)	(50.7)	(46.5)	(51.4)
Material costs total	103.8	121.1	111.0	107.2	80.7	79.5	84.9	77.9
- Automatization[d]	64.6	51.7	32.1	20.1	16.3	33.1[e]	36.7[e]	49.2[e]
- Managerial overhead[f]	19.3	13.6	15.1	27.0	18.1	22.7	24.5	31.0
- Communications[g]	19.9	23.0	26.0	30.8	26.0	14.0[h]	12.5[h]	12.7[h]
- Depreciation	n.a.	n.a.	n.a.	n.a.	8.8	9/7	11.1	10.5

n.a. Not applicable

[a] Includes salaries and other benefits to all employees
[b] Increase caused by increase in number of employees
[c] Decrease caused by hiving of of a division
[d] Includes purchase of computerized services
[e] Includes costs of hiring external computer experts (formerly included in salaries)
[f] Such as costs of office space
[g] Includes telecommunications (phone and mail) of regional offices
[h] Excludes regional offices

Source: Jaarverslag Informatiseringsbank (1990-1993); *Jaarverslag Informatie Beheer Groep* (1994-1997)

Annually, some 4 million calls are made to IB-Groep's central office and regional bureaus, mostly by students. The regional bureaus receive over 300,000 visitors per year. Most clients, however, try to contact IB-Groep by telephone. Despite several investments, the call centre still cannot answer nearly 45% of all calls (cf. table 5.2A).[21] Customer surveys between 1993 and 1997 confirm that IB-Groep is difficult to reach by phone. Customers also complain about the processing time of application forms, which are distributed by the regional bureaus or the central office in Groningen (for the amount of mail, see table 5.2A).

From 1994 on, IB-Groep has undertaken a number of activities to improve its reponsiveness. New indicators have been developed of the quality of service. A Quality Charter was published, which specifies the right of clients to good customer service, expressed in indicators like: the number of days or weeks it takes IB-Groep to respond to applications, letters and appeals; the waiting time to being served in the regional offices or for the telephone to be answered; clarity of information; complaints procedures, *et cetera*. A study of the Netherlands Court of Audit shows that IB-Groep has invested more in customer service than other public organizations have (Algemene Reken-kamer, 1997:19).

Performance of separate divisions IB-Groep consists of three policy imple-menting divisions (cf. figure 5.1). The division Student Loans and Grants is the largest of those three. Approximately 38% of IB-Groep's personnel work in this division. The division accounts for almost 70% of total programme revenues and almost 40% of the total running costs. The policies on student loans and grants have been changed over 70 times since 1986, which has complicated implementation enormously.

The division Tuition Fees and Indemnifications collects tuition fees and grants low-income parents of schoolchildren indemnification of schooling costs. It is a small division, and spends approximately 10% of the programme costs while it collects almost half of the programme revenues. Limitation of the right to a student grant has led to an increase in the output of this divi-sion.

The division Educational Services is increasingly carrying out tasks for other principals than the parent department. It mainly develops and maintains large databases, registering and providing information to other divisions. For further details on the performance of the separate divisions, see the case study report (Van Thiel, 1999a).

Changes in efficiency and effectiveness between 1990 and 1997 Figure 5.2 offers a picture of the development of the total output of IB-Groep before and after quango establishment. Total output is the sum of the number of awarded grants, loans, indemnifications, collected tuition fees, exam candidates, registered and prospective students, and granted teacher benefits.[22] Total output is contrasted with running costs and the revenues from commercial activities, which together equal the company's turnover.

Figure 5.2 shows a decrease in output, which is probably the main cause of the decrease in programme costs displayed earlier, in table 5.2A. Because running costs have not decreased as well after 1994 (cf. table 5.2B), it has to be concluded that the costs of policy implementation have increased. Cost-efficiency has therefore not improved since the establishment of the quango (cf. Ter Bogt, 1997; Van Berkum & Van Dijkem, 1997). However, three issues make it difficult to draw simple, straightforward conclusions.

First, programme costs are only one measure of output and, since they are determined by policy makers, not necessarily the best indicator of performance of the quango. For example, a decrease in the size of the average grant or benefit could also lead to a decrease in programme costs. Such effects, resulting from policy changes, should be taken into account as well.

Second, the services as delivered by IB-Groep have become more complex because of new policies and changes in existing ones,[23] and of a higher quality. The costs made to enable implementation of changes are booked only once, but not separately from other programme or running costs. The same holds for the costs of feasibility tests and the acquisition of new tasks and/or commercial activities. It is very difficult to single out all these costs. Therefore, they are included in the calculation of cost-efficiency. For example, the costs of awarding one student grant has increased by almost 10% since 1994, which well exceeds inflation.[24]

Despite the decrease in cost-efficiency, surpluses were obtained (and retained) after the establishment as a quango, except in 1994. IB-Groep has explicitly stated that it is not after high nett surpluses, because this would not agree with the public nature of the organization and its tasks. Indeed, after deduction of capital reserves and depreciation costs, surpluses are small. One cannot help but notice, however, that it is also not in the interest of the quango to obtain high surpluses, as this would undermine negotiations on the budget for running costs. High surpluses would show that services could be supplied much cheaper, which would lead to the parent department deciding to cut budgets.

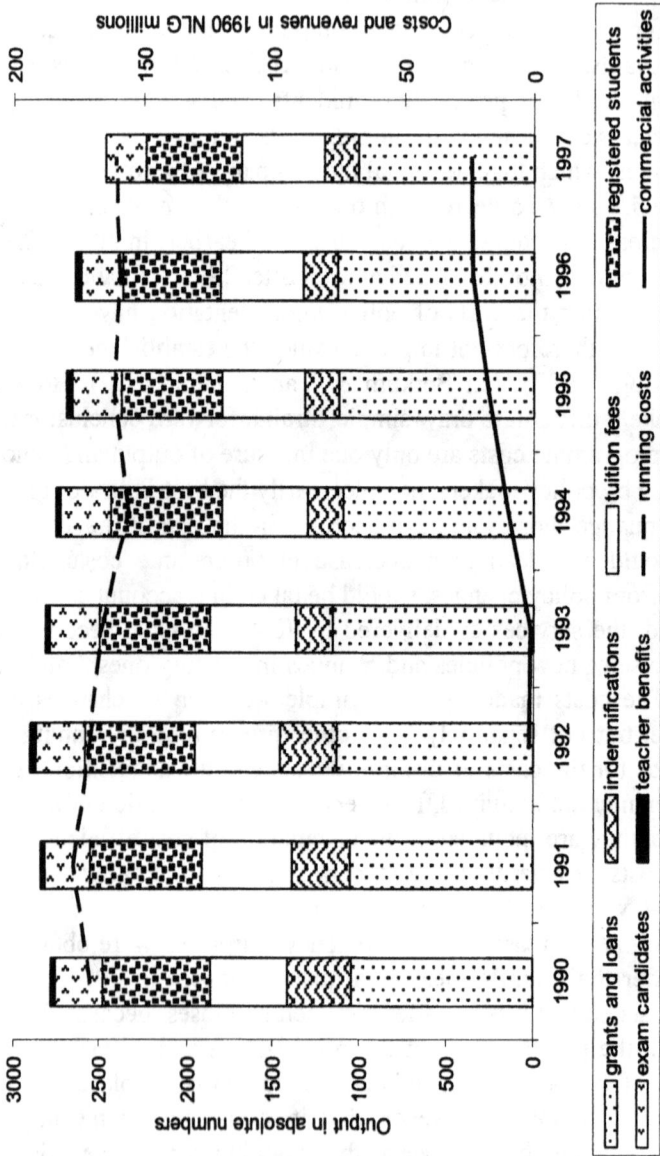

Figure 5.2 Performance of IB-Groep 1990-1997 in output, running costs and commercial activities (*Sources*: annual reports)

The fact that since the establishment as a quango, IB-Groep's deficits have become smaller or have even turned into surpluses could be the result of better management, which was one of the goals of the hiving off. It is now of more interest to the quango to avoid deficits, because the organization has to pay for itself. It could also be that the new accounting system, introduced in 1994, does indeed provide better insight into expenditures and projecting budgets, as intended. Informants from IB-Groep claim the latter, but there is no way of telling from just the annual reports and annual accounts.

IB-Groep has countered the decrease of policy related activities - for example the hiving off of one of its divisions in 1996 - by increasing its commercial activities (mainly in the educational sector). Figure 5.2 shows that, in particular between 1994 and 1996, revenues from such activities have increased. However, given the limited information in annual accounts and annual reports on running costs per division, it is not possible to ascertain the profitability of these activities. There will be much discussion on this topic between the quango and the parent department, especially considering the new guideline on market activities of public organizations. A further restriction of the possibilities of IB-Groep to undertake commercial activities seems likely.

Whereas cost-efficiency may have decreased, the quality of services has increased. Since 1994, IB-Groep has made large investments in the quality of customer service (e.g. by opening a call centre). There is some evidence to support the conclusion that these investments have indeed led to an improvement of the quality of services, such as the report by the Netherlands Court of Audit (Algemene Rekenkamer, 1997). Figure 5.3 summarizes the development of some performance indicators of the quality of services.

Figure 5.3 shows the improvement in the percentage of telephone calls answered and a slight improvement in the image of the division Student Grants and Loans (on a scale from 1-10). The number of complaints about IB-Groep lodged at the National Ombudsman[25] has decreased strongly, but more important most complaints are nowadays solved more swiftly through mediation. Annual reports show a reduction in the processing time of applications for student grants and a decrease in the percentage of registration errors (not shown in figure 5.3). Only the number of appeals to decisions about student grants has not declined significantly, but this can be due to policy changes.

Conclusions In sum, after the establishment of IB-Groep as a quango, policy implementation has become more expensive, but the responsiveness to clients has improved. Small surpluses have been obtained and the number of commercial activities has increased. Both informants from IB-Groep and the parent department agree that (small) efficiency losses are outweighed by improvements of the quality of customer service. In 1999 an official departmental evaluation - prescribed by the statutes - was undertaken by IB-Groep, the parent department and a consultancy firm. Regrettably, this was too late for the results to be incorporated in this case study. In the interviews, informants from IB-Groep and the parent department stated that they would consider the establishment of the quango successful, if the official evaluation would lead to the same conclusions as this case study.[26]

Performance Paradox

All conclusions about IB-Groep's performance are based on the information provided by the quango itself, mainly annual reports and annual accounts. However, as was argued in chapter 3, reports of performance may suffer from a performance paradox (Meyer & Gupta, 1994), i.e. performance indicators (PIs) loose their discriminatory value, or only concern certain aspects of performance (see chapter 3 for more explanation).

A performance paradox does not necessarily mean that performance is worse than reported, although sometimes information can be misrepresented deliberately. However, it is important to try to ascertain whether a performance paradox is present, because it poses a threat to the validity of conclusions about performance. Therefore, this subsection deals with the account given by IB-Groep of its performance. Information was obtained by analyzing existing documents and from interviews with informants from IB-Groep, the parent department and an expert in accountancy (cf. table 5.1). No evidence was found that IB-Groep (deliberately) gives an under- or overestimation of its performance, but there are some circumstances that could induce a performance paradox and warrant further discussion.

The statutes prescribe an audited account of programme costs, programme revenues, and running costs, and an annual report of activities to the parent department. Besides these documents, IB-Groep regularly compiles reports on its performance for internal use, which are discussed with the parent department.

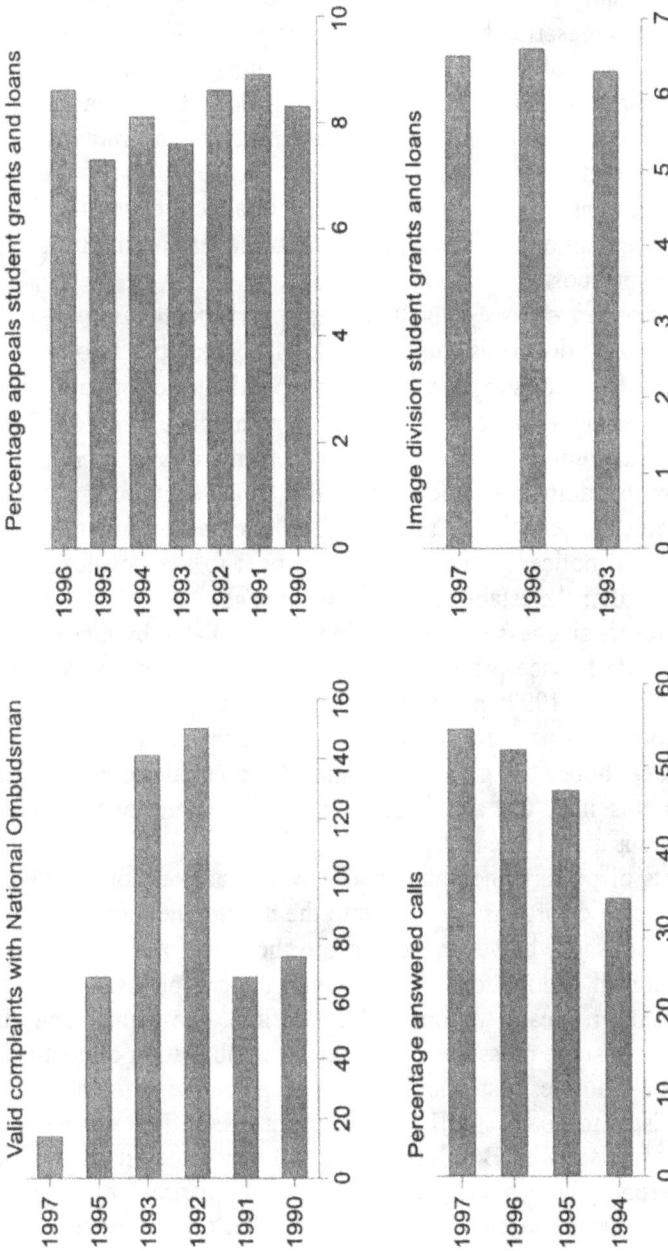

Figure 5.3 Quality indicators 1990-1997. Based on annual reports. *Additional sources:* **Imago onderzoek Studiefinanciering (1993-1997); Jaarverslag NOM (1990-1997)**

Moreover, annually negotiated management contracts and so-called information protocols prescribe budget and performance requirements in terms of PIs. The previous subsection presented indicators used in these documents, such as the number of products (e.g. grants, indemnifications), the costs associated with production (both programme costs and running costs) and the quality of performance (e.g. the number of appeals, and the processing time of applications). Also, some new indicators were constructed, such as the percentage commercial activities of total turnover and the percentage running costs of total costs.

The major problem of assessing IB-Groep's performance is that it is a monopolist. Not only does this imply a lack of comparable information,[27] more importantly the only supplier of information about performance is the quango itself. This might create opportunities to manipulate or hide information damaging to the reputation of the quango or its interests. It is *not* implied here that IB-Groep manipulates information. But, when examining the report on performance, it is interesting to see how IB-Groep has used its discretionary authority. Most noticeable is the attention paid to the development of quality indicators after the establishment of the quango.

A focus on responsiveness fits the mission as formulated by the organization: to become *the* service providing organization in the educational field (source: annual report 1997, p.6 [my translation, SvT]). By stressing the quality of customer service and deploying a lot of means to improve that quality, IB-Groep hopes to gain name among potential new principals. Thought along this line, the ample attention paid to the development of quality indicators is quite logical.

Other aspects of performance have been given less attention. For example, since 1994 some effort has been put into the development of cost-prices. These are not published, however, neither are they used as a management tool, or in the annual negotiations. While, given the complexity and size of tasks, it is certainly not easy to construct cost-prices, one cannot deny that IB-Groep also faces some pressures that makes the publication of cost-prices unappealing. For example, cost-prices enable the parent department or other external supervisors to detect inefficiencies or potential efficiency gains the quango has not realised yet. Both effects can influence the annual negotiations on the terms of the management contract. In particular, the parent department might decide to cut budgets, arguing that efficiency can be improved. Moreover, cost-prices allow for a comparison with other organizations performing similar tasks. As yet, there is no immediate replacement for (the monopolist) IB-Groep, but new technologies could lead to serious competition in the near future and perhaps loss of tasks by IB-Groep. The calculation of cost-prices could therefore have undesired consequences from IB-Groep's point of view. By shifting the focus to the quality of service, IB-Groep keeps the parent department satisfied; it shares the interest in customer service, and at the same time builds a good reputation for itself that might attract new principals.

The monopolist position of IB-Groep has a second major implication for performance assessment. Not only does the parent department depend almost entirely on the quango for information, it has also little power to force the quango to comply with rules and contracts because alternative organizations to perform the tasks in question are lacking. Ill performance can go unpunished (or perhaps even undetected) for a long time. The way in which quangocrats deal with non-compliance with PIs was mentioned as one of the causes of a performance paradox (cf. table 5.1). In the case study, questions were asked on how errors or failure to meet an indicator were dealt with.

Without questioning the integrity of the employees of IB-Groep, it has to be said that ill performance has little serious consequences. Failures and errors are discussed in a relatively open way, but sanctions are seldom imposed. Informants from IB-Groep and the parent department agree that errors or failures in policy implementation need to be handled with care. It is considered more important that people learn from errors, than their being punished for making errors. When detected, ill performance is discussed and analysed. However, it is not always easy to ascertain the cause of errors or failures, because changes in policies can lead to changes in the value of indicators as well. For example, when new legal restrictions are imposed on the supply of grants, the number of appeals made by clients will no doubt increase. This does not mean, however, that the performance of IB-Groep has deteriorated.

After establishing the causes of ill performance, measures are proposed to improve performance and, after some time, the effect of those measures is evaluated. This cycle of assessment can continue for a long time without performance actually improving.

Two more characteristics of the system of performance assessment are of importance here. First, there is a general belief in IB-Groep that *all* aspects of performance can be measured and that PIs are important instruments in the control of the organization and the production processes. That in itself creates a risk of measure fixation, i.e. performance is only aimed at maximizing the indicators and other aspects are neglected (Smith, 1995) - although the open, non-sanctioning culture counteracts this risk.

Second, IB-Groep uses an extensive system of performance assessment. Management contracts contain a great number of PIs. Indicators have been developed for each separate task and new tasks usually lead to new indicators. There is, however, a great deal of overlap between PIs. Box 5.1 shows that five main categories of (the same) indicators can be distinguished.

This set of indicators was developed by IB-groep in 1989 and subsequent years. Apart from a number of new quality indicators introduced after 1994, it has not changed much. It measures both quantitative and qualitative aspects of performance. Norms are often included, for example, budget information must be delivered within x days, and the percentage of appeals should be lower than y. According to an expert on accountability it is a well-developed system of performance assessment,[28] albeit that most information typically concerns client contacts (or: responsiveness) and not the efficiency of the supply of services or other internal processes (e.g. running costs per division, service or product). Information on those topics is often lacking, as is information on the profitability of commercial activities.

1.	**absolute numbers of input and output**
	e.g. the number of services that are supplied to clients and principas (grants, loans, indemnification, tuition fees, registration), the number of applications (cf. incoming mail), the number of decisions about applications (cf. outgoing mail) and the total amount of money to be paid or collected (programme costs and revenues);
2.	**accuracy (or legality) of decisions**
	e.g. the percentage of (successful) appeals against decisions, the number of complaints lodged at external supervisory bodies like the Ombudsman, and the percentage errors or incompleteness of information distributed to clients and principals;
3.	**timely supply of services**
	e.g. the processing time of applications, the time needed to respond to requests for information from clients and principals, and the time necessary to collect debts or fees;
4.	**customer service (or responsiveness)**
	e.g. the percentage of calls that is answered, client satisfaction (measured on a scale from 1 to 10), principal satisfaction, and the image of the organization (compared to other organizations);
5.	**financial soundness**
	e.g. auditors' approval of the annual account of divisions and IB-Groep.

Box 5.1 Performance indicators used by IB-Groep (based on annual reports and internal reports, 1990-1998)

Conclusions IB-Groep provides an extensive account of its performance. The quality of services is reported better than cost-efficiency, but besides that there is no evidence of an under- or overestimation of performance, either deliberately or unintended. The emphasis on quality aspects is consistent with the goal IB-Groep has set itself and approved by the parent department. However, more attention for cost-efficiency in the reports on performance could improve those reports. The fact that IB-Groep is a monopolist hinders comparison of performance with other organizations; there is no benchmark. More attention could be paid to IB-Groep's performance as compared to other organizations and quangos.

The results of this case study will be summarized and confronted with the theoretical expectations in the final section of this chapter. Now we turn to the second case study.

Case Study 2: The Regional Training Centre (ROC)

ROCs are schools for senior secondary and vocational education, which have come into existence through mergers of formerly independent schools. There are 46 ROCs in the Netherlands, one of which was selected for this study. The research was carried out in 1998, two years after the establishment of the selected ROC. In this section, the performance of the ROC in 1996 an 1997 is reported and compared to the average performance of all Dutch ROCs. The performance of the former schools up till 1996 was investigated (see the case study report for a more extensive description); the conclusions will be summarized in this section as well.

First, we start with a case description, following the categories that were discerned before. Next, the performance of the ROC is described and compared to other ROCs. Finally, evidence will be discussed pertaining the presence and workings of a performance paradox. The results of this case study will be confronted with the theoretical expectations in the final section of this chapter.

Case Description

Origin Autonomy for schools has been a major focus of almost all recent educational policies in the Netherlands (Ministerie van Onderwijs, Cultuur en Wetenschappen, 1998). In the field of adult and vocational education this has resulted in the establishment of Regional Training Centres (in Dutch:

Regionale OpleidingenCentra, henceforth ROCs).[29] ROCs resulted from large scale mergers of schools for adult education and senior secondary vocational education. Their autonomy is apparent from, among other things, the use of lump sum budgets and the relative freedom in the development of new curricula. The establishment of ROCs seems to be the end-result (for now) of the increased government interest in schools for adult and vocational education which first arose in the 1970s.

Government interest in senior secondary vocational education comes mainly from its important economic function; to deliver skilled workers for the labour market. Following the economic recession in the 1970s, a large number of mergers of schools for vocational education took place in the late 1980s, during the so-called 'sectorization' and innovation operation. Schools were re-organized to correspond with sectors of industry, such as electronics, architecture, trade, health services and social work, and economics and administration - this to improve the chances of students of graduating and finding a job (Boef-van der Meulen, Bronneman-Helmers, Eggink & Herweijer, 1995:120-121). Between 1988 and 1990, the number of schools was reduced from 1431 with an average of 325 students to 306 with an average of 1475 students. The introduction of a new budgeting system in 1993 was the first step towards more autonomy for vocational schools. This new system introduced lump sum budgets, replacing the former system of claiming expenses on the parent department. From then on, schools became responsible themselves for expenses, deficits and surpluses. The participation of vocational schools in the establishment of ROCs, as described below, further enhanced their autonomy.

Adult education dates back as far as the late 1800s (Van Zon, 1990:17-53). Government interference was absent, however, until until after World War II. The economic crisis of the 1970s increased government interest. While on the one hand the economic crisis induced retrenchments, also on education, it created new social problems as well. There was an increase in unemployment. Moreover, a large number of migrant labourers became permanent residents, and they had to assimilate (e.g. learn Dutch). Education could provide a solution for these problems. The government started to heavily subsidize schools for adult education, which were - by tradition - often privately founded. Following the rise in expenditures on adult education, the government began to develop policies on adult education. Because several departments were involved, it was decided that, to improve government co-ordination, adult education had to be organized in a more coherent way and eventually be integrated with vocational education for adults (Veld,

1994:10). Different law proposals were made and accepted by parliament during the 1980s. However, when these laws were implemented in the early 1990s, they were already dated because of new social-economic developments, such as a decrease in unemployment and a further increase in the number of refugees and immigrants. Therefore it was decided that all existing legislation on adult and vocational education would expire in 1996, when *the* law on vocational and adult education would be implemented (*Wet Educatie en Beroepsonderwijs* (WEB), 1995).

The WEB covers senior secondary vocational education for adults and apprentices, and three types of adult education: adult basic education; adult general secondary education; and non-formal adult education. It takes ROCs as the basic units of all policies and finances. In other words, schools were forced to merge. Schools began negotiating as early as 1992. Negotiations were completed in 1996, long before the prescribed date of January 1998 (cf. Boef-van der Meulen *et al.*, 1995: 129-134; for an overview, see BVE-Procescoördinatie, 1997).

Despite that schools had been anticipating the establishment of ROCs, informants from the selected organization do not perceive it as a gradual process but rather a radical change. This can perhaps be explained by the fact that the initiative to change has almost always lain with the government, i.e. the parent department. Schools are reluctant to change and would not themselves have come up with the idea of ROCs, even though these days they are no longer opposed to it.[30]

To conclude, one could say that, as a result of growing government interference, in the 1970s adult and vocational education were *hived into* the public sector. Schools became more and more dependent on government funding and the accompanying legislation for the execution of tasks that became more and more important to society.[31] The establishment of ROCs in the mid-1990s did not end the dependency of schools on government funding, but it gave the schools more autonomy. The establishment of ROCs can thus be considered a form of quangocratization.

Compared to the former schools, ROCs are expected to be better able to respond to changing societal demands, such as changes in the labour market, technological developments, the increasing number of immigrants, *et cetera*. Moreover, they offer students a wide(r) range of educational programmes and unlimited choice of combinations of courses and certificates.

There are now 46 licensed ROCs in the Netherlands, mergers of 89% of all formerly independent schools for vocational and adult education.[32] The ROC selected for this case study was established in 1996 - after two years of negotiation - through the merger of five schools: three schools for secondary vocational training, one school for basic- and adult education and a centre for non-formal adult education. For reasons of anonymity, it will be referred to as "the ROC".

The average number of students in ROCs is estimated at 12,000 (range from 2,500 to 38,000), which makes some schools even larger than the average polytechnic or university. The selected ROC is slightly larger than average and has approximately 14,500 students (see also below). ROCs are large employers and a major supplier of labour. Despite their size, there has been little attention for ROCs from politicians, academics and the media. This is partly due to a general lack of interest in particularly vocational education, but also to the fact that interest groups of schools, teachers and students have been scattered for a long time (Boef-van der Meulen *et al.*, 1995:153-156). It was not until 1996 - after the completion of the ROC formation - that all interest groups representing schools joined one Vocational and Adult Education Council called *BVE-raad* to represent their interests during the negotiations with the Minister of Education.

Policy objectives and tasks The main goals of adult and vocational education are: (i) to improve the personal development of adults and increase their societal participation, and (ii) to qualify and prepare adults for jobs (WEB, article 1.2.1 [my translation, SvT]). Especially the second goal is agreed upon by all informants from the ROC and the parent department, and usually coincides with a strong emphasis on the need for education to be accessible to all target groups (i.e. participation by minority or students from disadvantaged backgrounds has to be improved).

Furthermore, the statutes pay much attention to so-called qualifications, or graduation guidelines. National guidelines have been developed for all programmes of vocational and adult education to ensure that all graduates of ROCs are trained in a uniform way. These guidelines have been implemented in 1997 for vocational education, and in 1998 for adult education. It is important to note that the uniformity resulting from these guidelines inhibits competition.

Market position The territory of ROCs coincides with regions in which employment exchange agencies are active, this to facilitate the co-operation between vocational education and the labour market. In these regions, ROCs offer educational programmes in several places. For example, the selected

ROC has four main locations in the region, but adult education and in particular basic education is also taught at a small scale in other places.

From a national perspective, ROCs are clusters of quangos. However, as the intention of the government was for one ROC to be established in each region, one could also argue that they are regional monopolists. Forty-six schools have been established in 28 regions. Therefore, in a number of regions there is more than one ROC which leads to competition between the ROCs in that region. In the case at hand, not all schools for adult education and vocational training in the region have merged into one ROC. There are other ROCs operating within and at the borders of the region. So, there is competition, and not a regional monopoly.

In reality, competition is often limited because ROCs form alliances with each other or draw up contracts stipulating which curricula are provided by whom and under which conditions new curricula are allowed to be developed. The ROC in this case study has also formed such an alliance with its competitors.

Besides competition from other schools, ROCs also face competition from private providers of adult and vocational education, especially for commercial activities. ROCs are allowed to undertake commercial activities - up to 49% of their total turnover - such as providing training programmes to business companies or other organizations. In the selected ROC, a special foundation has been established to acquire and carry out commercial activities.

Private providers are allowed - and can be licensed - to offer the same curricula as ROCs because they have been incorporated into the same legal framework, a novelty in education policy. Opinions differ, however, whether this will lead to more competition. Informants from the ROC expect that this will lead to a serious increase of competition, in particular for vocational education. Not only will companies have more providers to choose from, they can also use this position to force ROCs to alter programmes or provide in-service training, which is not profitable for the schools because they have invested in school buildings and equipment. Experts outside the ROC do not expect that private providers will pose a threat, as they cannot offer the same range and quality of curricula (see also Vrancken & de Kemp, 1996:23-28).

Legal position of employees ROCs have been given full responsibility in matters of personnel. A national collective labour agreement has been drawn up as a general framework while details of personnel policies, in particular fringe benefits, are subject to internal negotiations. This explains why almost all informants from the selected ROC mention labour unions and the works council as a major stakeholder in the organization. Their influence has increased strongly since the establishment of the ROC.

Organizational structure and composition of board The statutes distinguish two types of ROCs: fully integrated institutes (20 out of 46); or federations of schools with representatives in one ROC board (26 out of 46). The selected case study started out as a federation but is now an institutionally integrated school that offers seven different educational programmes, as required by law.[33] It employs around 1,000 people and educates some 14,500 students (BVE-procescoördinatie, 1997).

The legal statutes do not contain any detailed prescriptions regarding the organizational structure of ROCs or the composition of the board. In practice, a large number of schools has adopted the same organizational structure, as the ROC at hand. Figure 5.4 shows the organizational structure that was implemented following the establishment of the ROC. The implementation of this structure was completed in 1998.

The Board of Supervisors is the official board of the ROC and consists of representatives of all former independent schools. They supervise the actions of the Board of Directors (BD) which is charged with the daily management of the ROC. There are three directors in the BD, all former directors of vocational schools.

The BD is supported by four divisions: General Management (charged with legal matters, public relations and quality care); Personnel; Finances; and Educational Support (charged with, amongst others, the proposals for new curricula). In addition, there is a separate division called Facilities, which is charged with tasks like the maintenance of buildings. From the supportive divisions of Personnel and Finances, employees are seconded to four decentralized service bureaus, one at each main location.

All educational matters are the responsibility of the unit directors, who form the third level in the organizational structure. Each unit comprises a particular educational programme. Eight units concern vocational programmes, divided along the lines of sectors of industry: graphics, electronics, mechanical engineering, architecture, health services and social work, trade, economic-administrative education, and catering. These eight units provide over 350 different courses. The ninth unit concerns adult education and offers general secondary and adult basic education.

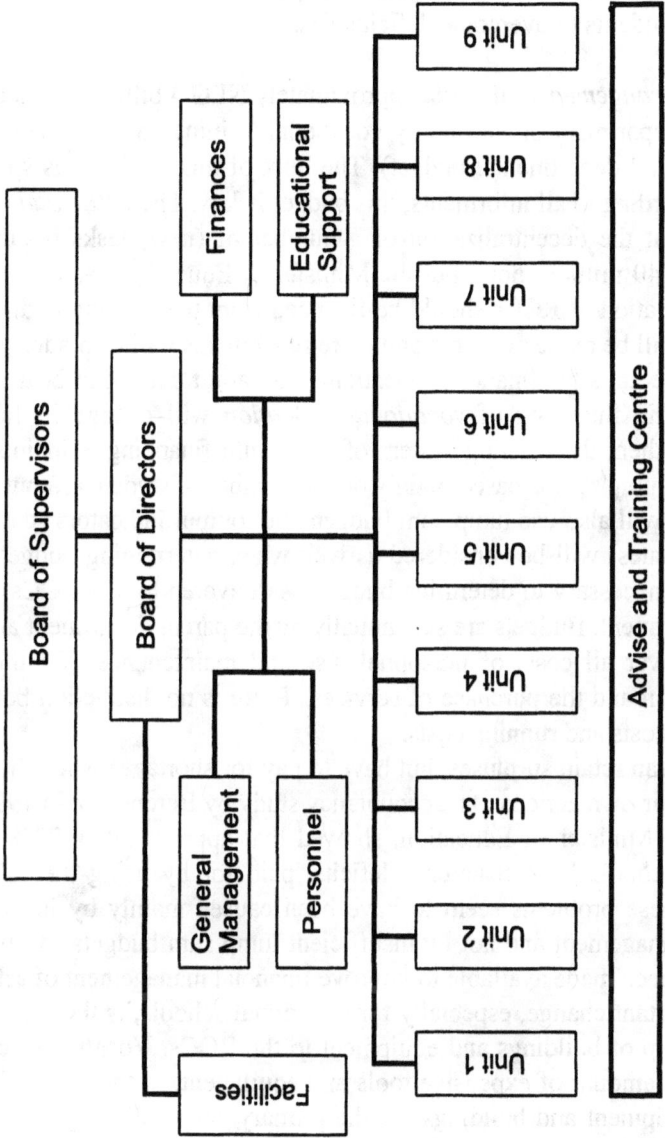

Figure 5.4 Organizational structure of the ROC (*Source*: Handboek Organisatiestructuur, 1997:9)

Besides the units, there is a special division called the Advice and Training Centre (formerly known as non-formal adult education). This centre advises students on their school career, helps drop-outs to return to school and assists students to overcome deficiencies.

Financial arrangements In 1998, approximately NLG 4 billion was spent by the parent department on secondary vocational training and adult education (10.8% of total departmental budget). The bulk of this money was spent on ROCs. According to all informants, this budget is low. The *BVE-raad* (1997) estimates that the decentralization of a number of (new) tasks requires at least NLG 240 million more, but the Minister of Education has determined that the formation of ROCs should be financed from the existing budget. No new funds will be made available and no retrenchments will be made.

The procedures for financing vocational and adult education bear a split character. The financing of *vocational education* will change in January 2000. Until then, the existing system of lump sum financing is maintained, wherein the lump sum is based mainly on the number of students (input). The new system will also use lump sum budgets, but output indicators (the number of graduates) will be considered as well when determining budgets. All information necessary to determine budgets is delivered by the ROCs to the parent department. Budgets are set annually by the parent department and are meant to cover all costs of personnel, use and maintenance of buildings, administration and the purchase of services. There is no distinction between programme costs and running costs.

Schools can retain surpluses, but have to pay for shortages when these result from their own actions. An accountancy study by Berenschot in 1996, by order of the Minister of Education, showed that approximately 23% of all vocational schools have structural deficits, paid for by using the schools' reserves. These problems seem to have been caused mainly by inadequate financial management and not by insufficient lump sum budgets. Additional funds have been made available to improve financial management of schools.

An important change, especially for vocational schools, is the transfer of the ownership of buildings and equipment to the ROCs. Vocational schools need a large amount of expensive tools and equipment. In the selected case, costs of equipment and buildings are the primary cause of budgetary shortages (see below).

The financing of *adult education* varies with the type of education. In 1994, the budgets for non-formal adult education were frozen by the parent department until 2000. After 1994, budgets were lump sum payments, no longer based on the number of students. The unit for non-formal adult education obtains additional funds from commercial activities. Senior secondary general education received lump sum budgets from the parent department in the period from 1993 to 1997. However, their budgets have been decentralized in January 1997 to (572) local governments, which already used to finance adult basic education. The education budgets are based on the number of inhabitants, the general level of education and the number of migrants in a municipality. Most local governments (89%) join their policies on adult education. A local government that does not spend the entire budget has to return the surplus, but ROCs do not have to do so.

ROCs have to negotiate with all local governments in their region to obtain budgets. In the case study at hand, annual negotiations are held with 16 municipalities. It was the legislator's idea that negotiations would increase efficiency, because they allow competitive private providers to participate as well. One can doubt if negotiating with large numbers of municipalities is really that efficient if it takes up much of the ROC's time and attention. Moreover, most local governments have not changed their policy and spend their budget entirely on the ROCs, not on other schools.

Accountability requirements ROCs have to account for different parts of their performance to different organizations. Each ROC has to account for its expenditures by way of an audited annual account to the parent department. Activities concerning adult education have to be accounted for as well to local governments. The school's performance in terms of the number of students, the number of graduates, examination procedures, drop-outs, school counselling, training of teachers, and such have to be accounted for in a so-called quality care report, which is audited by the Educational Review Office that is legally appointed as supervisor of ROCs. Finally, most schools have an internal Board of Supervisors as well (cf. figure 5.4), which has to approve all reports and accounts.[34]

Accountability did not have priority immediately after the establishment of ROCs, which meant that in the case study at hand annual reports, annual accounts and quality care reports were not always available. Negotiations are underway between the parent department and the *BVE-raad* on the development of a performance assessment system, under which ROCs provide the information necessary for the parent department to determine budgets and intervene in cases of ill performance. An accountancy firm has been charged with the development of a financial monitoring system (Moret, Ernst & Young, 1998). The *BVE-raad* wants to use the information from that system to persuade the Minister of Education to reduce the financial stress of ROCs (BVE-raad, 1997). See below for more information on the accountability of ROCs.

Property rights   ROCs have been given more autonomy than the former schools used to have. For example, the financing system of lump sum budgets allows ROCs to make autonomous decisions on expenditures concerning personnel, buildings and equipment (which have become their property as well). The right to retain surpluses was already mentioned, as was the responsibility for all personnel matters.

Furthermore, ROCs have been given relative freedom of developing new training programmes or educational curricula. An application to that end can be sent to the Minister of Education who honours it if it does not create inefficiencies at the national level, such as an overlap of courses or over-unemployment in certain sectors. All curricula are listed in a central register.[35] Only curricula that are listed can award legally valid certificates or diplomas.

Perceptions   As mentioned before, the idea of establishing ROCs was initiated by the parent department. At first schools were apprehensive and perceived the idea as yet another in a long line of policy changes. When asked, however, informants now seem pleased with the increase in autonomy and would not want to return to the former situation.

The reduction of the number of schools and the autonomy of ROCs have changed the relationship with the parent department. Informants from the ROC refer to the new relationship with the parent department as professionalized and more business like, although ROCs remain, of course, financially dependent. The number of contacts between schools and the Ministry of Education has decreased strongly. The *BVE-raad*, the council that represents ROCs, is now the first spokesman. In the department itself, the number of departmental divisions dealing with adult and vocational education has dropped significantly (as intended; Boef-van der Meulen *et al.*, 1995:135). The department is working on the establishment of new ways of consultation and negotiation with ROCs and the *BVE-raad*.

Efficiency and Performance since 1996

In 1998, ROCs were still adapting to their new situation. For example, in 1998 the ROC of this study was working on a new organizational structure (see before), a new financial system, and the introduction of management contracts between the board of directors and unit directors, aimed at decentralizing responsibilities concerning personnel and financial management to unit directors. Participants still have to get used to their new responsibilities but also to each other. The different types of education now incorporated into one organization have different backgrounds, visions and beliefs. Integration will take some time.

During the transition, accountability was not a priority. Annual reports and accounts have not been published regularly. Collection of information on performance was therefore sometimes difficult - even more so, because there hardly exists a tradition of using performance indicators and performance assessment systems in vocational and adult education (see also below). However, two years have passed since the ROC's establishment and some effects on performance should be visible, all the more because preparations for the merger already began in 1994. Moreover, some of the schools that merged had had the autonomy of lump sum financing since 1992.

Among informants from the ROC and the parent department, there is a strong belief in the positive effects of the establishment of ROCs in general and that of the case at hand in particular. They all think that, in the long run, efficiency gains will be obtained and education will become more accessible to students. The latter goal is valued even higher than the first.

Total performance In this subsection, the performance of the ROC since its establishment in 1996 is discussed. Three sources were available: the audited annual account of 1996, the quality care report (1998) and data collected for the financial monitoring system of the *BVE-Raad* about the performance in 1997 (Moret *et al.*, 1998). To improve our insight into the ROC's performance, information from the Ministry of Education on the average performance of all 46 Dutch ROCs will be used to compare the total performance of the ROC with (Ministerie van Onderwijs, Cultuur en Wetenschappen, 1999). Table 5.3 presents the information on the performance of the ROC in 1996 and 1997.

The available information mainly concerns financial indicators. Table 5.3 shows programme revenues, i.e. the budgets from the parent department, total costs and costs per student, surpluses or deficits, and the percentage revenues from commercial activities.

Table 5.3 Costs, revenues, input and output of the ROC in 1996 and 1997, compared to the national averages of all ROCs

	ROC 1996	Average 1996	ROC 1997	Average 1997
Programme revenues[a]	73.4	*77.8*	82.2	*88.2*
Commercial activities[a]	2.1	*2.8[b]*	2.8	*3.3[b]*
(% of total turnover)	(2.8)	-	(3.5)	
Total costs[a]	76.7	-	81.8	-
(% spent on salaries)	(73.7)		(71.6)	
Surplus[a]	-2.5	-	0.5	-
Costs per student[c]	5.2	*8.1[d]*	5.7	*8.3[d]*
Number of fte[e]	650	*685*	710[f]	*710*
(% management)	(27.3)	*(31.0)*	(27.9)	*(31.0)*
Number of students	14,775	*13,375*	14,280	*13,750*
(% in vocational education)	(76.3)	*(67.0)*	(80.4)	*(68.0)*
Ratio students/teacher[g]	31.0	*28.0*	27.8	*28.1*
Number of curricula	300	-	400	-

- No (reliable) information available
[a] amounts in NLG million (not adjusted for inflation)
[b] Additional subsidies for Dutch lessons to immigrants
[c] Costs in NLG 1000
[d] Only senior secondary vocational education
[e] fte = full-time equivalent
[f] Increase due to mergers
[g] Total number of students divided by total number of teachers in fte

Sources: Jaarrekening ROC (1996; 1997), BVE-Monitor (Moret *et al.*, 1998), Kwaliteitszorgverslag ROC (1998), Ministerie van Onderwijs, Cultuur en Wetenschappen (1999)

The selected ROC is slightly larger than average in terms of the number of students and employees. Revenues are slightly smaller than average as are commercial activities. This last finding could be the result of it being especially adult education that receives additional funds for Dutch lessons to immigrants. Because the ROC in question has a lower percentage of students in adult education than average (19.6% versus 32% in 1997), revenues from commercial activities tend to be relatively low as well. Moreover, a large percentage of students in vocational education are apprentices, who have to attend school only one day a week, which makes their education relatively cheap.

The ROC provides commercial services via two channels: first, through the adult education unit and second, a separate foundation that was established to operate in the market, and compete with private providers. This foundation employs teachers from the units to offer courses to business companies and other organizations. Revenues from these commercial activities go to the units that supplied the teachers. ROC informants project that eventually 20% of total revenues will be obtained from the activities of the foundation.

The main cause of the high total costs, which in 1996 even led to a deficit,[36] are the costs of equipment and buildings, particularly those used for (technical) vocational education. Such costs account for approximately 20% of total costs. The average costs per student in vocational education (see table 5.3) are also high (over NLG 8,000 per student per year). That the costs per student of the ROC in table 5.3 are much lower, is due to the fact that these include the costs of students in adult education and vocational education for apprentices, both of which are lower. The increase in the number of students in vocational education has led to a strong increase of the costs per student, exceeding the average increase of costs per student.

The number of students and the number of personnel of the selected ROC are higher than average.[37] Table 5.3 shows, however, that the average number of students has increased, contrary to the selected ROC where it has decreased slightly. This trend contradicts the expectation of informants from the ROC and the parent department, who expect the number of students to stabilize as a result of the ageing population. The increase in the number of personnel between 1996 and 1997 is caused by additional mergers with other schools. According to informants from the ROC, a large part of the staff is relatively old, leading to high salary costs. They expect centralization of personnel policies to bring a solution.

Despite the fact that a higher than average percentage of total personnel is charged with non-educational tasks (see the percentage management in table 5.3), the students/teacher ratio is lower than average. It should be noted, however, that this ratio varies very with type of education. For example, in 1995 the average ratio in senior secondary vocational education was 19.8, while in vocational education for apprentices it was 35.6 (Ministerie van Onderwijs, Cultuur en Wetenschappen, 1999). The ratios in table 5.3 are based on the total number of students and of teachers, and do not take such differences between types of education into account.

In 1998, information on the number of drop-outs and graduates were not available for the selected case.[38] On average, 62.8% of students in vocational education graduates (Ministerie van Onderwijs, Cultuur en Wetenschappen, 1999). The average number of graduates of adult education was not available.

Performance of former schools before 1996 A comparison of the performance of the former schools with that of the ROC is hindered by a lack of tradition in making performance assessments at the old schools. Schools had to provide different types of information, usually restricted to financial indicators. There are also differences in accountability and financing systems. For example, vocational education, adult general secondary education and non-formal adult education all used to be financed with lump sums, but these were based on different criteria. The budgets for senior secondary and basic adult education are determined by external criteria, such as the number of inhabitants and the level of education in the municipalities of the region. The schools can exert no influence on these indicators. This could account for the lack of information on, for example, output indicators in the annual reports and annual accounts of the schools that merged into the ROC in 1996. The introduction of national qualification guidelines in 1998 is expected to improve the accountability of adult education in this respect.

Information that was available shows that vocational schools already had to cope with deficits prior to the establishment of the ROC, due to the high costs of equipment and buildings. These deficits were usually paid from the schools' capital reserves. The school for adult education had less financial problems and even allocated money to prepare for the merger into the ROC.

Non-financial aspects of performance were underreported. For one, annual reports on non-formal adult education do not contain (consistent) information on the numbers of students. For adult basic education, the numbers of students are counted, but because graduation guidelines were absent before 1998, drop-out rates or the number of graduated students are not reported. The numbers of students and graduates that vocational schools had to provide to the parent department, had to be drawn up in a particular format, with very detailed information that is difficult to aggregate.

Analysis of the available information leads to the following conclusions (see the case study report for more details [Van Thiel, 1999b]). Vocational education constitutes the largest part of the ROC; it uses 90% of the total budget, and has 80% of all students, and eight of the nine units (cf. figure 5.4). Vocational schools already suffered from deficits prior to the establishment of the ROC, due to high costs of equipment. This explains the strain on the total budget of the ROC, which, in 1996, even led to a deficit. Surpluses and additional revenues from commercial activities in the education unit cannot make up for the deficits of the vocational education units.

It does not seem likely that budgets are going to be increased by the parent department, despite it geneally being acknowledged that budgets are low. To improve efficiency, the ROC aims to find other ways to reduce the costs of equipment and buildings by, for example, creating one location for all education, and reducing the under-utilization of buildings.

Another way for the ROC to improve efficiency would be to expand its commercial activities, which are now below average (cf. table 5.3), or to increase its share of adult education. An increase of the share of adult education in the ROC will be especially important with respect to the new financing system for vocational education, to be introduced in 2000. The number of graduates will become a major determinant of the budget for vocational education. Adult education can attract students from new target groups[39] and prevent vocational education students from dropping out of school. As the situation is now (in 1998), only the unit for non-formal adult education has profited from the merger. The number of students in this type of education has doubled after 1996.

Conclusions Based on the available information, it is difficult to draw a simple, clear conclusion on changes in the efficiency and effectiveness of the selected ROC after its establishment. There is no strong evidence to support the belief of informants from the ROC and the parent department that the establishment of the quango will lead to efficiency gains. The deficit of 1996 is overcome in 1997 by a small surplus, but the financial strain remains high, mainly due to the high expenses on equipment and buildings of vocational education. More important than efficiency gains to informants are the expected gains in the *effectiveness* of adult and vocational education, in particular the accessibility of the ROC to all students and the opportunities for students to get the education they need. In that respect a small improvement is reported for non-formal adult education.

At the moment of the research, the ROC still is in transition. The five former schools have to integrate structurally as well as culturally. Investments are being made in, for example, a new system of financial management, while at the same time the schools have to continue educating students. Besides extra costs, the process of investment also creates a double workload for the management and the teachers. As no additional funds have been made available by the parent department, and current funding is considered to be low, one might expect an increase in costs - and a decrease in efficiency -

before efficiency gains become visible. Moreover, informants see the increasing centralization as a result of the larger scale of the organization as a potential threat to efficiency, because it might lead to bureaucratization and loss of commitment of the management to daily activities.

There are two other potential threats to efficiency. First, the staff is on average relatively old.[40] Moreover, table 5.3 showed that the percentage non-teachers is quite high. Not only does this bring higher costs, there is also a risk of more organizational resistance to changes, such as the adoption of educational innovations and the exchange of expertise between different types of education within the ROC. The centralization of means may offers new possibilities for employees in the form of more mobility, and opens the way to new policies on, for example, seniority. As the costs of personnel take up a large part of the total budget (over 70%), it is important that the ROC deals with this problem.

The second potential threat to efficiency is - paradoxically - the presence of competitors. ROCs have to negotiate with large numbers of municipalities on the budgets for adult education. The time and costs associated with these negotiations make policy implementation more expensive. Or non-monopolist ROCs enter 'non-competition pacts' with other ROCs operating in or at the border of the region. These alliances are meant to avoid overlap (i.e. inefficiency) in the courses schools offer or want to develop. However, the negotiations to form such alliances cost time and money as well. So, while the WEB intended competition to increase the efficiency and effectiveness of ROCs, it may also increase the costs of policy implementation and reduce efficiency and effectiveness.

The lack of information on the performance of the ROC limits drawing conclusions. Moreover, ROCs will need more insight into their performance themselves now that they have become responsible for the budget. Financial indicators alone are not enough. The pending introduction of output-based financing of vocational education requires that schools have information on their output as well. The parent department, the BVE-raad and the ROCs are working on new accountability systems, to enable ROCs to deliver information on their performance, and to allow the parent department to exert supervision and determine budgets. Note that this implies a significant change for the parent department as well. It has to adjust its relationship with schools in the field of adult and vocational education to the new situation. The next section will deal more extensively with the current and future accountability requirements that ROCs face.

Performance Paradox

Table 5.3 listed a number of performance indicators (PIs) to assess the performance of the ROC, for example, the amount of revenues and costs, the
number of students and the number of personnel. In addition, new PIs were
calculated using existing information, such as the students/teacher ratio or
the percentage commercial activities in total turnover. To what extent do
these indicators give a valid image of performance? It was noted that information on certain aspects was missing (e.g. on the number of graduates in
adult education), which would imply that performance is under-reported.
Chapter 3 identified this as a performance paradox (Meyer & Gupta, 1994):
reported performance does not reflect actual performance. A performance
paradox does not (necessarily) imply ill performance, but it should be noted
that a paradox can also be evoked intentionally - through manipulation or
suppressing information - to disguise ill performance. Therefore, the performance assessment system of the ROC was evaluated, regarding the
amount and type of accountability requirements, the number and type of
performance indicators, the relationship between goals and indicators, supervisory activities, *et cetera*. Data were obtained through the analysis of documents and interviews (see table 5.1).

Analysis of the available information on the ROC's performance shows
that it is mainly finance-driven. PIs are either of a financial nature (such as
revenues, costs, surpluses, capital reserves), or relate straightforwardly to
criteria by which budgets are set (e.g. the number of students in vocational
education) or the units in which budgets are expressed (e.g. the number of
hours of adult education). Apart from these main indicators, there is some
minor information on personnel, such as the number of full-time equivalents,
the number of teachers, absenteeism, and some statistics like the age and
gender of teachers. Output indicators, such as the percentage of graduates
and drop-out rates, are less numerous. Non-financial aspects of performance
can therefore said to be under-reported. It is important to understand that this
does not mean that the ROC's performance is better or worse than reported,
but rather that the information is insufficient to obtain a comprehensive view
of performance. One could argue that there is a performance paradox, i.e. a
partial under-representation of performance in the annual reports. There is no
reason to believe that the ROC is any different from other ROCs in this
respect. Annual reports and annual accounts are drawn up according to legal
instructions, given by the parent department, which are imposed upon all
schools.

There is no evidence that information is withheld on purpose or manipulated. Still, schools sometimes present their information in a strategic way. Take, for example, the reports on the number of graduates in secondary vocational education. The legal instructions of how to deliver information on the number of students, (per year, per curriculum and including the students' progress) have as a consequence that annual reports consist mainly of very detailed and complex tables, which makes aggregation of information difficult. This allows schools to 'hide' information on total output. Only one vocational school offered a summary (see case study report, Van Thiel, 1999b). According to informants from this school, the increased responsibilities as a result of the financial freedom of lump sum budgets (introduced in 1993/4) made it imperative for the school (now one unit) to gain insight into total performance. Other vocational schools and units do not present such a summary. While it is not obligatory to report this type of information, it has to be acknowledged that schools might be reluctant to give summaries, because the average percentage of students that obtains a diploma can be perceived as relatively low; approximately 60% - which is not very different from the national average. However, the pending introduction of output based financing will force schools to make their success rates public.

A second example of strategic presentation of information relates to the deficits caused by the costs of equipment and buildings used for vocational education. In several instances informants admitted that these deficits could in fact be easily undone by 'balancing the books', i.e. using capital reserves. While other ROCs use this (legitimate) method frequently, in the case at hand it was preferred to report a deficit in 1996 rather than manipulating information. This seems noble, but it should also be pointed out that the ROC has a strong interest in reporting deficits because it wants to try to persuade the parent department to increase its budget.

The main cause for the one-sided reports of performance (i.e. focussing on finances) is that before the establishment of ROCs there was no need to report more than what was legally required. As long as information was available to determine budgets, schools could function, and as long as there were no problems, there was no need for intervention by supervisors, such as departmental accountants and the Educational Review Office. The culture with respect to accountability in the field of adult and vocational education did not encompass extensive performance assessment.

The introduction of lump sum financing in 1993/4 made schools more aware of the need for knowledge on performance, to be able to make full use of the financial freedom they were granted. This need was amplified when

ROCs were established, charged with new responsibilities, tasks, and more autonomy. It seems reasonable, therefore, to expect improvements of the performance assessment system in the field of adult and vocational education in the near future, especially when considering the numerous changes in the accountability requirements ROCs have to meet, such as the introduction of an obligatory quality care report, the decentralization of responsibilities in personnel matters, and of budgets for adult education to local governments. Schools are now obliged to deliver, at the least: (i) a quality care report to the Educational Review Office, (ii) an audited annual account to the parent department, (iii) an account of the performance of adult education to local governments, and (iv) reports on personnel matters to the unions. Accountability has thus become fragmented and complex, leading to an increased need for ROCs to improve their performance assessment systems.

Performance assessment is, however, still in its infancy. The development of a financial monitor, initiated by the *BVE-raad*, is a first step, although information is required on more than just financial matters. The quality care report of the ROC has only recently been published and contains mainly plans to improve the quality of education, for example, the introduction of national graduation guidelines (the so-called qualifications). It will take several years before the first results of these activities will be published.

Other changes in this respect are the newly integrated financial system and the pending introduction of management contracts. These contracts between the Board of Directors and the unit directors contain agreements on the performance of units, expressed in performance indicators and targets. Informants from the ROC expect that the contracts will become an important instrument within the organization. They are of the opinion that non-compliance with indicators should have serious consequences. Dismissal because of ill-performance should, however, only be a last resort.

The current performance assessment system has been in use since 1990 and has not changed much since. The question rises if new indicators should be developed and, if so, which and by whom. Their limited experience with performance assessment makes it difficult for informants to answer this question. Most of them prefer a top-down approach, with the *BVE-raad* taking the lead, drawing up guidelines for all ROCs. Within ROCs, the Board of Directors is expected to take the initiative to develop a performance assessment system. Ideas for new indicators are scarce. General agreement exists on the validity of (existing) indicators, such as the number of students, the number of graduates and drop-out rates. Besides these, new financial indicators are expected to become more important, such as the costs per student.

Annual reports contain hardly any information on the quality of education. In some cases, educational innovations are listed, announced or described, but there is little systematic collection or presentation of information. The quality care report, which was published for the first time in 1998, will have to provide more information on this topic. Also, the Educational Review Office is developing a quality inspection system for ROCs.[41]

A final note on performance assessment concerns the need for norms (or targets) and comparative evaluations.[42] Both serve as a frame of reference for performance indicators, without which indicators would only reveal information on one topic at one moment in time (static assessment). Setting targets is often aimed at the future. For example, a target could be that the percentage of personnel in management has to decrease by 1%. Such targets help organizations to gain insight into their performance and make improvements. Comparative evaluations can be made over time, between ROCs, and between units. They give insight into the development of, for example, costs and revenues. Comparisons between ROCs are necessary to find out whether developments pertain to a particular school or are caused by national trends. For example, a decrease in the number of students can be caused by the ageing of the population, or by a bad reputation of vocational and adult education. So far, the reports of the ROC have not included norms or comparative evaluations.

To sum up the main findings, information on the performance of the selected ROC is somewhat one-sided, because it concerns mainly financial indicators. There is no reason to assume that this is only the case with the ROC in this study. Accountability requirements are the same for all ROCs and the results from other studies on the performance of vocational education point to similar problems (see Vrancken & De Kemp, 1996; BVE-raad, 1997). The focus on financial indicators can be explained by the fact that former schools for adult and vocational education used to be required to provide this type of information only. Furthermore, because of the long-standing dependence on the parent department, there was little or no tradition in extensive performance assessment.

The introduction of lump sum financing in 1993/4 triggered the interest of some schools in more detailed reports on performance, but the autonomy of ROCs, the presence of competitors, the pending introduction of output based financing, mandatory national guidelines for graduations, and the quality care report makes comprehensive performance assessment even more necessary.

Comparison of Cases

In this chapter two case studies were conducted on the consequences of quangocratization. Changes in the efficiency and effectiveness of policy implementation due to the establishment of a quango were investigated. Table 5.5 summarizes the findings.

In the case of IB-Groep, evidence was found that the cost-efficiency of policy implementation has decreased after the quango was established. However, overall small surpluses have been obtained as well. Moreover, the quality of output has increased. To conclude, the performance of IB-Groep has improved in some respects and deteriorated in others after its establishment as a quango in 1994.

For the case of the ROC, insufficient information was available to make a comparison between performance before and after its establishment. The financial strain of the costs of equipment and buildings, and the one-off costs of the merger and the current transition into a new, integrated school make it unlikely that efficiency and effectiveness have already improved significantly since its establishment. Only the unit for non-formal adult education displayed an improvement in effectiveness; the number of students doubled.

With regard to the presence of a performance paradox, in both cases conditions were found that could induce such a paradox. However, there is no evidence to support the conclusion that there is indeed a performance paradox. IB-Groep provides an extensive public account, but emphasizes some aspects, in particular quality of service, more than others, like cost prices and commercial activities. The ROC has little tradition in performance assessment. Available reports provide an under-estimation; financial aspects are over-reported while non-financial aspects are not reported or only to a limited extent.

This section seeks to explain these findings, using the hypotheses that were developed in chapter 3. Table 5.5 confronts the results of the two cases with the hypotheses. The limited number of cases makes (statistical) testing of the hypotheses impossible. Below, for each hypothesis it will be discussed whether the case study results contribute to the proposed explanation of the consequences of quangocratization. See also the overview in table 5.6 at the end of this chapter. If necessary, recommendations are made for future theory development and research.

Ownership of production rights Ownership of production rights was expected to stimulate the efficiency and effectiveness of policy implementation and to prevent the occurrence of a performance paradox (hypothesis 2.1[P]). The case study results show that both organizations own some of the production rights, but not all. Take, for example, financial arrangements. Although both organizations own the right to retain surpluses, IB-Groep has more influence on the size of its budget than the ROC. The annual negotiations on the management contract and the relevant budget are based on the information IB-Groep gives about its performance. In the case of the ROC, the parent department unilaterally determines the budgets for all ROCs. There are no negotiations between the schools and the parent department. ROCs provide only part of the information that is used by the Ministry of Education to divide the total budget between the ROCs and the local governments. The budgets for ROCs and local governments are included in the departmental budget.

With respect to the right to hire and fire employees, the ROC appears to be a little more autonomous than IB-Groep, whose employees still have the same legal position (and salaries) as they had before IB-Groep became a quango. ROC employees fall under the new national collective labour agreement, which creates possibilities for each ROC to design its own personnel policy. However, the power and influence of the labour unions in ROCs have also increased.

The Minister of the parent department has kept the right to intervene in case of ill performance. He also has the right to appoint the members of the Board of Supervisors of IB-Groep, and he has charged the Educational Review Office with supervision of the ROCs (see also accountability requirements below).

How do these findings fit the predictions about efficiency and effectiveness of policy implementation? In the case of IB-Groep, it can be argued that the ownership of production rights has led to some improvement in performance. Although the costs of policy implementation have increased, the quality of services has improved. Small (nett) surpluses have been gained and retained since IB-Groep's establishment as a quango. So, only after IB-Groep obtained the right to retain surpluses, have these been realized; prior to the establishment as a quango deficits were booked and paid for by the parent department.

For the increase in the cost prices of goods and services several explanations have been forwarded, such as the increased complexity of policies and the additional investments made in the quality of performance and client service. However, without comparative information, it remains difficult to attribute the drop in cost-efficiency to the establishment of the quango.

In the case of the ROC, performance does not seem to have improved much. This could be explained by the limited influence ROCs have on their financial arrangements. Only once budgets have been set by the parent department, do they have any autonomy in deciding how to use their money. Furthermore, ROCs have to compete with each other for budgets. Therefore they have nothing to gain from reporting surpluses, which might induce politicians to reduce their future budgets. To conclude, the restricted ownership of production rights, in particular of financial arrangements, has not led to an improvement of the efficiency and effectiveness of policy implementation.

In general, it can be concluded that the transfer of production rights when a quango is established does not lead to an *immediate* improvement of performance, it might take some time. Moreover, if quangocratization leads to improvement, this may be limited to particular aspects of performance. The case study results support hypothesis 2.1 only moderately. It is recommended to adjust the hypothesis and include a time lag.

The role that the selected quangos play in the determination of budgets also explains the presence of conditions that may induce a performance paradox. The findings in both cases are therefore considered to support hypothesis 2.1P. Quangos will report that information that gives them the best opportunities to maintain (or even increase) their budgets. For example, because IB-Groep has a lot of influence on its budget, it can afford to provide extensive information, particularly on aspects of performance, such as quality and customer service, that have improved since its establishment. The ROC has less influence and will therefore stress financial indicators that confirm deficits and the need for larger budgets. Other aspects of performance are less relevant in this respect and are under-reported. The same holds for reporting surpluses; when quangos have less interest in reporting surpluses - perhaps because they fear that the budget for next year will be cut as a result - they will try to report no or only very small (nett) surpluses.

Table 5.5 Summary of case study results in terms of the hypotheses about efficiency and effectiveness of policy implementation and about the occurrence of a performance paradox

| No. | Hypothesis | Expected effects: | | Results | |
		E & E	PP	Case study 1 (IB-Groep)	Case study 2 (the ROC)
2.1(P)	Ownership of production rights	+	-	Ownership of right to retain surpluses, budget based on mutual annual negotiations but included in state budget, quangocrats have secure legal position similar to civil servants	Ownership of right to retain surpluses, budget is determined unilaterally by parent department and included in state budget, competition for budget within cluster, legal position personnel laid down in national collective labour agreement
2.2(P)	Competition	+	+	Monopolist, restricted commercial activities, highly specific assets	Member of cluster, no regional monopoly, commercial activities allowed, fairly specific assets
2.3(P)	Corporatism	+	+/-	Board consists of independent experts (appointed); many contacts with interest groups outside quango	Board members from old schools, influence of unions has increased within organization
2.4(P)	Accountability requirements	+	?	Annual report and audited account are mandatory, frequent contacts with parent department, extensive internal reports, external scrutiny by e.g. Ombudsman and judicial courts, high profile in media	Accountability is fragmented, financial reports to parent department and local government are mandatory, as is educational report to Educational Review Office and consultation with trade unions

Continued

No.	Hypothesis	E &E	PP	Expected effects: Case study 1 (IB-Groep)	Results Case study 2 (the ROC)
2.5(P)	Size	-	+	Budget is approximately NLG 5 billion (running costs 4% of total budget); number of personnel is approx. 1,400 full-time equivalents	Budget: approximately NLG 80 million; number of personnel: approximately 1,000 full-time equivalents
2.6(P)	Closeness to politicians	+	-	Close to parent department; hived-off departmental unit, frequent contacts, status quangocrats resembles that of civil servants	Not close to parent department; hived into public sector, few contacts (via inter-mediary), legal position laid down in collective labour agreement
2.7(P)	Risk perception	+	-	Willing to take risks and initiative, seldom sanctions for ill performance	Passive, seldom sanctions for ill performance
2.8P	Diversity PIs		-	Diverse and extensive system of PIs on output, costs and quality, has been in use for some time	Limited diversity; little tradition in and experience with PIs, mostly financial indicators
2.9P	Clear policy objectives		-	Discrepancy between mission and official objectives	No discrepancy; mission coincides with official policy objectives
2.10P	Emphasis on efficiency, PIs		+	Strong emphasis on PIs, quality more important than cost-efficiency	Little emphasis on efficiency or PIs; accessibility of education is more important than either
2.11P	Supervision		+/-	Board of Supervision	Educational Review Office

E&E = Efficiency & Effectiveness; PP = Performance Paradox; - = negative effect; + = positive effect; +/- = mixed prediction; ? no prediction

Competition Competition was expected to increase the efficiency and effectiveness of policy implementation (hypothesis 2.2). However, to survive in a competitive environment, quangos might choose to manipulate information on their performance, thus evoking a performance paradox (hypothesis 2.2P). The market position of the two selected quangos is one of the most striking differences between them.

IB-Groep is a monopolist. Not only does it have a monopoly on the implementation of a number of educational policies, it also owns many specific assets, such as knowledge, equipment and information. These sunk costs make it very difficult and expensive for the principal to resort to another executive agent, let alone that such a transfer requires a change of law.

The case study showed that the performance of IB-Groep improved in some aspects and deteriorated in others. This would contradict the expectation formulated in hypothesis 2.2. Yet, it is difficult to reject the hypothesis because of a lack of comparative information on the quango's performance. Perhaps the development of its performance is part of a general trend in the sector where the quango operates, or of the type of task it executes.

The lack of competition also makes it difficult to evaluate the accounts IB-Groep gives of its performance, which increases the risk of an (unintended) performance paradox. Moreover, with a monopolist quango, the parent department depends entirely on the quango for information on its performance, which creates opportunities for a (deliberate) performance paradox. On the other hand, because there are no alternative executive agents, a monopolist quango has no need to manipulate information and report better efficiency or effectiveness than it actually achieves. So, monopolist quangos can afford to account for their performance more extensively, and spend more means on accountability. This might explain why IB-Groep provides extensive reports on its performance; the lack of alternative agents and comparative information reduces the risk that inefficiencies will be sanctioned (see also 'risk perception' and 'emphasis on efficiency' below). This is in line with the prediction formulated in hypothesis 2.2P.

The selected ROC is member of a cluster of quangos, and has no regional monopoly. Due to a lack of data on performance, no conclusions can be drawn about the effect of competition on the ROC's performance. Although all informants firmly believe in the efficiency gains that the ROC will make, there is no evidence of that. Hypothesis 2.2 is not supported. Moreover, it was noted that one element of the establishment of ROCs could pose a threat to the efficiency and effectiveness of policy implementation. The introduction of competition means that ROCs have to negotiate with local governments on budgets. Negotiation costs will increase the costs of policy implementation. If this is indeed the case, hypothesis 2.2 needs to be reformulated.

In theory, the performance of ROCs could be compared between schools. This might also reduce the risk of a performance paradox, but not if ROCs agree beforehand on what they will report to the parent department. For example, information on the percentage of graduates in vocational education was not transparent. Although schools were required to give information about this, apparently they felt no need to present information in a clear way - except for one school in the selected case - which would enable them to make better use of the information themselves. An explanation for this behaviour was sought by suggesting that the average percentage of graduates of approximately 60% may be considered low, and not something schools would like to publish. Such agreements may thus evoke a performance paradox, as predicted in hypothesis 2.2P.

A similar agreement has been made to reduce regional competition. Several ROCs have entered into alliances with other schools in the same region. This also happened in the case study region. Schools have made agreements about which schools are allowed to offer certain curricula. Thus these alliances have led to specialization and the re-instalment of monopolies (actually, cartels).

While this may reduce the overlap in curricula and so decrease the risk of spending means in an inefficient way, it also diminishes the accessibility of education because it limits the freedom of choice of students in those regions. Because accessibility is an important objective of the establishment of ROCs, such forms of co-operation may threaten effectiveness. This would contradict the expectation of hypothesis 2.2.

To conclude, while competition may in theory lead to higher efficiency and effectiveness, in practice the effects of competition can be counteracted when quangos join forces (cf. Flache & Macy, 1996). Such forms of co-operation should get more attention in future research. For example, it would be interesting to study the effects of co-operation on the competition for budgets in clusters of quangos, or in internal markets.

Corporatism The participation of interest groups in quangos through, for example, membership of the board, was expected to affect the efficiency and effectiveness of policy implementation in a positive manner (hypothesis 2.3). Corporatism was expected to increase the chance of a performance paradox occurring only if the goals of the participating interest groups differ strongly from the goals of the politicians (cf. hypothesis 2.3[P]).

In neither of the case studies are there interest group members on the company's board, however. The Board of Supervisors of IB-Groep consists of independent experts appointed by the minister. IB-Groep does maintain intensive contacts with interest groups that represent, among others, students and schools. IB-Groep claims to use these contacts to improve its customer service. The impact of these contacts is, however, not measured or otherwise substantiated.

The board of the ROC is made up of members of the former school boards. In the ROC, the works council, which represents all teachers who are employed by the school, has gained an important position after the decentralization of personnel policies. All important policy decisions have to be discussed with the work council. It is unknown, however, what the effects of this are on performance.

The absence of interest groups in the quangos studied implies that no conclusions can be drawn on the influence of corporatism. To investigate the effect of corporatism on the performance of quangos, future research could perhaps select cases in different policy sectors with different degrees of corporatism (cf. the analyses in chapter 4). Instead of testing the participation of interest groups in *individual* quangos, the focus would then be on characteristics of the policy *sector* in which a quango operates.

Accountability requirements Hypothesis 2.4 stated that the more accountability requirements are imposed upon quangos, the more efficient and effective policy implementation will be. IB-Groep has to publish annual reports and audited accounts, which are sent to the parent department. Besides these documents, annual negotiations result in management contracts stipulating the estimated performance and budgets, both in terms of running and programme costs. Moreover, in information protocols agreements are made on the exchange of information and the information flow between the quango and the parent department. It can be concluded that IB-Groep delivers extensive and frequent reports on its performance. These reports are discussed with the departmental management, in order to reach mutual agreement on IB-Groep's performance.

The accountability requirements imposed on ROCs have increased and are more complex than the requirements for individual schools of adult and vocational education used to be. ROCs have little experience with such extensive performance assessment and will have to develop an assessment system. PIs are expected to become important instruments in managing the organization, for example, in the management contracts with unit directors. The current information on performance is limited to financial aspects.

The effect of accountability measures on performance is not unequivocal. Reported performance does not always reflect actual performance. In the case studies attention was paid to conditions that might induce such a performance paradox (see below). The findings on these conditions need to be taken into account before conclusions can be drawn about the effect of accountability requirements on the performance of the selected cases. No conclusion can be derived for hypothesis 2.4.

Size Smaller quangos were expected to perform more efficiently and effectively, and to be less prone to a performance paradox (hypothesis 2.5[P]). IB-Groep is clearly the larger quango of the two cases. The development of the performance of IB-Groep and the ROC both show *partial* improvement; IB-Groep's quality of service has increased and the number of students in the ROC's unit for non-formal adult education have increased. In other areas, particularly the costs of policy implementation, both cases show a decrease of performance. Hypothesis 2.5 is therefore only partly supported by the case study findings.

With regard to the occurrence of a performance paradox, it was found that IB-Groep offers a full account of its performance, emphasizing the quality of service. This would support hypothesis 2.5P. In the case of the ROC, an under-estimation of performance was found. This could indicate the presence of a performance paradox, which would refute hypothesis 2.5P. The fact is, though, that ROCs in general have little tradition in extensive performance assessment. The underestimation of performance will probably be found in other schools as well. The *BVE-raad*, which represents all ROCs, has therefore initiated the development of a system of PIs. With the information rendered by such a system, ROCs can be compared amongst each other to ascertain the effect of size of a quango on its performance. A limited comparison was made, which showed that the selected ROC is larger than average and in some respects is indeed less efficient and effective than other ROCs (see reported deficits and commercial activities). This would support hypothesis 2.5. More such comparative research is necessary, however, to improve the validity of the conclusions about the effect of the size of quangos on their performance and the occurrence of a performance paradox.

Closeness to politicians Closeness to the principal was expected to induce compliance, and hence efficient and effective policy implementation (hypothesis 2.6), and reduce the risk of a performance paradox (hypothesis 2.6P). Quangocrats in hived off former departmental units were expected to be closer to politicians because they used to work at the parent ministry. This might also show in the legal position of these quangocrats, in particular when it is the same as that of civil servants. Closeness is evident as well if contacts between the quango and the parent department are intensive.

IB-Groep is a hived-off departmental unit and still has strong ties with the parent department, which expresses itself in frequent contacts and negotiations. As both the quango and the parent department claim to value quality improvement higher than efficiency gains, the strong focus on quality indicators in the performance accounts can be perceived as an expression of IB-Groep's desire to please its main principal (this is in line with hypothesis 2.6). However, IB-Groep may also be making investments in quality and customer service to attract new principals, in its quest for extension of commercial activities. According to informants, the acquisition of new tasks is hindered by the strong association between the quango and the parent department, especially in the media, with IB-Groep coming across as a departmental division. By building a good client-oriented reputation, IB-Groep could be hoping to attract new principals. PIs would then be used for another purpose than that of pleasing the parent department. Such a conclusion would point to the presence of a performance paradox and refute hypothesis 2.6P.

Schools for adult and vocational education were never part of the department but when they became more dependent on government funding, they were incorporated into a legal framework and hived in into the public sector. The relationship with the parent department was characterized by an overall dependence of the schools. Quangocratization (the establishment of ROCs) offered the schools new autonomy, but the financial dependence remained. As a result, the relationship between ROCs and the parent department has changed. These days, communication is professionalized and formalized, with the *BVE-raad* representing the interests of the semi-autonomous schools. The number and frequency of contacts between individual schools and the department have decreased significantly, which explains why informants do not consider the Ministry of Education a major stakeholder in the ROC. Closeness has decreased, but this has not led to an overall deterioration of performance (partly supporting hypothesis 2.6).

Informants from the ROC and the parent department value effectiveness of education (in particular accessibility) higher than efficiency. Nevertheless, financial indicators are more numerous in reports than non-financial ones. This under-estimation of performance points to the presence of a performance paradox and refutes hypothesis 2.6P. The under-estimation seems to be caused by tradition rather than intention, however. The schools - and the parent department, for that matter - have little tradition in reporting on non-financial aspects of performance.

Risk perception Hypothesis 2.7(P) argued that quangocrats will be inclined to comply with the principal's goal as they perceive the risk of getting caught at deviant behaviour higher. Policy implementation will then be more efficient and effective, and quangos will not evoke a performance paradox. To measure risk perception, attention was paid to, among others, the willingness of quangrocrats to initiate changes, and the use of sanctions for ill performance.

IB-Groep appears to be much less afraid of taking risks than the ROC. For example, it was actively involved in taking the initiative to become a quango, it anticipated the change even better than the parent department. Over time, it has shown to be willing to take on ever more tasks and responsibilities. Finally, IB-Groep wants to expand its activities for other principals in the nearby future. The focus on quality indicators can be seen as a way to increase customer relations with the current and possible future principals and is therefore consistent with this attitude.

To sum up, IB-Groep seems to perceive the risk of getting caught at deviant behaviour low. Performance has not - as predicted by hypothesis 2.7 - decreased overall; efficiency has decreased, but quality of service has improved. Hypothesis 2.7 is therefore only partially supported. The decrease in efficiency is not sanctioned, because the quango and the parent department agree that quality improvement is more important (see also below on 'emphasis on efficiency and PIs'). Moreover, the principal has no real alternatives for IB-Groep, which reduce the risk of sanctioning even further. Hypothesis 2.7P appears to be supported by the first case study.

Compared to IB-Groep, the ROC takes a much more passive attitude. For example, informants thought of its establishment in 1996 as a radical change, even though it had been known for four years that ROCs were to become the main unit of policies and negotiations to merge were well underway. There is little anticipation on policy changes; the dominant attitude is 'to wait and see'. Politicians are considered fickle, changing their ideas all the time. That is not to say that the informants want to reverse the merger, having gotten used to their new autonomy. Although they claim not to be afraid to take responsibility for the ROC's performance, they think there is no need to expand the ROC's discretionary authority. Only with regard to financial arrangements does the ROC actively seek change; by reporting a deficit - instead of balancing it with capital reserves - it hopes to persuade the parent department to increase its budget. This latter observation would refute hypothesis 2.7P. However, it is not the most typical example of the ROC's behaviour.

Based on these findings, it can be imagined that the effects of risk perception are mediated by other conditions. For example, the more production rights (cf. hypothesis 2.1) a quango owns (see IB-Groep), the lower it perceives the risk of getting caught at deviant behaviour. Or, when competitive quangos (cf. hypothesis 2.2) perceive the risk of getting caught to be high, they may decide to join forces rather than compete (as was found in the case of the ROC), by making agreements about performance or about their reports on performance. These suppositions demand further study.

Diversity of performance indicators   Meyer and Gupta (1994) describe a performance assessment model that is to prevent the occurrence of a performance paradox. PIs have to be diverse with respect to the range of the indicators and have to vary over time, but must be comparable as well (cf. hypothesis 2.8P). Meyer and Gupta labelled this a paradoxical model of performance assessment. In the case studies, attention was therefore paid to the system of performance assessment, the range and variety of PIs and changes in PIs over time.

Since 1989, IB-Groep has developed an extensive system of PIs. After the establishment as a quango in 1994 several new indicators have been added, mainly of the quality of customer services. This has led to a slight over-representation of quality aspects, which could be considered indicative of a performance paradox (supportive of hypothesis 2.8P). However, IB-Groep has a large number of comparable indicators. A comparable set of indicators can be found for each policy implemented by IB-Groep. Examples are: output, the percentage of errors or appeals, the time required to process information, and the number of answered calls (see box 5.1). This set of PIs has been in use for almost ten years now. Both quantitative and qualitative aspects of performance are being measured. Only information on cost prices and profitability of commercial activities is not published.

Contrary to IB-Groep, the ROC has little experience of performance assessment. The number of performance indicators is limited, has not changed much over time, and consists mainly of financial indicators. The reported under-estimation of the ROC's performance supports hypothesis 2.8P. The establishment as a quango has forced the school to develop a system of indicators. Some first initiatives have been undertaken already.[43]

Clarity of policy objectives Executive agents, such as quangos, are often confronted with vague policy objectives, multiple goals or even contradictory goals. This creates leeway for quangocrats to diverge from the policy objectives as intended by politicians. Moreover, quangocrats can also use their discretionary authority to display deviant behaviour, for instance by manipulating information to upgrade the account of their performance. Hypothesis 2.9P predicted that if policy objectives are not clearly and unambiguously formulated, the chance of a performance paradox occurring is relatively high. In the case studies, the mission of the organizations was compared with the official policy objectives as mentioned in the statutes.

IB-Groep's mission is to become *the* service provider in the educational field (cf. annual report 1997). Among informants, consensus on this mission is strong. The stated mission is, however, not the same as the official goal the statutes mention, which is to implement policies in an efficient and impartial manner. Apparently, IB-Groep has re-interpreted the official goal to allow it to serve other principals as well. That also explains why quality is emphasized so strongly in the accounts of performance (in line with hypothesis 2.9P).

There is little divergence between the statutory goals of ROCs and the objectives informants specify: personal development, preparation for paid labour and accessibility of education to all students are mentioned as the most important goals. However, these aspects of performance are less intensively reported on than financial aspects. So, although the quango and the parent department agree on the objectives of adult and basic education, these are not used to assess the performance of ROCs. Congruence of the agent's and principal's objectives is therefore no guarantee that a performance paradox will not occur. Hypothesis 2.9P is not supported. Perhaps this can be explained by what Torenvlied (1996a,b) refers to as the tolerance level of politicians for deviant policy implementation. The ambiguity of policy objectives is created deliberately to allow executive agents some leeway with respect to policy implementation. In other words, while politicians claim to consider particular objectives to be most important, they have other objectives when assessing the performance of executive agents.

Emphasis on efficiency, effectiveness and Performance Indicators The more quangocrats value efficiency, effectiveness and PIs, the higher the chance that a performance paradox will occur (hypothesis 2.10P). Typically, in both case studies cost-efficiency is considered less important than, for example, the improvement of the quality of services (IB-Groep) or better accessibility of education to students (ROC). In neither case did informants consider the lack of efficiency gains a reason to limit the quango's autonomy or undo quangocratization. Effectiveness is valued higher. In the case of IB-Groep, this is matched by an emphasis on quality indicators in performance accounts. In the ROC, the lack of a tradition in performance assessment has led to little interest in PIs in general. Doubts are even expressed about the measurability of the quality and accessibility of education. Perhaps the implementation of the quality care report will offer new opportunities.

The system of performance assessment of IB-Groep being far more advanced than that of the ROC, the role of and importance attached to indicators is bigger as well. There is a strong commitment to (or belief in) the necessity and possibility of measuring performance, even of those elements that seem difficult to quantify such as the quality of customer service. Performance is frequently reported and discussed at length. Ill performance is evaluated and tackled, but sanctions are not imposed.

The development of new indicators in the ROC combined with decentralization of responsibilities and budgets are expected to increase the importance of PIs as a management tool. It is the intention of the management of the ROC to also use indicators to evaluate performance and, if necessary, sanction ill performance. At the moment this is not the custom, however.

To sum up, the case study results give only partial evidence in support of hypothesis 2.10P. It appears that those aspects of performance which are considered most important by the quango and the principal, are also the aspects on which is most extensively reported. Therefore, *if* efficiency and effectiveness are highly valued (which was not unequivocal in the case studies), this will be reflected in the reports on performance. Hypothesis 2.10P should therefore be reformulated into the prediction that if particular aspects of performance are considered more important than others, a performance paradox can occur, because the aspects that are valued most highly will tend to be over-reported.

Supervision The presence of a supervisor or regulator makes it more difficult to hide or manipulate information (hypothesis 2.11P). In both cases, supervisors were present, both within and outside of the quango.

Supervision of IB-Groep is executed by the Board of Supervisors (BS) and departmental accountants. Moreover, the Minister can order additional audits. Such external audits have been carried out and annual accounts are scrutinized by independent accountants. Interventions by the BS have taken place in the past. An example is the support of measures to decrease absenteeism among employees. However, the fact that the board is also part of IB-Groep may corrupt its supervisory role. Instead of an independent regulator, it could become an intermediary and, in case of a performance paradox, an accomplice.

Supervision on the ROC is the task of the Educational Review Office. In addition, the Educational Review Office has been given new tasks, in particular the supervision of quality care in schools following the introduction of national graduation guidelines. However, these activities have only just begun, and the full influence of the Educational Review Office cannot be determined yet.

Besides the Educational Review Offices, most ROCs have a Board of Supervisors. However, these boards consist of former school board members, who will be less independent than the Review Office. Informants from the ROC could not agree on the role the Board of Supervisors played in the school.

Because in both cases the role and position of the supervisor is unclear in some respects, no conclusions are drawn with respect to hypothesis 2.11P. Regulators were not part of the research design. I recommend that they are included in future research.

Tables 5.6 and 5.7 summarize to which extent the case study results have provided (partial) support for the hypotheses. If one case provided support and the other case did not, it is said that support is mixed. Only when both cases contradict the hypothesis, is the hypothesis refuted. It should be kept in mind that a (statistical) test of the hypotheses is not possible with the evidence gained from the two cases.

Some implications of the results have been discussed already, both with regard to the theoretical model as developed in chapter 3, and with respect to future research. In Chapter 6 the discussion will be continued by integrating the results from chapter 4 and 5, to find the answer to the two main research questions of this study.

Table 5.6 Degree of support for the hypotheses about the efficiency and effectiveness of policy implementation; case study results

No.	Hypothesis	Expected effect on Efficiency	Support for hypothesis
2.1	Ownership production rights	+	supported
2.2	Competition	+	refuted
2.3	Corporatism	+	?
2.4	Accountability requirements	+	?
2.5	Size	-	supported
2.6	Closeness to politicians	+	supported
2.7	Risk perception	+	supported

- = negative effect; + = positive effect; ? = no decision

Table 5.7 Degree of support for the hypotheses about the occurrence of a performance paradox; case study results

No.	Hypothesis	Expected Performance Paradox	Support for hypothesis
2.1P	Ownership production rights	-	supported
2.2P	Competition	+	supported
2.3P	Corporatism	+/-	?
2.4P	Accountability requirements	*	
2.5P	Size	+	mixed findings
2.6P	Closeness to politicians	-	refuted
2.7P	Risk perception	-	supported
2.8P	Diversity PIs	-	supported
2.9P	Clear policy objectives	-	mixed findings
2.10P	Emphasis on efficiency, PIs	+	supported
2.11P	Supervision	+/-	?

- = negative effect; + = positive effect; +/- = mixed prediction;
* = no prediction; ? = no decision

Notes

[1] Ideally, to test the claim of the practitioner theory, the performance of quangos should be compared to that of government bureaucracy. For practical reasons this is not possible. First, the legal monopoly on policy implementation implies the absence of competitors and hence of comparative information. Moreover, a task is often charged to one type of agent only, which makes a comparison between agents impossible. Finally, due to low accountability (see chapter 2), data on the performance is not available for all quangos and their predecessors. Therefore, an intra-quango comparison was made between a quango and its predecessor, which *might* have been government bureaucracy, but also a private organization or another type of quango.

[2] Of each case study an extensive case study report was made (Van Thiel, 1999a,b). This chapter contains only parts of those reports. A research log was included in those reports.

[3] Quangos in a cluster can be seen as competitive organizations, even though they are often regional monopolists. Their performance could be mutually compared, especially because they are charged with the same tasks and have to adhere to the same statutory prescriptions. However, quangos in a cluster can also take advantage of their cluster membership by co-operating when it comes to the presentation of information on their performance. For example, if the quangos in one cluster all report on particular aspects of their performance only, the principal has no comparable information to show that reports are incomplete or manipulated. A performance paradox is thus deliberately evoked, aimed at misguiding the principal.

[4] Note that new indicators can also suffer from a performance paradox.

[5] Because the cases are active in the same policy sector, hypothesis 2.5(P) cannot be tested, where the size of the sector is concerned. In 1993, there were 65 quangos in this policy sector (Algemene Rekenkamer, 1995), which makes it one of the sectors with the highest number of quangos. The parent department, i.e. the Ministry of Education, is also one of the largest ministries; total expenditures in 1998 are projected as NLG 38.9 billion, approximately 16% of total government expenditures (Rijksbegroting, 1998). In the 165 divisions (count of 1992; Carasso *et al.*, 1994), over 2,700 civil servants were employed (count of 1996; Staatsalmanak, 1996).

[6] The legal status of IB-Groep is that of a so-called *zelfstandig bestuursorgaan*, a public body (cf. table 1.1). IB-Groep was not included in the survey of the Netherlands Court of Audit (Algemene Rekenkamer, 1995; see chapters 2 and 4) because it was established only after 1993. IB-Groep participated several times in the contest organized by Arthur Andersen on the best annual report (see also chapter 2). It won the first prize in 1996 and came second a year later.

[7] In 1999 an official departmental evaluation was published (Deloitte & Touche, 1999). The results of this evaluation are not incorporated in this case study report. Conclusions of the official evaluation and this case study are very similar, despite differences in the availability of data and the methods used for analysis.

[8] In April 1990 the dissension about this law and its implementation finally led to the occupation and vandalization by students of the Groningen offices.

[9] The change of name was necessary because the use of the word bank is legally restricted.

[10] The motives given by politicians for the establishment of the quango IB-Groep confirm the assumptions of the practitioner theory about expected efficiency gains (cf. chapter 1). Moreover, the reduction of political risks for the Minister by hiving off the Groningen divisions corroborates the assumption made in chapter 3 that politicians will try to prevent loss of political support. The fact that only the implementation of policies was hived off, whereas the development of policies remained the prerogative of the Ministry seems in line with hypothesis 1.5 about collective goods; because policy development resembles a collective good to a greater extent than policy implementation does, policy development is not charged to quangos.

[11] The case of USZO is interesting, because it raises the question whether the principal, i.e. the Minister of Education, can actually dismiss a quango. When USZO's performance was criticized strongly, the Minister threatened to dismiss the quango - but did not do so (*De Volkskrant*, 1997).

[12] Moreover, political pressure often led the parent department to demand from IB-Groep to give priority to changes in the implementation process. A number of managerial improvements was repressed or delayed because of this pressure.

[13] IB-Groep's central office is located in Groningen but there are also 16 regional bureaus where clients can get information and application forms. However, because these bureaus are formally integrated in the organizational structure of IB-Groep and have limited responsibilities, they cannot be considered separate quangos. Hence, IB-Groep cannot be described as a cluster of quangos.

[14] 'Commercial' activities refer to tasks that do not concern the implementation of policies with which IB-Groep is charged by the parent department. Some examples are: the collection of debts from external students on behalf of the University of Amsterdam; the payment of benefits to employees at the Agricultural University Wageningen, mandated by the Ministry of Agriculture (until 1996); the development of a chipcard for students, which functions as both a credit and a student card; the establishment of a foundation charged with the coordination of examinations in adult education; and the development of a registration system of alumni for higher education institutions.

[15] In response to the findings of the official departmental evaluation (DeLoitte & Touche, 1999), the Minister of Education has indeed formulated stricter regulations on commercial activities by IB-Groep (*Brief van de Minister*, 1999).

[16] The statutes do not explicitly preclude the appointment of civil servants from the parent department as members of the Board of Supervisors.

[17] A special project team was charged with the acquisition of commercial activities.

[18] Some of IB-Groep's current clients (schools, universities) are potential future principals as well.

[19] The development of salaries of employees of IB-Groep equals that of civil servants (cf. CBS, 1998f). See also the findings of the Netherlands of Court of Audit study on the development of the costs of salaries for a number of quangos (Algemene Rekenkamer, 1995:48).

20 Turnover is the total budget received from principals to execute tasks. The parent department provides budgets for both programme costs and running costs, but only running costs are included in turnover.

21 In the annual report of 1996, IB-Groep states that answering all calls would be too expensive. The aim now is to answer 80% of the 2500 calls received per hour within 30 seconds by means of the (automated) voice-mail response system (see also *Kwaliteitshandvest*, 1998).

22 The total number of indemnifications was not available for 1992 and 1997. For 1992, the average number of 1991 and 1993 was imputed, and for 1997 the value of 1996 was taken. Teacher benefits were included until 1996 only, because the relevant division was hived off in 1996.

23 Paradoxically enough, most changes made were meant to cut budgets, i.e. to decrease programme costs.

24 In the official evaluation (Deloitte & Touche, 1999:70) an example is shown in which the costs of implementing policy changes are separated from the total costs of awarding a student grant. The example shows that the nett costs of awarding a grant have decreased, but because of the many changes total (gross) costs have increased.

25 Figure 5.3 includes only complaints the Ombudsman found valid.

26 In fact, the main conclusion of the official evaluation is similar to that of the case study. The evaluation report states that the *effectiveness* of policy implementation has improved since 1994. However, the *efficiency* of policy implementation has decreased for those tasks that were subject to numerous policy changes (Deloitte & Touche, 1999:4-5 [my translation, SvT]).

27 Some comparable information is present, though. For example, in customer surveys clients have been asked to compare the customer service of the quango with that of other organizations, such as the Tax Bureau and private banks (IB-Groep's performance is rated better than the first organization, but worse than the second). Furthermore, clients can file complaints with externally appointed supervisors, such as the National Ombudsman (see figure 5.3).

28 In 1996, IB-Groep won the contest for the best annual report between public agencies and local governments, organized by the accountancy and consultancy firm Arthur Andersen (1996). See also chapter 2.

29 Internationally, the Dutch ROCs can be best compared to the British Training and Enterprise Councils (TECs) which have been established from 1980 on (see, for example, Vickerstaff & Parker, 1996). There are 82 TECs in the United Kingdom (Hall & Weir, 1996:5).

30 This also could be interpreted as a general resistance of schools to change.

31 There is much disagreement about the question whether schools can be regarded as quangos. In my opinion *all* schools - including ROCs - meet the criteria listed in the definition in chapter 1: a public task is executed at arm's length but funded by public means. Schools should therefore be considered quangos. However, in the study of the Netherlands Court of Audit on Dutch quangos, only *public* universities and polytechnics were listed (Algemene Rekenkamer, 1995). The disagreement on the position of schools and their relationship with the government can be traced back to the school funding controversy of the late 1900s. In particular representatives of confessionally based

schools strongly resist the idea of their schools being controlled by the government, claiming their constitutional right of freedom of education.

[32] Independent schools may continue to exist but only under specific conditions. Also, they have far less autonomy than ROCs. Thirteen schools have been transformed into professional schools. Two schools based on a particular religion are excluded from the obligation to participate in an ROC. Some twenty schools are still searching for potential merging partners and have to find one before January 2000.

[33] Each ROC preferably consists of at least 7 components: at least three sectors of senior secondary vocational education, vocational education for apprentices, adult general secondary education for adults, adult basic education and non-formal adult education. The absence of one component is allowed, while the inclusion of non-formal education is optional.

[34] Between informants, opinions differ strongly with regard to the role of the Supervisory Board. According to the statutes, the SB has to supervise the ROC, but informants rather consider it an integral part of the ROC, even though it is operating at a distance.

[35] The central register (CREBO) is kept by IB-Groep, the first case study. Besides curricula, it lists which institutes are allowed to design examinations. In vocational education, 51% of all examinations have to be designed and supervised by other institutes than the ROCs, such as professional assocations.

[36] The difference between costs and revenues in table 5.3 does not exactly match surpluses, because funds were drawn from the capital reserves as well, and because of interest revenues (not listed in the table).

[37] All numbers of personnel and students are rounded off.

[38] In 1999, the ROC published a quality care report that does list the number of students and drop-outs for all nine units. However, the report did not include information on the number of graduated students.

[39] On average, 63% of students in adult education belong to an ethnic minority. Most of them are taking Dutch lessons.

[40] Vrancken and De Kemp (1996:7) also mention the high average age of staff as one of the major causes of inefficiencies in Dutch vocational education.

[41] In 1999, the Educational Review Office published the guidelines of the supervision on ROCs.

[42] Meyer & Gupta (1994) stress the need for various, comparable performance indicators, to allow for variations over time and comparisons between organizations or divisions of the same organization. In this manner, ROC-units could be compared.

[43] In the case study report (Van Thiel, 1999b) some recommendations are made for PIs that could be used in addition to existing indicators. Examples are: the number of students as a percentage of the total population of eligible students in the region, satisfaction of companies and tertiary schools with graduates, and the cost price per student or curriculum.

6 Conclusion

This book began with two observations. First, western governments are increasingly using quangos,[1] instead of government bureaucracy, for policy implementation. The proliferation of quangos is labelled quangocratization. In chapter 2 this trend was shown for the Netherlands. The number of Dutch quangos has increased strongly after World War II. They are charged with an ever increasing diversity of tasks and operate in all policy sectors.

My aim was to go beyond description, however. I want to *explain* the increase in the number of quangos as well. Using a rational actor approach, a theoretical model was developed in chapter 3, which indicated under which circumstances politicians choose quangos rather than government bureaucracy for the implementation of policies (the first research question). These specified circumstances were assumed to be the causes of quangocratization. Hypotheses were developed and tested in chapter 4. Below, the main results will be summarized and discussed.

The second observation concerns the motives politicians themselves mention for choosing a quango as an executive agent - that is, if politicians do mention motives, for in more than half the cases they do not (cf. Algemene Rekenkamer, 1995:19). Together these motives were called the practitioner theory. Several advantages are ascribed to quangos by politicians. In general, the performance of quangos is expected to be better because they operate closer to the citizen than government bureaucracy, away from meddling politicians.

From 1980 on, the dominant motive for choosing a quango as an executive agent stems from the neo-liberal belief in the superiority of the market. Quangos are considered more 'market-like' than government bureaucracy, and hence to be more efficient and effective agents. However, there is not much evidence to substantiate this claim. Chapter 5 therefore paid attention to the consequences of quangocratization, with a focus on quango performance.

A theoretical model was developed to predict under which conditions quangocrats - i.e. quango employees - implement policies in the most efficient and effective way (the second research question), and in compliance with the intention of the politicians who established the quango - or the opposite: when do they deviate from the intentions of the politicians?[2] Deviant behaviour is assumed to threaten the efficiency and effectiveness of policy implementation. Hypotheses were formulated on quango performance and put to the test in two case studies (see chapter 5 for the results).

This chapter concludes the study of the *trends, causes* and *consequences* of quangocratization. A separate section is devoted to each of these topics. The research findings, possible implications for the theoretical model in chapter 3, and recommendations for future research and policy development will all be discussed.

Trends

The number of quangos has increased throughout the western world in the past few decades. In this study the empirical focus is on quangos of the 'public body' type in the Netherlands, between 1950 and 1993. Chapter 2 described the increase in the number and variety of quangos. Also, a comparison was made between quangocratization and bureaucratization. This section will summarize the main findings of chapter 2. Also, the question raised in chapter 1 on how to characterize the process of quangocratization (as rationalization or not) will be dealt with below.

For a long time, there was little political debate on or scientific interest in quangos. Recently, however, a number of reports on quangos have been published (for an overview, see chapter 1). One of these reports was used in this study as the primary data source, namely the survey by the Netherlands Court of Audit on Dutch public bodies (NCA survey; Algemene Rekenkamer, 1995). In general, the interest of politicians and academics in quangos has increased after these reports were published, in particular with respect to the accountability of these organizations. In this study, ample attention was given to the accountability of quangos. Below a summary of the main findings is discussed. This section will conclude with some recommendations for future research.

Quangocratization in the Netherlands between 1950 and 1993

In chapter 2 the NCA survey was used to describe quangocratization in the

Netherlands. In particular after 1950, the number of quangos has increased. Nowadays, there are approximately 600 public bodies, employing more people (130,000) than there are departmental civil servants. Almost 20% of the State Budget is spent on quangos. Quangos are charged with an increasing variety of tasks, ranging from supervision, regulation, quasi-judicature, the granting of benefits, to research and co-ordination. Chapter 2 gave several examples of quangos and their tasks, also for other countries such as the United Kingdom, Denmark, Sweden, Finland and New Zealand (Hood & Schuppert, 1988; Modeen & Rosas, 1988; Hall & Weir, 1996; Flinders & Smith, 1999).

Quangos are not new types of organizations, though. In the Netherlands, as well as in other countries, such as the UK and Denmark, quangos have been used for centuries (Greve *et al.*, 1999). In the late 1970s and early 1980s, quangos were rediscovered as instruments of administrative reform (Pollitt, 1999). This led to an increase in the number of quangos in many western states, although there were differences with regard to the pace, institutional context and the means that were deployed to achieve reform (Van Waarden, 1992:158; Unger & Van Waarden, 1995:11). For example, privatization occurred on a much larger scale in the United Kingdom than in the Netherlands. Besides the fact that there were fewer state-owned companies in the Netherlands, differences in political tradition and administrative system also played a part in this disparity (Pollitt & Bouckaert, 2000:42).

Trends after 1993

The empirical parts of this study concentrated on the establishment of quangos in the Netherlands between 1950 and 1993. At face value, there does not seem to be a decline in the use of quangos *after* 1993 (as claimed by some researchers, see e.g. Hakvoort & Veenswijk, 1998:1). However, the publication of reports such as the NCA survey, triggered a hot political debate on the desirability of using quangos. Politicians now seem more inclined to use less extreme types of quangos, for example, contract agencies instead of public bodies, or public bodies instead of privatization (cf. table 1.1).[3]

The increasing use of quangos and private organizations for policy implementation has led to a blurring of the boundaries between state, market and society. Consequently, the national government is rapidly changing from a hierarchical, centralistic body to a horizontal, cooperative one.

Governments are looking for new ways of governance (Kooiman, 1999). For example, in the UK, the Blair administration has produced a white paper on 'Modernising Government' (1999), which stresses the importance of a so-called *joined-up* government. In collaboration with local governments, interest groups, executive agencies, and private organizations the government aims to improve the quality of policy development and implementation. Such plans do not entail a retreat from the use of quangos for policy implementation, however (Leeuw, Jenkins & Van Thiel, forthcoming).

Quangocratization and Bureaucratization Side by Side

This study has shown that, contrary to what the practitioner theory claims, the increase in the number of quangos has *not* led to a decrease in the size of government bureaucracy. Figure 2.3 showed that, until 1980, bureaucratization and quangocratization took place alongside each other. After 1982, the number of departmental divisions has decreased, but the number of civil servants has risen, as have government expenditures (adjusted for inflation).

The analysis in chapter 4 confirmed these trends. Tables 4.4 and 4.6 showed that quangos are established more often after an increase in the size of government. This means that politicians first take on more tasks, and only after that start using quangos for policy implementation. One would expect that the use of quangos as executive agents reduces the size of the government bureaucracy; quangos take over tasks that would otherwise have been carried out by government bureaucracy. Moreover, quangos are sometimes hived-off former departmental units, which would mean a reduction in governments size has taken place. This expectation was refuted by the analysis, however.[4] Government bureaucracy will continue to exist. As LeGrand and Bartlett (1993:7) predicted, governments will change the *way* in which policies are implemented, rather than abolishing the policies in question.

Rationalization or De-rationalization?

In this study, quangocratization - i.e. the proliferation of quangos - is considered a recent stage in the development of western states. In chapter 1 the question was raised whether quangocratization could be seen as a next step in the process of rationalization, or if it is rather a form of de-rationalization with quangos replacing government bureaucracy. I hold the opinion that quangocratization is a form of rationalization, for the following reasons.

First, the findings of this study show that quangos have not replaced government bureaucracy but have become *supplementary* executive agents. Quangos and government bureaucracy exist side by side. Moreover, quangos can be equally bureaucratic as government bureaucracy when it comes to, for example, using standard operating procedures (Wilson, 1989:221). Also, in quangos the focus lies more often on input than output (see results on performance indicators in annual reports of quangos, chapter 2), and in some quangos the legal position of quangocrats is comparable to that of bureaucrats (see the first case study in chapter 5). Weber considered bureaucracy the most rational form of organization and therefore labelled its proliferation rationalization. If quangos have equally bureaucratic features, their proliferation could also fit that label (cf. Nonet & Selznick, 1978).

Second, the analysis of the practitioner theory in chapter 1 showed that the main motive of politicians for the establishment of quangos is to make efficiency gains. This is a typical rational aim (Van der Loo & Van Reijen, 1997:167).[5]

Third, the transfer of executive power to quangos fits the idea of continued specialization, or division of labour, typical of the rationalization process in western societies. In chapter 1 it was described how citizens transfer part of their individual rights to politicians, who provides these citizens, in their turn, with collective goods (cf. North, 1981). To implement the policies promised, politicians transfer part of the citizens' rights to executive agents. A cascade of principals and agents results from this process (see box 1.1). The preference of politicians for executive agents may have changed from government bureaucracy to quangos, the continued partitioning of rights is typical of a process of rationalization. Therefore, quangocratization is, in my opinion, the next step in the process of rationalization.

Despite the rational characteristics of quangocratization, it has led to some 'irrational' outcomes as well.[6] Most notably, as a result of quangocratization in many western countries, today's public sector is characterized by a plethora of organizations, which impedes a simple and logic ordering of that sector (Leeuw, 1992:20-22). There are but few similarities between different types of quangos, although an effort was made in this study (see table 1.1) to draw up a typology of quangos. Comparative research will remain a difficult task.

Policy Developments: the Accountability of Quangos

In the Netherlands and the UK, reports on the number of quangos and their democratic accountability (Weir & Hall, 1994; Algemene Rekenkamer, 1995; Hall & Weir, 1996) show that the accountability of quangos is poorly regulated. My study demonstrates that many quangos are under no obligation to report on their performance. But if they are, reports are often considered incomplete by experts (see table 2.6), or tend to concentrate on particular aspects of performance only. This was also the case with the two quangos studied in chapter 5.

In response to the reports on the accountability of quangos, politicians have tried to reassert their political authority and increase regulation and auditing (*Herstel van het primaat van de politiek*, 1995; Rhodes, 1997:89-93). For example, committees have been set up to advise the government on the behaviour of quangocrats (Nolan Committee in UK) or the market activities of quangos (Commissie Cohen in the Netherlands). Guidelines have been drawn up on the decision-making process surrounding the privatization or hiving off of departmental units (*Aanwijzingen*, 1996), and a law proposal is presented on the accountability requirements that should be imposed on. Regulators have been appointed for the supervision of quangos and privatized companies in, for example, the policy sectors of telecommunications, and water and electricity. Some of these regulators are quangos themselves. The effects of these new policies and regulations are as yet unknown.

An explanation for the lack of interest of politicians in imposing accountability requirements on quangos falls outside the scope of this study, although the findings do offer some suggestions. For example, policy implementation may be put at arm's length by politicians in order to avoid accountability for that implementation. Politicians may not *want* to know what is going on in the quango, because they no longer wish to be responsible. Moreover, legally they are not responsible any longer.[7] As long as there are no signs of ill performance - not because ill performance does not occur, but because it is not being reported - there is no need to intervene (Leeuw, 1995). Without external intervention, this cycle can go on for a long time.

On the other hand, the findings also suggest that in some cases accountability requirements *are* imposed, sometimes even over the full range of the accountability scale. It would be interesting to explain such patterns. For example, it was found that in years when a large number of quangos is established, more accountability requirements are imposed on average (contrary to what was expected; see table 4.7). This finding could be attributed to the desire of politicians to minimize monitoring costs, - and thus increase the efficiency of policy implementation (for a more extensive argument, see chapter 3). If imposing accountability requirements on one quango alone is relatively more expensive than imposing them on several quangos at a time, politicians will only impose requirements when larger numbers of quangos are established. This explanation has not been tested in this study, however.

Another pattern found is that of quangos in corporatist policy fields facing fewer accountability requirements (see table 4.7). It was suggested that in corporatist policy areas, such as Agriculture and Welfare, more informal monitoring devices are available (because of more intensive contacts between politicians, interest groups and executive agents), that can replace the need for formal ones. Further study is necessary on such 'soft controls'.

Future Research

Unfortunately, the NCA survey does not contain information on the origin of quangos. Although it was established that quangos are seldom abolished (3%), re-organizations and mergers do occur in one out of five cases. To improve the descriptive research of quangos, more study is necessary on the lifetimes of quangos. For instance, information is needed on whether a certain quango has been newly established, or results from a merger, has been set up by hiving off a former departmental unit, or by hiving in a former private organization into the public sector. Also, quangos can change over time from, for example, a contract agency to a public body, and *vice versa*. This is called quango-drift (Greve *et al.*, 1999).

Another option could be to refine the level of analysis to policy sectors, instead of confining it to national government level. The number of quangos in policy fields varies strongly (see figure 2.6), as does the rate of growth in different sectors. The establishment of quangos in policy sector A could coincide with an expansion of the size of the parent department in policy sector B, leading to both more quangocratization and bureaucratization. By examining one policy sector at a time, such counter-effects can be excluded and the *nett* effect of quangocratization on the size of government bureaucracy studied.

Causes

The first research question dealt with the causes of quangocratization. In chapter 3, a theoretical model was developed to explain why, under certain conditions, politicians will choose quangos as an executive agent. Hypotheses were formulated that were tested in chapter 4. In this section the model and the analyses are discussed and the main findings summarized. Also, some recommendations for future theory development and research are given.

Theoretical Model to explain Causes of Quangocratization

In order to explain quangocratization, a theoretical model was developed to predict the choice of politicians for a quango as an executive agent, as opposed to government bureaucracy. See chapter 3 for a full analysis and formulation of the model; here, I shall confine myself to a basic outline. The model is based on assumptions from rational choice theory (Coleman, 1990; Lindenberg, & Frey, 1993). Politicians are actors who aim to maximize particular goals, in the present case, that of getting re-elected (public choice theory; Mueller, 1989; Dunleavy, 1991). To achieve that goal, politicians will try to please voters by promising them new policies. Implementation of these policies is charged to an executive agent. In this study, it is assumed that politicians have the choice between a quango and government bureaucracy as an executive agent.

The choice for a quango has two advantages to politicians. First, the responsibility of politicians for policy implementation by quangos is limited. The risk of being held accountable for ill performance is reduced. Second, the establishment of quangos offers politicians the opportunity to let interest groups (which represent large numbers of voters) participate in, for example, quango boards. This has been labelled patronage. However, the establishment of a quango has an important potential disadvantage to politicians as well. If policies are implemented in an inefficient or ineffective way, politicians have less opportunity to intervene. And, although their responsibility is limited, they can, in the end, still be held accountable for choosing a quango for policy implementation and supervising it.

In a rational actor model, it is assumed that politicians are able to assess all these advantages and disadvantages when choosing an executive agent. Their choice will depend on situational characteristics and the potential gain in electoral support. For example, when competition for votes is fierce, politicians are expected to choose quangos, because of the afore-mentioned benefits. Also, when policies are considered very important to voters, as in the case of collective goods, politicians will not want to put implementation at arm's length, which would lead to a situation in which they cannot intervene. See table 3.1 for a full overview of all hypotheses.

On the other hand, it does not seem realistic to assume that politicians can size up *all* this information and make the most rational choice. There-fore, the model was expanded with some assumptions on *bounded ration-ality*. Politicians can use information and experience from other politicians to improve their decision-making. This is called imitation.

Another alternative is to monitor the performance of quangos set up in the past. In the latter instance, however, extra costs will have to be made. These 'monitoring costs' will increase the costs of policy implementation - and decrease efficiency.

All hypotheses from the rational actor model and bounded rationality model were tested in chapter 4. Below, the main findings are discussed.

The Rational Actor Model

As explained before, the choice of politicians will be influenced by situa-tional characteristics. Six circumstances (or conditions) were tested on their impact: (i) political ideology; (ii) economic conditions; (iii) electoral competition among politicians; (iv) corporatism; and the degree to which the policy to be implemented concerns the provision of (v) collective goods or (vi) requires many specific investments (hypotheses 1.1 to 1.6). The results of the analyses were shown in tables 4.3 and 4.4. Below, only those conditions are discussed that contributed to the explanation of quangocrati-zation.

Political ideology Contrary to what common sense would suggest, politi-cal ideology was not expected to be of decisive influence on the choice of politicians for quangos. The advantages and disadvantages of choosing quangos were thought to be valid for *all* politicians no matter what their political beliefs are. The analyses confirm this expectation.

Actually, this is not surprising. It was pointed out before that quangos have been in use for a long time, and consequently have been established by different political administrations. The increase in the number of quan-gos in the 1980s was a widespread one. Public sector reform took place in countries with conservative governments (e.g. the UK) and social-democratic ones (e.g. Sweden). The neo-liberal belief in the market has been followed by western governments of all sorts of ideological backgrounds. There are, perhaps, differences in the pace of administrative reform and the preference for certain types of quangos (Van Waarden, 1992:158; Unger & Van Waarden, 1995:11; Pollitt & Bouckaert, 2000), but quangocratization has taken place throughout the western world.

For the Netherlands, it would be interesting to investigate quangocratization for the period after 1993. Between 1950 and 1993, cabinet coalitions (left-wing and right-wing) were dominated by the christian-democratic party. This may have distorted the analysis. If Christian-Democratic politicians favour quangos for ideological reasons, a lot of quangos will have been established in this period, no matter which other political party participated in the governing coalition. Christian-Democratic politicians may have used their power and resources to force other politicians to take the same policy position (Stokman, 1994). In the analyses in chapter 4, such an effect could have been ruled out. However, after 1993, cabinets have come into office in which the Christian-Democrats do not participate. It would be interesting to see whether this had an effect on the number of decisions to establish a quango.

Economic conditions Common sense would probably suggest that politicians will choose quangos more often in times of economic down-swing. Politicians expect efficiency gains from the use of quangos - at least according to the practitioner theory - and they may wish to downsize the administrative system by hiving off departmental units into quangos. However, one could just as well argue that in times of economic upswing, when government tasks and budget are expanding, more policies have to be implemented by executive agents, which include quangos. Therefore, economic conditions were not expected to be decisive to the choice of politicians for quangos. The analyses showed that quangos are no more (or less) frequently established in periods of economic up-swing, suggesting that economic conditions indeed are not decisive to the choice of politicians for quangos. However, the testing of the hypothesis on economic conditions was incomplete due to a lack of data. Conclusions should therefore be drawn with some reservation.

It would be interesting to investigate the effect that quangocratization, in its turn, has on economic conditions. For example, if the practitioner theory is valid, efficiency gains due to quangocratization will lead to a decrease in government expenditures. So far, there is little evidence to support this claim (see also the results of case studies below).

Electoral competition In the model, politicians are said to strive after (re)-election. Therefore, it is expected that in situations where competition for votes is fierce, for example, in election times, politicians will use quangos to enhance their electoral support. The analyses refuted this expectation; elections lead to fewer quangos being established. During election campaigns politicians promise new policies to voters. These new policies will have to be implemented by executive agents, such as quangos. However, policies cannot be implemented directly. The development of policies and the passing of laws takes time, on average seven years (Algemene Rekenkamer, 1994:6). Therefore, the *total* number of decisions on executive agents, quangos included, is expected to decrease in election times and increase in the years after. This could not be tested in this study, because only data on the decisions to establish a quango were available.

Tasks of quangos: collective goods and specific investments Quangos were expected to be charged less often with tasks that require investments in specific assets, such as knowledge or equipment. Two drawbacks for politicians were identified that could result from putting specific tasks at arm's length (for a more elaborated argument, see chapter 3). First, efficiency losses may occur because specific assets can be less easily re-deployed by a quango than by government bureaucracy. Second, the principal (i.e. politicians) might unwillingly become dependent upon the agent due to the sunk costs connected with specific assets. The findings do not corroborate these expectations, however (see table 4.6). Most quangos are charged more often with specific tasks, such as supervision, certification, quasi-judicature and regulation development (see figure 2.4 for an overview of tasks of quangos).

Apparently, the drawbacks of charging quangos with specific tasks do not outweigh the advantages. Three advantages were listed in chapter 4. First, the risk that politicians will be held accountable for ill performance is reduced. Second, the risk of high investments in non-recurrent assets is transferred to the quango. And third, specific tasks can no longer disrupt the bureaucratic routines of government bureaucracy. On the basis of these arguments, a new hypothesis can now be formulated: the more specific the investments required for policy implementation are, the more likely it is that politicians will choose a quango as the executive agent.

Conclusions with respect to the rational actor model The rational actor model offers no explanation of quangocratization. Apparently, political ideology and economic conditions do not influence the choice of politicians for quangos. Quangos are established to implement policies that have been promised to voters, in particular policies that require specific investments. This does not, however, explain the *increase* in the number of quangos in the Netherlands between 1950 and 1993. Below, I shall show that the explanation of quango proliferation can be improved by using the bounded rationality model.

The Bounded Rationality Model

To reduce uncertainty about the effects of their choice of an executive agent, politicians can use two strategies to gain information or experience with agents and develop guidelines for decision-making. The first strategy is imitation, or the repetition of decisions. By repeating the decisions of other politicians, or previous ones they made themselves, politicians gradually obtain more information and experience.

Politicians do indeed repeat their decisions for quangos as executive agents. No conclusive evidence was found, however, to support the expected increase in the diversity of tasks quangos are charged with and the policy fields they operate in. Only in the case of clusters, the rate of establishment has decreased in policy sectors that provide collective goods, such as Defence, Finance, Justice and the Home Office. It has to be noted, though, that the number of quangos in these sectors is generally low (see figure 2.5).

The second strategy politicians can apply is monitoring. Information on the performance of quangos can be used to evaluate the effects of past decisions. However, monitoring costs inflate the costs of policy implementation, something which is considered undesirable by politicians. Therefore, politicians were expected not to choose quangos if many investments are necessary for monitoring. This expectation was refuted. Apparently, the choice of politicians for a quango is not discouraged by a need for monitoring. This seems awkward when remembering the few accountability requirements imposed on quangos in general (shown in chapter 2). Perhaps under certain conditions, politicians can make a choice for a quango only if they also impose monitoring demands onto the organization. Further study into such conditions is recommended.

To conclude, the bounded rational actor model provides a better explanation of quangocratization than the rational actor model. The increase in the number of quangos is caused by politicians repeating (or imitating) decisions. Quangocratization is indeed a trend, in vogue. This raises the question whether this trend occurs in other countries as well. That is a question for future research.

Future Research: Convergence or Divergence?

Quangocratization is taking place in several western countries (Pollitt, 1999), although there are differences in the rate with which quangos are established and the types of quangos that result. There is some debate about whether this trend will lead to a convergence between western states or a divergence (see, e.g. Unger & Van Waarden, 1995). To find an answer to this question, more insight is needed into the process of imitation. For example, the differences in the rate of establishment of quangos in different policy sectors (shown in figure 2.6) are of interest. Imitation could take of one policy field by another. One could also go beyond the scope of this study and look at imitation between different types of quangos (e.g. agencies and state-owned enterprises) or between levels of government (e.g. local government). The focus of such imitation studies should be on three issues.

First, there are different types of imitation. Powell and DiMaggio (1991) mention three types: coercive, normative and mimetic isomorphism. Coercive isomorphism refers to the process in which politically superior bodies oblige subordinate bodies to copy decisions or structures. Unger and Van Waarden (1995:21), for example, point to the possibility of multinationals using their influence and position to force governments of different countries to use the same organizational setting for negotiations. They call this type of imitation 'enforcement'. Normative isomorphism refers to situations where (professional) norms are copied in order to achieve legitimization of ideas or organizational structures. Mimetic isomorphism is the phenomenon of organizations copying other organizations that are considered most successful (cf. Tolbert & Zucker, 1982). As a result, organizations resemble each other more and more.

A second issue is the source of imitation; who is the first to use quangos? This study has suggested, amongst others that imitation takes place between policy fields, or between quangos with certain tasks. There are other possibilities as well. Imitation can occur between the private and public sector (see Fligstein [1985] on the spread of the multi-divisional form of organization).

The third issue to be studied is how the imitation process comes about. Rogers' (1995) theory on the diffusion of innovations can be useful. It offers ideas on, for example, first adopters and the way in which new ideas or technologies spread through networks.

Methodological Problems

The analysis of the causes of quangocratization was hindered by a lack of data on decisions to charge government bureaucracy with the implementation of policies (cf. the control group in the design). Out of necessity, the analyses therefore focussed on the number of decisions to establish quangos *per year*. In that way, the causes of quangocratization could be inferred; if a certain condition caused a large number of decisions to establish quangos, it was considered to have caused quangocratization.

However, this research design does not allow the incorporation of - *individual* characteristics of decisions to establish a quango. To solve this problem, the number of decisions was aggregated for each year. Several weighting formulas were used, in particular for the explanatory variables 'corporatism', 'collective goods', 'specific investments' and 'monitoring' (see chapter 4), which led to some sub-optimal operationalizations. The conclusions of this study should therefore be approached with some reservation. For example, the complete interpretation of the findings on the tasks with which quangos are charged is that quangos are often charged with specific tasks. However, it cannot be determined whether quangos are charged more often with specific tasks *than government bureaucracy*, which was the original prediction.

Theoretical Implications

The theoretical model in this study is but a first step towards an explanation of quangocratization. I have made a number of simplifying assumptions. Moreover, the model limits itself to only two corporate actors, between whom no interaction is allowed. This makes the model rather static and abstract. To improve the model, one could add new elements (cf. method of decreasing abstraction; Lindenberg, 1992), in particular other actors and by interaction between actors.

There is a number of actors which could be incorporated. The most obvious candidates are civil servants and interest groups. Civil servants play an important role in the decision-making process surrounding policies and the implementation of policies. According to Dunleavy (1991: ch.6) and Christensen (1999), bureaucrats can increase their status and acquire more autonomy by, for example, becoming the executive of a quango. On the other hand, bureaucrats are expected to act in the general interest and serve their ministers. The hiving off of a departmental unit can be in the interest of a minister, for instance, if the political risks are high or if hiving off is accompanied by budget cuts. If, however, hiving off a departmental unit is not advantageous to the minister but has a positive effect for bureaucrats, the latter face a conflict of interests. This raises the question under which conditions bureaucrats will make a certain choice.

Interest groups were discussed at several points in the previous chapters. Politicians were expected to use quangos for patronage purposes, for example, by appointing members of interest groups as members of quango boards. The fact that interest groups were present did not, however, contribute to the explanation of quangocratization. An alternative explanation was proposed, which stated that politicians have other means than patronage to enhance the commitment of interest groups in corporatist policy sectors.[8] Frequent contact and membership of official advisory boards can substitute patronage by quango board membership. This also enables politicians to do equal favour to all interest groups in a particular policy sector - and maxime electoral support - instead of giving preference to one group over another (no monopoly rents; Mueller, 1989; Tollison, 1997). Therefore, the *presence* of interest groups may be of importance for the explanation of the behaviour of politicians and quangocrats, but for the study of quangocratization it is *not* necessary to include these groups as (corporate) actors in the model.

Another possibility for adding actors to the model, is to refine the distinguished corporate actors (cf. Coleman, 1990:541, Scharpf, 1997:21). For example, no distinction was made between politicians from different parties or between politicians in office and in opposition. Differences in power position, possible conflicts, and the need to compromise and co-operate are, however, important factors in the decision-making process (see, e.g., Bueno de Mesquita & Stokman, 1994; Stokman, 1994; Stokman & Van Oosten, 1994; Stokman & Zeggelink, 1996).

Interaction between politicians and quangocrats could be added to the model by including a feedback loop. For example, if politicians have chosen a quango as an executive agent, they can use information on its performance to improve their next choice of an executive agent. In fact, the imitation and monitoring hypotheses implicitly assume such feedback loops already. I will continue the discussion on the potential advantages of allowing interaction into the theoretical model in the next section.

Consequences

The second research question concerned the consequences of quangocratization, in particular quango performance. A theoretical model was developed to explain under which conditions quangos will implement policies in the most efficient and effective manner. Hypotheses were formulated and put to the test in two case studies (in chapter 5). In this section, the model and the findings of the case studies are summarized and discussed. Implications from the findings for both the practitioner theory and the theoretical model developed in this study are discussed below. Finally, some recommendations are given for future research.

Theoretical Model on Quango Performance

The practitioner theory claims that quangos are more efficient and effective than government bureaucracy when it comes to policy implementation. This claim is, as yet, not substantiated (chapter 1 gives an overview of the research on quango performance up till now). Therefore, this study paid attention to the performance of quangos. In fact, the practitioner theory can be said to have been put to the test. To that end, a theoretical model was developed to predict quango performance. The practitioner theory itself is *not* used as the theoretical framework. In the theoretical model developed in chapter 3, assumptions were used from rational choice theory (Coleman, 1990), neo-institutional economics (in particular principal agent theory; Pratt & Zeckhauser, 1991) and public choice theory (Mueller, 1989; Dunleavy, 1991). The model was described at length in chapter 3; here, I shall only discuss its main features.

Politicians want quangocrats to implement policies in the most efficient and effective manner. However, quangocrats may pursue their own goals as well (e.g. to gain fringe benefits, social approval, or strengthen their own policy position). If the goals of politicians (the principal) and quangocrats (the agent) diverge, quangocrats have to choose which goals to pursue, i.e. whether they will comply with the principal's goals or whether they will deviate from those goals in pursuit of their own. In the latter case, the efficiency and effectiveness of policy implementation is in danger - at least from the politicians' point of view.

The choice of quangocrats between compliance and deviance is - conditioned by situational constraints. For example, the more autonomy a quango has, the more it has to gain by performing efficiently and effectively. Autonomy was defined in this study as the ownership of production rights, for example, whether quangos can determine their own input, output and budget (cf. chapter 1). A quango that has the right to retain surpluses will try to perform as efficiently as possible. Another condition that - influences quango performance is its market position. Monopolists are expected to be less efficient and effective than competitive quangos. A final example of situational constraints that influence the choice between compliance and deviance is the perception of quangocrats of the risk of being caught at deviant behaviour. The higher the chance of getting caught, the more inclined quangocrats are to comply with the principal's goals. Hypotheses were formulated about the expected effects of these and other conditions. See table 3.2 for a full overview.

The model assumes that politicians are able to assess whether a quango is performing efficiently and effectively. This need not always be the case, however. Not only can it be questioned whether politicians are capable of collecting and processing all information on quango performance (cf. bounded rationality), but performance assessment itself can be subject to limitations. For example, accounts of performance can suffer from a so-called *performance paradox* (Meyer & Gupta, 1994). Performance indicators may - instead of providing good insight into performance and stimulating it - lead to distorted accounts of performance. Indicators may 'run down' and loose the ability to discriminate between good and bad performers. Or indicators can focus on certain aspects of performance only, such as easily quantifiable aspects (cf. also Smith, 1995). In such cases performance is - unintentionally - under-reported. Indicators can also be deliberately manipulated to hide ill performance (over-reporting). It is important to keep in mind that a performance paradox does not necessarily mean that performance is worse than reported. It merely indicates that reported performance is not an accurate reflection of actual performance. Chapter 3 deals with this phenomenon extensively, and offers examples.

A performance paradox can contaminate the information on performance and invalidate conclusions on the consequences of quangocratization. It is therefore important to pay attention to conditions that can evoke such a paradox. According to Meyer and Gupta (1994), certain characteristics of the performance assessment system are important in this respect. For example, a limited variety of performance indicators and a strong emphasis in the organization on using performance indicators can lead to a performance paradox, unintended or deliberately. A deliberately evoked paradox can be seen as a type of deviant behaviour of quangocrats. The conditions that were expected to lead to deviant behaviour - mentioned above - can therefore also lead to a performance paradox occurring. Hypotheses about the occurence of a performance paradox were summarized in table 3.2.

Quango performance was studied by means of case studies (see chapter 5). Two quangos were selected for an intra-quango comparison of performance, both before and after their establishment as a quango. Annual reports and annual accounts were analyzed, and informants from the quangos and the parent department interviewed. Based on the results of two case studies, hypotheses cannot be (statistically) tested, but the findings were discussed with respect to the amount of support they provided for the hypotheses (i.e. analytical generalization; Yin, 1994:30). See chapter 5 for an extensive summary and discussion of the results of the case studies.

Consequences of Quangocratization: Quango Performance

The first case study was IB-Groep, a quango established in 1994, which is charged with the implementation of a number of educational policies. After 1994, its performance has improved with regard to the quality of service, but efficiency has deteriorated slightly, because the costs of policy implementation have increased. Similar conclusions were drawn in the departmental evaluation of the establishment of IB-Groep as a quango, the report of which was published after this case study was done (Deloitte & Touche, 1999).

The second case study was the ROC, a school for adult and vocational education, established in 1996. A full comparison of performance before and after the ROC's establishment was not possible due to a lack of information and incomparability of the performance data of the former schools. However, two conclusions could be drawn. First, the deficits of the former vocational schools - which make up almost 90% of the ROC - strongly influence the ROC total performance. As a result, there has been no significant improvement in efficiency since the school's establishment as a quango. Second, adult education, in particular non-formal education, seems to have profited most from the merger, which is shown by an increase in the number of students. This will improve the accessibility of education, one of the main goals of ROCs, and could therefore be interpreted as an improvement in the effectiveness of the quango (although there are more aspects to effectiveness).

To sum up, both case studies show that the establishment as a quango has not led to an immediate or an overall improvement in performance. In chapter 3, eleven hypotheses were formulated to explain quango performance or predict the occurence of a performance paradox. These hypotheses were tested in the case studies. To facilitate the case descriptions, the hypotheses were re-grouped into four categories (see chapter 5). These categories will be used here to describe the main findings of the case studies.

Unfortunately, not in all cases could clear, unambiguous conclusions be drawn with respect to the hypotheses (cf. tables 5.6 and 5.7 for a summary). For example, sometimes the findings of the case studies contradicted each other. In other instances, there were insufficient data or informants disagreed. More research is therefore necessary. The discussion below will only deal with conclusions that are clearly supported by the case study evidence.

Production rights It was expected that the more production rights a quango owns, the more it stands to gain from efficient and effective policy implementation. For example, one of the production rights is the ability to influence the size of budgets and the right to retain surpluses. Quangos that own such rights will profit from gains in efficiency and effectiveness and will therefore perform better. The case studies confirm this expectation.

IB-Groep negotiates with the parent department on its budget every year and can thus influence its budget. Consequently, the performance of IB-Groep has improved; the quality of customer service has increased and, after its establishment as a quango, IB-Groep has obtained - and retained - small nett surpluses almost every year. The increase in the costs of policy implementation is considered less detrimental than the aforementioned improvements, both by the quango and the parent department.

The ROC, on the other hand, has little if no influence on its budget. In one particular year, this led to the decision to report a deficit rather than using reserves to solve the problem. By reporting the deficit, the quango hoped to persuade the parent department to increase its budget. It lacked other means to influence budgetary decisions.

The more production rights a quango owns, the more autonomous it is (cf. definition of autonomy in chapter 1). The case studies prove that autonomy influences which aspects of performance are reported on most. The more production rights a quango owns, the lesser the need to manipulate information (no performance paradox). This is in line with expectations. IB-Groep, which owns many production rights, gives an extensive account of its performance. The emphasis it places on the quality of customer service is fully approved of by the parent department. Performance assessment in ROCs, on the other hand, was only recently developed. For a long time the former schools had little interest in performance assessment. They provided only information requested by the parent department, in the prescribed format. Because the requested information concerned only financial indicators, the schools had little insight into other aspects of performance. The autonomy obtained after the establishment of the ROC - e.g. the ROC is now responsible for shortages itself - has increased the need for performance assessment. So, the fewer production rights a quango owns, the less information it will provide on its performance (under-reporting).

Organizational characteristics Two organizational characteristics proved to be important for the explanation of quango performance. The first characteristic is the market position of a quango. Competition was expected to enhance quango performance. In reality, however, quangos face little real competition. IB-Groep is a monopolist, as are many other quangos (approximately 139 out of the 545 in the NCA-survey; Algemene Rekenkamer, 1995 [own calculations]).

The ROC does face a few competitors in its region, but it has eliminated the pressure of competition by entering into an alliance with those competitors. These types of co-operation are an *unintended* consequence of quangocratization. Although the absence of competition does not immediately lead to ill performance, the lack of comparative material makes it difficult to assess how efficient and effective policy implementation by quangos is. In the case of co-operating competitive quangos, it is even possible that the quangos make agreements on what information to report to the principal. If that is the case, reports on performance become unreliable; a performance paradox is present.

The second organizational characteristic that proved important is the origin of the quango, in particular whether it is a hived-off former departmental unit (like IB-Groep) or a hived-in former private organization (like the ROC). Quangos established through hiving off are closer to the parent department. A close relationship was expected to induce compliance, and thus lead to efficient and effective policy implementation. The case study evidence supported this expectation. A close relationship does not, however, preclude the occurence of a performance paradox, which was expected to happen. Apparently, how many and what kind of information a quango provides on its performance depends on other factors than its relationship to the parent department. Autonomy already proved to be important (see above), but accountability requirements and the perceptions the quango has of which aspects of performance are important proved to be of influence as well (see below).

Accountability requirements The emphasis that both quangos place on certain aspects of performance (IB-Groep stresses the quality of customer service and the ROC financial matters) is reflected in the performance indicators they use. IB-Groep employs a large number of quality indicators, in an otherwise elaborate performance assessment system. For ROCs, a performance assessment system is being developed to replace the current one, which confines itself to financial indicators. According to Meyer and Gupta (1994), a more diverse system of indicators, with a large variety of comparable indicators, will reduce the chances of a performance paradox occurring.

Another probable cause of the performance paradox lies in the clarity of policy objectives. The extent to which quangos succeed in reaching the objectives of the policies they implement - within budgetary contraints - reflects their effectiveness and efficiency. As such, policy goals are important in the assessment of quango performance. However, policy goals are often vague, multiple and sometimes even contradictory (Wilson, 1989:45-48),[9] because politicians want to please as many voters as possible. In practice, it is up to the executive agent to translate the official policy goals into operational ones (cf. Torenvlied, 1996a,b).

In both case studies such a translation has occurred. IB-Groep is charged with the implementation of a number of educational policies. IB-Groep itself has formulated its mission as offering good customer service. This explains why such a lot of attention is paid in the annual reports to quality indicators. In the case of the ROC, full accessibility of education and a high quality of the education offered are the goals of the school itself, whereas performance assessment focusses almost entirely on financial indicators. In both organizations, performance indicators stress other aspects of performance than the official policy objectives - which does *not* mean that the quangos are performing poorly. The vagueness and multiplicity of policy objectives threatens the clarity of performance reports, which could result in a performance paradox.

Perceptions The case studies showed that quangos report most extensively on those aspects of performance that are considered vital to the continuation of their existence as an executive agent. Other aspects of performance will not or to a lesser extent be reported on. Therefore, if the focus within a quango is one-sided, its performance reports will be so as well, and a performance paradox results. These findings are in line with the expectations.

In the case of IB-Groep, the quango considers quality of customer service vital to its survival (see the mission statement), which explains the ample attention for quality indicators. The parent department agrees with this, because it values quality as well. However, the quango wants to use the improvement of customer service to attract new principals, in case the parent department reduces the amount of tasks to be carried out. The parent department does not agree with those plans and intends to restrict the regulations on commercial activities of IB-Groep (*Brief van de Minister*, 1999:8).

In the case of the ROC, the emphasis so far has been on financial indicators only, despite the general agreement between the quango and the parent department that the effectiveness of education (i.e. accessibility to all students) is, in fact, the main objective of ROCs. However, the parent department has for a long time only requested financial information, and the schools provided only that kind of information. Now that schools have been given more autonomy regarding budgets and educational programmes, performance assessment will become more extensive. Some first initiatives have been undertaken already by, among others, the *BVE-raad* (the council that represents all ROCs) and the Educational Review Office (see chapter 5 for further explanation).

Quangos can afford to report only on particular aspects of performance when the chance of getting caught at and sanctioned for this kind of behaviour is low. For example, in the case of IB-Groep the parent department has no (immediate) substitute executive agents. The lack of competitive information reduces the chance of getting caught, while the dependency of the parent department on the quango reduces the chances of being sanctioned for deviant behaviour. White (1991) referred to this latter type of dependency as the 'reversal of control' between principal and agent.

In other cases, quangos have found ways to avoid getting caught out. For example, ROCs were meant to compete, which would enable the parent department to compare the performance of ROCs. Instead of competing, ROCs have entered into alliances that reduce the pressure from competition. If ROCs also make agreements on the information they report to the principal - and thus deliberately evoke a performance paradox - alliances can reduce the possibility for comparison of performance as well. Reversal of control and circumvention of competition are unintended consequences of quangocratization. As in the case of a performance paradox, these unintended consequences do not necessarily lead to a deterioration of quango performance, still, from the politicians' point of view, they pose a threat to the efficiency and effectiveness of policy implementation.

Conclusions To sum up, the case studies show that quangocratization does not automatically, or immediately, lead to more efficient and effective policy implementation, as claimed by the practitioner theory. Moreover, the case studies revealed a number of unintended consequences of establishing quangos. So far, these consequences have been overlooked by politicians: reversal of control, circumvention of competition, and performance paradoxes. The practitioner theory should therefore be adjusted.

Policy Developments: Modification of the Practitioner Theory

The practitioner theory claims that quangos are more efficient and effective than government bureaucracy when it comes to policy implementation. This study has shown that the establishment of quangos *may* lead to an improvement in policy implementation, as compared to implementation prior to establishment of quangos (note: not necessarily by government bureaucracy), but the effect is not an immediate one, nor does it concern *all* aspects of performance, i.e. costs, output, and quality.[10] Therefore, the practitioner theory should be moderated to allow for a transitional period. Moreover, the establishment of a quango also costs money. The budget restrictions, or even budget cuts, often coinciding with the establishment of a quango can undermine the realization of efficiency and effectiveness gains.

The practitioner theory assumed that competition would increase quango performance: quangos are forced to beat their competitors in order to acquire budgets and their performance can be compared. First of all, this study shows that there is little competition among quangos. A large number of quangos are monopolists. Secondly, quangos have found ways to circumvent the pressure of competition. This is an unintended, and perhaps unforeseen, consequence of quangocratization that needs to be taken into account by the practitioner theory.

The case studies suggest that it is not so much competition that influences quango performance, but autonomy, i.e. the ownership of production rights. The more production rights a quango owns, the more efficiently and effectively it performs. So far, this finding is in line with the practitioner theory. Recently, however, politicians seem to prefer to establish quangos with *lower* degrees of autonomy. The claims of the practitioner theory with regard to efficiency and effectiveness of policy implementation should then be mitigated.

Autonomy also strongly influences the manner in which quangos report on their performance. Quangos tend to report most extensively on those aspects of performance that are relevant to the continuation of their existence as an executive agent. This may lead to an over- or under-representation of actual performance. Reports on performance should therefore not be taken for granted by politicians, nor by academics for that matter (Leeuw, 1996). The current debate on quango accountability shows that politicians are getting more interested in this issue. So far, however, this does not seem to have had any consequences for the practitioner theory.

Theoretical Implications

A real statistical test of the hypotheses cannot be performed on the basis of two case studies. Most hypotheses seem to be supported by the case study findings. Replication of case studies is necessary to draw more valid conclusions.

With regard to theoretical model, the same remarks can be made as - before. The model is but a first step towards an explanation of the consequences of quangocratization. It is a simple and static model that needs to be elaborated further. Two improvements were suggested earlier, which will be discussed again here.

First, the model can be improved by allowing interaction between quangocrats and politicians. The case studies gave a number of examples in which interaction led to consequences not anticipated by politicians. For example, the co-operation between ROCs to circumvent competitive pressure is a typical example of interaction, in this case between quangos.[11] The case study of IB-Groep showed that the closeness of the relationship between the quango and the parent department is responsible for, for example, the way in which performance is reported.

The theoretical model developed in chapter 3 assumes that there is no interaction; the decision of politicians to establish a quango is followed by the quango carrying out its task (or not). Interaction between politicians and quangocrats gives politicians more information on the consequences of their decision. Not only can they use that information to improve future decisions (as argued in the previous section), they can also try to adjust decisions already taken. For example, monitoring devices may indicate that a particular quango is not performing efficiently. Such a quango can be dismissed, at least in theory. In practice, there are often no substitute quangos.[12] Therefore, it is most likely that politicians will (threaten to or) impose budget cuts, or develop new regulations for the quango, as was done in the case of IB-Groep.

Nowadays, communication between the parent department and quangos is often formalized in so-called *interfaces* (Verhaak, Bagchus & Van Twist, 1996: 33-37; Kickert et al., 1998:17). Interfaces can be contracts or protocols specifying the exchange of information on both policy and managerial matters. Interfaces can also be departmental divisions charged with all contacts between quangos and the parent department, a procedure followed by the Ministry of Education (see chapter 5).

To make the model more dynamic, interface organizations could be included as an actor. Appointed regulators could also be incorporated, for that matter. While the presence of interfaces and/or regulators is meant to improve quango performance, it may also have perverse effects. For example, it limits the autonomy of a quango, which - according to earlier findings - can negatively influence performance (see above). Moreover, quangocrats may consider the appointment of regulators or interface organizations as a sign of distrust and try to sabotage these types of monitoring (cf. Breton & Wintrobe, 1982) by, for example, deliberately manipulating performance assessment information (i.e. evoke a performance paradox).

Future Research: the Performance Paradox in Public Organizations

In the case studies, several strategies were used to try to uncover a performance paradox. Besides an analysis of the performance assessment system of the two quangos, information from external sources was used as well to evaluate performance. For example, information from the National Ombudsman on IB-Groep was used and data from the Ministry of Education on all Dutch ROCs. Also, new performance indicators were developed, based on the indicators the quangos use themselves. The results, however, can be no more than indicative of conditions or mechanisms that could evoke a performance paradox. In both cases, such conditions were found to be present, leading to an over-estimation of quality aspects of performance in the annual reports of IB-Groep and of financial indicators in the reports of the ROC. It proved to be very difficult, however, to actually verify the existence of a performance paradox. The ambiguity of policy objectives and the lack of competitors - typical characteristics of public sector organizations - made it difficult to assess and evaluate performance.

On the other hand, one could argue that the chance of a performance paradox occurring is greater in the public sector, as compared to the private sector. A performance paradox is the result of a discrepancy between the policy objectives set by politicians and the goals of executive agents (Smith, 1995). The translation of the executive agent of official policy objectives into operational goals leaves room for deviations in policy implementation, which can lead to a performance paradox. It should be noted, though, that in some cases room for interpretation is given intentionally because politicians want to leave implementation to the experts, i.e. the executive agents (cf. Torenvlied, 1996a,b). Other factors that could increase the chance of a performance paradox in the public sector are the lack of potential bankruptcy (dismissal) and the disjunction between costs and revenues (LeGrand, 1991). Both factors create leeway for organizations to manipulate information *and* get away with it.

More research on the performance paradox in public sector organizations - including quangos - is warranted, especially when one considers the amounts of money spent on and by those organizations. Because there is still so little information available on the performance paradox and its workings in the public sector, I recommend that in the first instance, more case studies be done, along the lines of those in this study. Next, a meta-analysis could be conducted, after the fashion of Meyer and Gupta (1994). Meyer and Gupta compared the performance of numerous organizations (e.g. banks, hospitals, nuclear plants) over several decades, using the same indicators for all organizations (see also Meyer & O'Shaughnessy [1993] on strategic business units of firms). Such a study does, as yet, not seem feasible in the public sector. Public organizations are, however, increasingly getting interested in the development and application of performance indicators (as was found in both of the case studies). In the near future it should be possible to perform this kind of research. The problem of incomparability of performance - because of the lack of competition - remains an obstacle to benchmarking, though.

A Final Word

This study has described and tried to explain quangocratization, in particular in the Netherlands. It has moved beyond the case studies done so far by developing a theoretical framework to explain the causes and consequences of quangocratization, and by using a combination of quantitative and qualitative research methods. More theory development and research are necessary, however, and several recommendations have been made to that end. My research has demonstrated that quangocratization is caused mainly by imitation, or repetition of decisions by politicians. Establishing quangos is in vogue. The motives of politicians for their choice of quangos (i.e. the practitioner theory) are not substantiated. An (immediate and overall) improvement in the efficiency and effectiveness of policy implementation is not found. The lack of interest politicians have shown for a long time in the accountability of quangos does, however, seem to indicate that politicians are not really interested in whether the creation of quangos will lead to an improvement of the performance. Perhaps the *political* efficiency of establishing quangos is more important to politicians than the *economic* efficiency.

Notes

[1] Quango is the acronym of *qu*asi-*a*utonomous *n*on-*g*overnmental *o*rganization (Barker, 1982). In chapter 1, quangos were defined as organizations, which, as their main task, are charged with the implementation of one or more public policies. They are funded publically but operate at arm's length of the central government, without an immediate hierarchical relationship existing with a minister or a parent department (Leeuw, 1992). There are different types of quangos - for example, contract agencies, public bodies, and state-owned enterprises - operating under different conditions and having different degrees of autonomy (see table 1.1). Private organizations can be charged with policy implementation as well by privatization, competitive tendering or outsourcing.

[2] Three types of deviant behaviour were discerned in chapter 3. First, quangocrats can minimize their efforts (shirking; Douma & Schreuder, 1998:109). Second, they can try to use means to further their own ends, for example, to maximize fringe benefits,or manipulate information to hide or upgrade their behaviour. And third, quangocrats can implement policies in a way consistent with their own policy position rather than those of politicians (cf. Torenvlied, 1996a,b).

[3] The inclination of Dutch politicians to use less extreme types of quangos can be illustrated by two recent examples. First, the privatization of the Dutch railroad company (*Nederlandse Spoorwegen*) has been temporarily suspended, awaiting the results of the political debate on this issue (see e.g. *De Volkskrant*, 1999b). Second, in November 1999 the Minister of Social Affairs published a new proposal on the implementation of social security policies, in particular policies regarding disability and unemployment benefits. In this proposal, the government reinstates her power and reduces the influence of unions, employers and the quangos currently implementing social security policies (*NRC Handelsblad*, 1999).

[4] In part, this is due to an operationalization poblem. Most quangos (60%) receive their budgets from the state, and in a large number of cases (30%) quangocrats are, in fact, seconded civil servants (see chapter 2 for more details). Budgets and the number of employees are therefore included in counts of government expenditures and the number of civil servants. It is even possible that former private organizations that have been hived in into the public sector and become quangos, are included; their establishment thus has led to an increase in expenditures and the number of personnel, instead of a decrease.

[5] For this line of reasoning it is irrelevant whether quangos are indeed more efficient and effective. It is the *wish* of politicians to use more efficient executive agents that makes quangocratization an example of rationalization.

[6] Irrational outcomes of a process of rationalization do not undo the rational character of the process. Bureaucracy has led to some irrational outcomes as well, such as bureaucratism. Another form of rationalization, the McDonaldization of society (Ritzer, 1993), aims at optimal efficiency by designing the production process in such a way that as many customers as possible are served in the shortest time possible. Irrational outcomes of this process are, for example, the de-humanizing of the work environment, resulting in a high degree of absenteeism and the breaking of contracts (Van der Loo and Van Reijen 1997:167).

[7] Politicians do remain responsible, though, for their choice of a quango as an executive

agent and also for the supervision of these quangos.

[8] A similar explanation was offered for the lack of accountability requirements imposed upon quangos in corporatist policy sectors.

[9] For example, quangos often are expected to meet goals such as equitable *and* efficient distribution of particular goods or services, or are confronted with an expansion of the workload and simultaneous budget cuts. In the latter case, some quangos decide to carry out only those tasks that will be successful. This phenomenon is called cream skimming (LeGrand & Bartlett, 1993:31-34) or cherry picking. Cream skimming can be illustrated by the dilemma of the Dutch Employment Agencies, whose performance is measured as the number of people for whom they find a job. As a result, th agencies tend to focus on those people for whom it is relatively easy to find a job, and skip the 'difficult cases' (*Volkskrant*, 1994). However, employment policies specify that it is precisely the second group on which they should concentrate. The agencies face the dilemma of choosing between carrying out the policies as intended but performing poorly on the indicators, or doing well on the indicators but carrying out the policies ineffectively.

[10] The absence of expected efficiency gains means that quangocratization does not lead to the (rational) aims politicians had in mind. However, this does not diminish the rational character of quangocratization as a process; rationalization can have irrational outcomes.

[11] The co-operation between quangos to reduce the effects of measures taken by politicians is in line with the findings of Flache and Macy (1996) on the cohesion of social networks. High cohesion in groups (in this case ROCs) may lead to deviance rather than compliance to the principal. See also chapter 3.

[12] Sometimes, the lack of subsitute agents can force the principal to accept a certain amount of deviant behaviour by the executive agent, without being able to take measures against it. White (1991) refers to this as a 'reversal of control' between principals and agents.

Bibliography

Aanwijzingen voor de regelgeving met aanwijzingen inzake zelfstandige bestuursorganen. *Staatscourant, 177*, 13 september 1996, pp. 16-21.

Algemene Rekenkamer. (1994). *Wetgeving: organisatie, proces en produkt*. Tweede Kamer, vergaderjaar 1993-1994, 23 710 nrs. 1-2. Den Haag, Sdu.

Algemene Rekenkamer. (1995). *Verslag 1994. Deel 3: Zelfstandige bestuursorganen en ministeriële verantwoordelijkheid*. Tweede Kamer, vergaderjaar 1994-1995, 24 130, nr. 3. Den Haag, Sdu.

Algemene Rekenkamer. (1997). *Klantgerichtheid publieke dienstverlening*. Tweede Kamer, vergaderjaar 1996-1997, 25 285, nrs. 1-2. Den Haag, Sdu.

Algemene Rekenkamer. (1999). *Verantwoording en toezicht bij rechtspersonen met een wettelijke taak*. [On-line: www.rekenkamer.nl]

Agresti, A. (1996). *An introduction to Categorical Data Analysis*. Wiley Series in Probability and Statistics. New York, John Wiley & Sons, Inc.

Aquina, H. (1988). The Netherlands. In T. Modeen & A. Rosas (eds.), *Indirect public administration in fourteen countries* (pp. 281-299). Finland, Abo Academy Press.

Arrow, K.J. (1991). The economics of agency. In J.W. Pratt & R.J. Zeckhauser (eds.), *Principals and agents* (pp.37-55). Boston, Massachusetts & Harvard Business School Press.

Arthur Andersen. (1995). *Verslaggeving en prestatieverantwoording bij de overheid: jury-verslag F.G. Kordestrofee 1995*. Den Haag.

Arthur Andersen. (1996). *Verslaggeving en prestatieverantwoording bij de overheid: jury-verslag F.G. Kordestrofee 1996*. Den Haag.

Arthur Andersen. (1997). *Verslaggeving en prestatieverantwoording bij de overheid: jury-verslag F.G. Kordestrofee 1997*. Den Haag.

Arthur Andersen. (1998). *Verslaggeving en prestatieverantwoording bij de overheid: jury-verslag F.G. Kordestrofee 1998*. Rotterdam.

Barkema, H. (1995). Prikkels en prestaties: agency theorie. *ESB, 75*, 228-230.

Barker, A. (ed.). (1982). *Quangos in Britain*. MacMillan Press Ltd., London.

Barron, D.N. (1992). The analysis of count data: overdispersion and autocorrelation. *Sociological methodology, 24*, 179-220.

Bendor, J. (1988). Review article: formal models of bureaucracy. *British Journal of Political Science, 18*, 353-395.

Berry, W.B. & Feldman, S. (1985). *Multiple regression in practice*. Series Quantitative Applications in the Social Sciences, No. 50. Newbury Park, SAGE Publications.

Berkum, J. van & Dijkem, K. van. (1997). Verzelfstandiging van rijkstaken in Nederland: de eerste schreden van drie zelfstandige bestuursorganen. Zoetermeer, Omslag Groep.

Blau, P.M. & Meyer M.W. (1987). *Bureaucracy in modern society* (3rd edition). New York, Random House.

Boef-van der Meulen, S., Bronneman-Helmers, H.M., Eggink, E. & Herweijer, L.J. (1995). *Processen van schaalvergroting in het onderwijs: een tussenstand.* SCP, Sociale en Culturele Studies, Cahier 121. Den Haag, Sociaal Cultureel Planbureau.

Bogt, H.J. ter. (1994). Verzelfstandiging van overheidsorganisaties, bezien vanuit de neo-institutionele economie. *Beleidswetenschap, 8,* 205-239.

Bogt, H.J. ter. (1997). Neo-institutionele economie, management control en verzelfstandiging van overheidsorganisaties. Capelle aan den IJssel, Labyrint Publication.

Boston, J. (1995). Lessons from the Antipodes. In B. O'Toole & G. Jordan (eds.), *The next steps: improving management in government?* (pp. 161-177). Aldershot, Dartmouth.

Bovenberg, A.L. & C.N. Teulings. (1999). Op zoek naar de grenzen van de staat: publieke verantwoordelijkheid tussen contract en eigendomsrecht. In W. Derksen, M.E. Kelenkamp, F.J.P.M. Hoefnagel, & M. Scheltema (eds.), *Over publieke en private verantwoordelijkheden* (pp.19-136). WRR Voorstudies en Achtergronden, V105. Den Haag, Sdu.

Boxum, J.L. (1997). Algemene wetgeving voor zelfstandige bestuurslichamen. Deventer, Uitgeverij Kluwer.

Boxum, J.L., Ridder, J. de & Scheltema, M. (1989). *Zelfstandige bestuursorganen in soorten.* Deventer, Uitgeverij Kluwer.

Boyne, G. (1998). Bureaucratic theory meets reality: public choice and contracting in US local government. *Public Administration Review, 58,* 474-484.

Braam, A. van. (ed.). (1969). *Sociologie van het staatsbestuur II: een keuze uit de internationale literatuur* (Weber: Gezag, bestuur en bureaucratie [pp. 482-497]). Rotterdam, Universitaire Pers.

Breton, A. & Wintrobe, R. (1982). The logic of bureaucratic conduct: an economic analysis of competition, exchange and efficiency in private and public organizations. Cambridge, Cambridge University Press.

Brief van de Minister van Onderwijs, Cultuur en Wetenschappen. (1999). Tweede Kamer, vergaderjaar 1998-1999, 24 724, nr. 35.

Bueno de Mesquita, B. & Stokman, F.N. (1994). Models of exchange and of expected utility maximization: a comparison of accuracy. In B. Bueno de Mesquita & F.N. Stokman (eds.), *European Community Decision Making: models, applications and comparisons* (pp. 214-228). New Haven and London, Yale University Press.

Bulder, B., Leeuw, F. & Flap, H. (1996). Networks and evaluating public-sector reforms. *Evaluation, 2,* 261-276.

Bulder, A., Wal, A. van der & Flap, H. (1997). Evaluatie besturingsmodel rechtsbijstand. Utrecht, Universiteit Utrecht.

BVE-procescoördinatie. (1997). *Sprong naar kwaliteit.* Bunnik.

BVE-raad (1997). ROC's in de branding. Financiële kaders in relatie tot maatschappelijke betekenis. De Bilt.

Carasso, L.C., Koopmans, J.M.P., Raadschelders, J.C.N. & Voermans, I.F.J. (1994). Organisatiedifferentiatie bij de rijksoverheid in historisch perspectief. *Bestuursweten-schappen, 6,* 483-495.

CBS: Centraal Bureau voor de Statistiek. (1994). *1899-1994: vijfennegentig jaren statistiek in tijdreeksen.* Den Haag, Sdu.

CBS: Centraal Bureau voor de Statistiek. (1998a). *Tijdreeksen niet-financiele instellingen: gewone uitgaven rijksfinancien.* [On-line: www.cbs.nl]

CBS: Centraal Bureau voor de Statistiek. (1998b). *Tijdreeksen economie: consumentenprijsindex*. [On-line: www.cbs.nl]

CBS: Centraal Bureau voor de Statistiek. (1998c). *Tijdreeksen mens en maatschappij: verkiezingen en kabinetten, 1950-1993*. [On-line: www.cbs.nl]

CBS: Centraal Bureau voor de Statistiek. (1998d). *Tijdreeksen economie: economische groei 1993*. [On-line: www.cbs.nl]

CBS: Centraal Bureau voor de Statistiek. (1998e). *Tijdreeksen arbeid: percentage werkloosheid op totale beroepsbevolking 1950-1990*. [On-line: www.cbs.nl]

CBS: Centraal Bureau voor de Statistiek. (1998f). *Tijdreeksen arbeid: CAO-lonen per maand, inclusief bijzondere beloningen, sector overheid*. [On-line: www.cbs.nl]

CBS: Centraal Bureau voor de Statistiek. (1998g). *Tijdreeksen gezondheid en maatschappelijk welzijn: ziekteverzuim overheid*. [On-line: www.cbs.nl]

Christensen, J. (1988). Denmark. In T. Modeen & A. Rosas (eds.), *Indirect public administration in fourteen countries* (pp. 65-85). Finland, Abo Academy Press.

Christensen, J. (1999). *Bureaucratic autonomy as a political asset*. Paper presented at workshop 'Politicians, bureaucrats and institutional reform', ECPR Joint Sessions of workshops. Mannheim, March 26-31.

Coleman, J.S. (1982). *The asymmetric society*. New York, Syracuse University Press.

Coleman, J.S. (1990). *Foundations of social theory*. Cambridge MA, The Belknap Press of Harvard University Press.

Commissie Cohen. (1997). *Eindrapport Werkgroep Markt en Overheid*. Den Haag, Ministerie van Economische Zaken, Commissie Marktwerking Deregulering en Wetgevingskwaliteit.

Commissie Sint. (1994). *Verantwoord verzelfstandigen*. Den Haag.

Coops, R.H. (ed.) (1995). *Van overheid naar markt*. Den Haag, Sdu.

Database Algemene Rekenkamer (1995). Abstracts and excerpts from laws underlying quangos. [Unpublished]

Deloitte & Touche. (1999). *Rapport evaluatie verzelfstandiging IB-Groep*. Den Haag, Deloitte Touche Tohmatsu.

DiMaggio, P.J. & W.W. Powell. (1983). The iron cage revisited: institutional isomorphism and collective rationality in organizational fields. *American Sociological Review, 48*, 147-160.

Doel, J. van den & Velthoven B.C.J. van. (1990). *Demokratie en welvaartstheorie* (3rd edition). Alphen aan den Rijn, Samsom H.D. Tjeenk Willink. Serie Maatschappijbeelden.

Douma, S. & Schreuder, H. (1998). *Economic approaches to organizations* (2nd edition). New York, Prentice Hall.

Downs, A. (1965). Non-market decision making: a theory of bureaucracy. *American Economic Review, 54*, 439-446.

Dunleavy, P. (1991). Democracy, bureaucracy and public choice: economic explanations in social science. New York, Harvester Wheatsheaf.

Dunleavy, P. (1994). The globalization of public services production: can government be 'best in world'? *Public Policy and Administration, 9*(2), 36-65.

Eggertson, T. (1990). *Economic behavior and institutions*. Cambridge, Cambridge University Press.

Fernhout, R. (1980). Incorporatie belangengroeperingen in de sociale en economische wetgeving. In H.J.G. Verhallen, R. Fernhout, P.E. Visser (eds.), *Corporatisme in Neder-*

land: belangengroepen en democratie (pp. 119-228). Alpen aan den Rijn, Samson Uitgeverij, Reeks Arbeidsverhoudingen.

Flache, A. & Macy, M.W. (1996). The weakness of strong ties: collective action failure in a highly cohesive group. *Journal of Mathematical Sociology, 21,* 3-28.

Flap, H.D. (1990). Patronage: an institution in its own right. In M. Hechter, K.D. Opp & R. Wippler (eds.), *Social institutions: their emergence, maintenance and effects* (pp. 225-244). New York, Walter de Gruyter Inc.

Fligstein, N. (1985). The spread of the multidivisional form among large firms, 1919-1979. *American Sociological Review, 50,* 377-391.

Flinders, M.V. (1999a). Quangos: why do governments love them? In M.V. Flinders & M.J. Smith (eds.), *Quangos, accountability and reform: the politics of quasi-government.* (pp. 26-39). London, Macmillan Press.

Flinders, M.V. (1999b). Setting the scene: quangos in context. In M.V. Flinders & M.J. Smith (eds.), *Quangos, accountability and reform: the politics of quasi-government.* (pp. 3-16). London, Macmillan Press.

Flinders, M.V. & Smith, M.J. (eds.). (1999). Quangos, accountability and reform: the politics of quasi-government. London, Macmillan Press.

Gardner, W., Mulvey, E.P. & Shaw, E.C. (1995). Regression analyses of counts and rates: Poisson, overdispersed Poisson and Negative Binominal models. *Psychological Bulletin, 118,* 392-404.

Gazendam, H.W.M. & Homburg, V.M.F. (1999). Efficiëntie en verzelfstandiging: economische en politieke efficiëntie als verklaring voor verzelfstandiging. *Bestuurskunde, 8,* 19-27.

Ghoshal, S. & Moran, P. (1996). Bad for practices: a critique of the transaction cost theory. *Academy of Management Review, 21,* 13-47.

Goorden, C.P.J., Boer, M.M. den & Buijn, F.K. (1997). *ZBO's, verzelfstandiging en privatisering. Pre-advies voor de Vereniging van Administratief Recht,* VAR-reeks 118. Alphen aan den Rijn, Samson H.D. Tjeenk Willink.

Graaf, H. van de. (1988). Beleid en de beoordeling van beleidstheorieën. *Beleid & Maatschappij, XV,* 7-19.

Granovetter, M. (1973). The strength of weak ties. *American Journal of Sociology, 78,* 1360-1380.

Greve, C. (1996). Quangos in Denmark and Scandinavia:. trends, problems and perspectives. PERC Occasional Paper No. 14. Sheffield.

Greve, C. (1999). Quangos in Denmark and Scandinavia: trends problems and perspectives. In M.V. Flinders & M.J. Smith. (eds), *Quangos, accountability and reform: the politics of quasi-government* (pp.83-108). London, Macmillan Press.

Greve, C., Flinders, M.V., & Thiel S. van. (1999). Quangos: what's in a name? Defining quangos from a comparative perspective. *Governance, 12,* 1, 129-146.

Groenendijk, J. (1998). *Overheidsinvloed in het openbaar vervoer.* Amsterdam, Thesis Publishers.

Hakvoort, J.L.M. & Veenswijk, M. (1997). *De dynamiek van cultuurverandering: een diagnostisch cultuurinstrument voor overheidsorganisaties.* Management in overheidsorganisaties, november, G3230-1/18.

Hakvoort, J.L.M. & Veenswijk, M. (1998). *Cultuurverandering bij verzelfstandigde organisaties.* Delft, Eburon.

Hall, W. & Weir, S. (1996). *The untouchables: power and accountability in the quango state*. The Democratic Audit of the United Kingdom. London, Charter 88 Trust.

Hardin, R. (1997). Economic theories of the state. In D.C. Mueller (ed.), *Perspectives on public choice: a handbook* (pp. 21-34). Cambridge University Press.

Hazeu, C. (2000). Institutionele economie: een optiek op organisatie- en sturingsvraagstukken. Bussum, Uitgeverij Coutinho.

Hemerijck, A.C. (1994). Hardnekkigheid van corporatistisch beleid in Nederland. *Beleid en Maatschappij*, 1-2, 23-47.

Hendrikse, G.W.J. (1993). Coördineren en motiveren: een overzicht van de economische organisatietheorie. Schoonhoven, Academic Service.

Herstel van het primaat van de politiek bij de aansturing van zelfstandige bestuursorganen. (1995). Tweede Kamer, vergaderjaar 1994-1995, 24 130, nr. 5. Den Haag, Sdu.

Hogwood, B. (1995). The 'growth' of quangos: evidence and explanations. *Parliamentary Affairs*, *48*, 207-225.

Hoed, P. den. (1992). De samenstelling van de overheid. *Beleid en Maatschappij, XIX*, 111-126.

Hood, C. (1984). *The hidden public sector: the world of para-government organizations*. Glasgow, Centre for the study of public policy, no. 133.

Hood, C. (1988). PGOs in the United Kingdom. In C. Hood & G.F. Schuppert (eds.), *Delivering public services in Western Europe* (pp.75-93). London, SAGE Publications.

Hood, C. & Schuppert, G.F. (eds.). (1988). *Delivering public services in Western Europe*. London, SAGE Publications.

Hoogerwerf, A. (1984). Beleid berust op veronderstellingen: de beleidstheorie. *Acta Politica, 19*, 493-531.

Jaarverslag Nationale Ombudsman. (1990). Tweede Kamer, vergaderjaar 1990-1991, 22 016, nrs. 1-2. Den Haag, Sdu.

Jaarverslag Nationale Ombudsman. (1991). Tweede Kamer, vergaderjaar 1991-1992, 22 550, nrs. 1-2. Den Haag, Sdu.

Jaarverslag Nationale Ombudsman. (1992). Tweede Kamer, vergaderjaar 1992-1993, 23 050, nrs. 1-2. Den Haag, Sdu.

Jaarverslag Nationale Ombudsman. (1993). Tweede Kamer, vergaderjaar 1993-1994, 23 655, nrs. 1-2. Den Haag, Sdu.

Jaarverslag Nationale Ombudsman. (1995). Tweede Kamer, vergaderjaar 1995-1996, 24 635, nrs. 1-2. Den Haag, Sdu.

Jensen, M.C. & Meckling, W.H. (1976). Theory of the firm: managerial behavior, agency costs and ownership structure. *Journal of Financial economics, 3*, 305-360.

Johnston, J. (199?). *Econometric methods*. (pp.304-330). New York, McGraw-Hill.

Kaufman, H. (1976). *Are government organizations immortal?* Washington, Brookings Institution.

Kickert, W.J.M., Mol, N.P. & Sorber, A. (eds.). V*erzelfstandiging van overheidsdiensten*. Geschriften van de Vereniging voor Bestuurskunde. Congrespublikatie 1992. Den Haag, VUGA Uitgeverij B.V.

Kickert, W.J.M. (ed.). (1997). Public management and administrative reform in western Europe. Cheltenham, Edward Elgar.

Kickert, W.J.M. et al. (1998). Aansturing van verzelfstandigde overheidsdiensten: over publiek management van hybride organisaties. Alpen aan den Rijn, Samsom.

Kiezer en Parlement. (1950-1993). Groningen, Wolters Noordhoff.

King, G., Keohane, R.O. & Verba, S. (1994). *Designing social inquiry: scientific inference in qualitative research.* New Jersey, Princeton University Press.

Kooiman, J. (1999). Social-political governance: overview, reflections and design. *Public Management: an International Journal of Research and Theory, 1*, 61-92.

Künneke, R.W. (1992). De verdeling van eigendomsrechten als bestuurskundig vraagstuk. *Bestuurskunde, 1*, 194-203.

Kuiper, G.M., Vliet, J.J. van, Boxum, J.L., Schreuder, C.A., Ridder, J. de & Scheltema, M. (1992). *Verzelfstandiging: publiek of privaat.* Deventer, Kluwer.

Land, K.C., McCall, P.L. & Nagin, D.S. (1996). A comparison of Poisson, Negative Binominal, and semiparametric mixed Poisson regression models. *Sociological Methods & Research, 24*, 387-442.

Leeuw, F.L. (1989). Beleidstheorieën: veronderstellingen achter beleid. In A. Hoogerwerf (ed.), *Overheidsbeleid* (4th edition, pp. 91-105). Serie maatschappijbeelden. Alphen aan den Rijn, Samsom H.D. Tjeenk Willink.

Leeuw, F.L. (1992). Produktie en effectiviteit van overheidsbeleid: institutionele analyse en effectmeting. Amsterdam, VUGA.

Leeuw, F.L. (1995). Onbedoelde gevolgen van bestuurlijke intenties. in H. van Gunsteren & E. van Ruyven (eds.), *Bestuur in De Ongekende Samenleving* (pp. 55-72). Den Haag, Sdu.

Leeuw, F.L. (1996). Performance auditing, new public management and performance improvement: questions and answers. *Accounting, Auditing and Accountability Journal, 9*, 92-102.

Leeuw, F.L. & Thiel, S. van. (1996). *Quangocratization in the Netherlands.* PERC Occassional Paper No. 13. University of Sheffield.

Leeuw, F.L., Thiel, S. van & Flap H.D. (1997). Quangocratie in Nederland? *Intermediair, 48*, 9.

Leeuw, F.L. & Thiel, S. van. (1999). Quangocratization in the Netherlands. In M.V. Flinders & M.J. Smith (eds.), *Quangos, accountability and reform: the politics of quasi-government* (pp.72-83). London, Macmillan Press.

LeGrand, J. (1991). The theory of government failure. *British Journal of Political Science, 21*, 423-442.

LeGrand, J. & Bartlett, W. (eds). (1993). *Quasi-markets and social policy.* London, Macmillan Press Ltd.

Lijphart, A. (1968). Verzuiling, pacificatie en kentering in de Nederlandse politiek. Amsterdam, De Bussy.

Lindenberg, S.M. (1983). The New Political Economy: its potential and limitations for the social sciences in general and for sociology in particular. In W. Sodeur (ed.), *Ökonomische Erklärung sozialen Verhaltens* (pp. 1-68). Duisburg, Verlag der sozialwisschaftlichen Kooperative.

Lindenberg, S.M. (1992). The method of decreasing abstraction. In J. Coleman & Th. Fararo. (eds.), *Rational choice theory* (pp. 3-19). Newbury Park, SAGE Publications,

Lindenberg, S.M. (1993). *Framing, empirical evidence and applications.* In Jahrbuch fur Neue Politische Ökonomie, vol. 12 (pp.11-38). Tubingen: Mohr.

Lindenberg, S.M. & Frey, B. (1993). Alternatives, frames and relative prices. *Acta Sociologica, 36*, 191-205.

Lipsky, M. (1979). Street level bureaucracy. New York, Russell Sage Foundation.

Loeff Claeys Verbeke. (1994). *Nederland privatiseert.* Den Haag, Sdu.

Long, J.S. (1997). *Regression models for categorical and limited dependent variables.* Advanced Quantitative Techniques in the Social Sciences. Thousand Oakes, SAGE Publications.

Loo, H. van der & Reijen, W. van. (1997). *Paradoxen van modernisering: een sociaalwetenschappelijke benadering.* Bussum, Uitgeverij Coutinho.

March, J.G. & Olson, J.P. (1983). Organizing political life: what administrative reorganization tells us about government. *The American Political Science Review, 77,* 281-296.

March, J.G. & Olson, J.P. (1984). The new institutionalism: Organizational factors in political life. *The American Political Science Review, 78,* 734-749.

Meer, F.M. van der & Roborgh, L.J. (1993). Ambtenaren in Nederland: omvang, bureaucratisering en representativiteit van het ambtelijk apparaat. Alphen aan den Rijn, Samsom H.D. Tjeenk Willink.

Menard, S. (1995). *Applied logistic regression analysis.* Series: Quantitative applications in the social sciences, no. 106. SAGE Publications.

Meyer M.W. & O'Shaughnessy, K. (1993). Organizational design and the performance paradox. In R. Swedberg (ed.), *Explorations in economic sociology* (pp. 249-278). New York, Russell Sage Foundation.

Meyer, M.W. & Gupta, V. (1994). The performance paradox. *Research in Organizational Behavior, 16,* 309-369.

Miles M.B. & Huberman A.M. (1994). Qualitative data analysis: een expanded sourcebook. London, SAGE.

Miljoenennota 1999. (1998). Den Haag, Ministerie van Financiën. [On-line: www.minfin.nl]

Ministerie van Financiën. (1998). Verder met resultaat: het agentschapsmodel 1991-1997. Den Haag.

Ministerie van Onderwijs, Cultuur en Wetenschappen. (1998). *Ontwikkelingen in het onderwijsbeleid in Nederland 1994-1996.* Nationaal rapport van Nederland voor de International Conference on Education, 45e zitting in Geneve 1996. [On-line: www.minocenw.nl].

Ministerie van Onderwijs, Cultuur en Wetenschappen. (1999). *OCenW in kerncijfers 1999.* [On-line: www.minocenw.nl].

Mintzberg, H. (1997). *Organisatie structuren.* Hemel Hempstead, Prentice Hall International.

Modeen, T. & Rosas, A. (eds.). (1988). *Indirect public administration in fourteen countries.* Finland, Abo Academy Press.

Modernising Government. (1999). [On-line: www.cabinet-office.gov.uk]

Moe, T.M. (1984). The new economics of organization. *American Journal of Political Science, 28,* 739-777.

Moret, Ernst & Young. (1998). Vragenlijst BVE-monitor, module financiën. Utrecht.

Mueller, D.C. (1989). *Public choice II.* Cambridge University Press.

Mueller, D.C. (ed.). (1997). *Perspectives on public choice: a handbook.* Cambridge University Press.

Naschold, F. (1996). Redefining public sector tasks at the interface between public and private service provision. In F. Naschold & C. von Otter (eds.), *Public sector transformation: rethinking markets and hierarchies in government* (pp. 21-38). Amsterdam, John Benjamins Publishing Company.

NAO: National Audit Office. (1994). *National Audit Office access to organisations receiving public money.* Note by the comptroller and auditor general to the committee on standard in public life. London, National Audit Office.

Niskanen, W.A. (1975). Bureaucrats and politicians. *The Journal of Law and Economics, 17,* 617-643.

Nonet, P. & P. Selznick. (1978). *Law and society in transition: towards responsive law.* New York, Harper Colophon Books.

Nooij, A. (1995). Variabelen en modellen: multi-variate analyse in het sociaal-wetenschappelijk onderzoek. Amsterdam, Boom.

Noordegraaf, M. & Kickert, W.J.M. (1993). Verzelfstandiging van de Informatiseringsbank. In W.J.M. Kickert (ed.), *Veranderingen in management en organisatie bij de rijksdienst* (pp. 183-196). Alphen aan den Rijn, Samsom Tjeenk Willink.

North, D.C. (1981). *Structure and change in economic history.* New York, W.W. Norton & Company.

NRC Handelsblad. (1999). *Crisis in overleg sociale zekerheid.* November 24.

OECD. (1993). *Managing with market-type mechanisms.* Public Management Studies. Paris.

Olson, M. jr. (1965). *The logic of collective action: public goods and the theory of groups.* Harvard economic studies, vol. 124. Cambridge, Mass. Harvard University Press.

Osborne, P. & Gaebler, T. (1992). Reinventing Government: how the entrepreneurial spirit is transforming the public sector. Reading MA, Addison-Wesley Publishing Company Inc.

Ostrom, E. & J. Walker. (1997). Neither market nor states: linking transformation processes in collective action arenas. In D.C. Mueller (ed.), *Perspectives on public choice: a handbook* (pp. 35-72). Cambridge University Press.

PERC: Political Economy Research Centre. (1996). *List of quangos and central government departments.* [Unpublished]. Sheffield.

Petren, G. (1988). Sweden. In T. Modeen & A. Rosas (eds.), *Indirect public administration in fourteen countries* (pp. 226-248). Finland, ABO Academy Press.

Pierre, J. (1995). Governing the welfare state: public administration, the state and society in Sweden. In J. Pierre (ed.), *Bureaucracy in the modern state. An introduction to comparative public administration* (pp.140-160). Aldershot, Edward Elgar.

Pollitt, C. (1999). *Reinvention and the rest: reform strategies in the OECD world.* Paper presented at the IDHEAP Colloquium 'L'aventure des réformes dans le secteur public: réalisations et consequences', Lausanne, 11th and 12th February.

Pollitt, C., Birchall, J. & Putman, K. (1998). *Decentralising public service management.* London, MacMillan Press Ltd.

Pollitt, C. & Bouckaert, G. (2000). *Public management reform: a comparative analysis.* Oxford, Oxford University Press.

Poot, J.K, Loo, R.R.A. te & Hengeveld., M.B. (1999). Verslaggeving en prestatie-verant-woording in de publieke sector: Kordes-Trofee op naar eerste lustrum. *Overheids-management, 12,* 107-109.

Powell, W.W. & DiMaggio, P.J. (eds.). (1991). *The new institutionalism in organizational analysis.* Chicago, The University of Chicago Press.

Pratt, J.W. & Zeckhauser, R.J. (1991). *Principals and agents.* Boston, Massachusetts & Harvard Business School Press.

Rapportage Doorlichting Zelfstandige Bestuursorganen. (1997). Den Haag, Ministerie van Binnenlandse Zaken en Ministerie van Financiën.

Rainey, H. (1997). *Understanding and managing public organizations* (2nd edition). San Francisco, Jossey-Bass Publishers.

Rhodes, R. (1997). Reinventing Whitehall, 1979-1995: hollowing out the state? In R. Rhodes (ed.), *Understanding governance* (pp. 87-111). Buckingham, Open University Press.

Rijksbegroting 1998. Ministerie van Financiën. [On-line: www.minfin.nl].

Ritzer, G. (1993). The McDonaldization of society: an investigation into the changing character of contemporary social life. Newbur Park, CA, Pine Forge Press.

Rogers, E.M. (1995). *Diffusion of innovations* (4th edition). New York, The Free Press.

Rosas, A. & Suksi, M. (1988). PGOs in Finland. In C. Hood & G.F. Schuppert (eds.), *Delivering public services in Western Europe* (pp. 120-133). London, SAGE Publications.

Rosas, A. & Suksi, M. (1994). Indirect public administration in Finland. In T. Modeen (ed.), *Public Administration in Finland.* (pp.73-86). Helsinki, Finnish branch of the International Institute of Administrative Sciences, Ministry of Finance, Adminsitrative Development Agency.

Rowan, B. & Meyer, J.W. (1979). Institutionalized organizations: formal structure as myth and ceremony. *American Journal of Sociology, 83,* 340-363.

Scharpf, F.W. (1997). *Games real actors play: actor-centered institutionalism in policy research.* Theoretical lenses on public policy. USA/United Kingdom, Westview Press.

Scheltema, M. (1974). *Zelfstandige bestuursorganen.* Groningen, H.D. Tjeenk Willink.

SCA: School Curriculum and Assessment Authority. (1997). *The value added national project: report to the Secretary of State.* University of Durham.

Schuyt, K. & Veen, R. van de. (eds.). (1990). De verdeelde samenleving: een inleiding in de ontwikkeling van de Nederlandse verzorgingsstaat (2nd edition). Leiden, Stenfert Kroese.

Siegers, J.J. (1992). Interdisciplinary economics. *De Economist, 140,* 531-547.

Smith, P. (1995). On the unintended consequences of publishing performance data in the public sector. *International Journal of Public Administration, 18,* 277-310.

Staatsalmanak voor het Koninkrijk der Nederlanden. (1950-1999). Den Haag, Sdu.

Stiglitz, J.E. (1988). *Economics of the public sector* (2nd edition). New York, W.W. Norton & Company.

Stokman, F.N. (1994). *Besluitvorming binnen beleidsnetwerken.* In L.W.J.C. Huberts & J. Kleinnijenhuis (eds.), *Methoden van invloedsanalyse* (pp. 165-187). Amsterdam, Boom.

Stokman, F.N. & Oosten, R. van. (1994). The exchange of voting positions: an object-oriented model of policy networks. In B. Bueno de Mesquita & F.N. Stokman (eds.), *European Community Decision Making: models, applications and comparisons* (pp. 105-128). New Have and London, Yale University Press.

Stokman, F.N. & Zeggelink, E.P.H. (1996). Is politics power or policy oriented? A comparative analysis of dynamic access models in policy networks. *Journal of Mathematical Sociology, 21,* 77-111.

Stone, B. (1995). Administrative accountability in the Westminster democracies: towards a new conceptual framework. *Governance, 8,* 505-526.

Swaan, A. de. (1989). Zorg en staat: welzijn, onderwijs en gezondheidszorg in Europa en de Verenigde Staten in de nieuwe tijd. Amsterdam, Bert Bakker.

Swanborn, P.G. (1996). *Case-study's: wat, wanneer en hoe?* Amsterdam, Boom.

Tarschys, D. (1988). PGOs in Sweden. In C. Hood & G.F. Schuppert (eds.), *Delivering public services in Western Europe* (pp. 63-74). London, SAGE Publications.

Thiel, S. van. (1999a). *Quangos in cases: IB-Groep.* Rotterdam.

Thiel, S. van. (1999b). *Quangos in cases: the ROC.* Rotterdam.

Thiel, S. van., Leeuw, F.L. & Flap, H.D. (1998). Quango-cratisering in Nederland? *Beleid & Maatschappij, XXV,* 143-151.

Thiel, S. van., Leeuw, F.L., Siegers, J.J. & Flap, H.D. (1999). Oorzaken van verzelfstandiging: een empirische verklaring voor de toename in verzelfstandiging. *Bestuurskunde, 8,* 28-43.

Tolbert, P.S. & Zucker, L.G. (1982). Institutional sources of change in the formal structure of organizations: the diffusion of civil service reform, 1880-1935. *Administrative Science Quarterly, 28,* 22-39.

Tollison, R.D. (1997). Rent seeking. In D.C. Mueller (ed.), *Perspectives on public choice: a handbook* (pp. 506-525). Cambridge University Press.

Torenvlied, R. (1996a). Besluiten in uitvoering: theorieen over beleidsuitvoering getoetst op sociale vernieuwing in drie gemeenten. Amsterdam, Thesis Publishers.

Torenvlied, R. (1996b). Political control of implementation agencies: effects of political consensus on agency compliance. *Rationality and Society, 8,* 25-56.

Torenvlied, R. (2000). *Political decisions and agency performance.* Dordrecht, Kluwer Academic Publishers.

Ultee, W., Arts, W. & Flap, H.D. (1992). *Sociologie: vragen, uitspraken, bevindingen.* Groningen, Wolters-Noordhoff.

Unger, B. & Waarden, F. van. (1995). Introduction: an interdisciplinary approach to convergence. In B. Unger & F. van Waarden (eds.), *Convergence or diversity? Internationalization and economic policy response* (pp. 1-36). Avebury, Aldershot.

Veld, Th.W.M. (1994). ROC-vorming: beleid voor een nieuw bestel. Een onderzoek naar de beleids- en meningsvorming inzake ROC's. De Lier, Academische Boeken Centrum (RISBO-reeks).

Veld, R.J. in 't. (1995). *Spelen met vuur: over hybride organisaties.* Den Haag, VUGA Uitgeverij BV.

Verhaak, F.O.M., Bagchus, R. & Twist, M.J.W. van. (1996). Kerndepartementen: analytisch kader. In M.J.W. van Twist, R. Bagchus & F.O.M. Verhaak (eds.), *Kerndepartementen op afstand? Een vergelijkend onderzoek naar departementale veranderingsprocessen binnen de Nederlandse rijksdienst* (pp. 23-40). Delft, Eburon.

Verhaak, F. (1997). Shifting frames of reference in Dutch autonomisation reforms. In W.J.M. Kickert (ed.), *Public management and administrative reform in western Europe* (pp.157-176). Cheltenham, Edward Elgar.

Vickerstaff, S. & Parker, K.T. (1996). TECs, LECs and small firms: differences in provision and performance. *Environment and Planning: Government and Policy, 14,* 251-267.

Volkskrant, de. (1994). Langdurig werkloze moet weg uit bestand. July 7.

Volkskrant, de. (1996). Linschoten gehavend door Ctsv-rapport. June 25.

Volkskrant, de. (1997). Uitkeringsorgaan USZO krijgt nog respijt van Ritzen. May 30.

Volkskrant, de. (1999a). *Topambtenaren?* September 28.

Volkskrant, de. (1999b). Parlement komt NS te hulp in strijd om HSL. June 14.

Vrancken, P.H.J. & Kemp, A.A.M. de. (1996). *Marktwerking in het secundair en tertiair beroepsonderwijs: een verkenning*. Den Haag, Instituut voor Onderzoek van Overheidsuitgaven.

Waarden, F. van. (1987). Vervlechting van staat en belangengroepen (1). *Beleid en Maatschappij*, *14*, 172-184.

Waarden, F. van. (1988). Vervlechting van staat en belangengroepen (2). *Beleid en Maatschappij*, *15*, 115-126.

Waarden, F. van. (1992). The historical institutionalization of typical national patterns in policy networks between state and industry: a comparison of the USA and the Netherlands. *European Journal of Political Research*, *21*, 131-162.

Waarden, F. van. (1995). Zal de markt voor openbaar vervoer werken? *ESB*, *80*, 866-869, 872.

Waarden, F. van. (1999a). Ieder land zijn eigen trant? In W. Bakker & F. van Waarden (eds.), *Ruimte rond regels: stijlen van regulering en beleidsuitvoering vergeleken* (pp. 303-339). Jaarboek 1999/2000 Beleid en Maatschappij. Amsterdam, Boom.

Waarden, F. van. (1999b). De institutionele grondslag van ambtelijke gewoonten. In W. Bakker & F. van Waarden (eds.), *Ruimte rond regels: stijlen van regulering en beleidsuitvoering vergeleken* (pp. 340-374). Jaarboek 1999/2000 Beleid en Maatschappij. Amsterdam, Boom.

Waldegrave, W. (1993). *The reality of reform and accountability in today's public service*. London, CIPFA, Public Finance Foundation.

Weimer, D.L. & Vining, A.R. (1992). *Policy Analysis: concepts and practice* (2nd edition). Englewood Cliffs, New Jersey, Prentice Hall.

Weir, S. & Hall, W. (1994*). EGO-trip: Extra-Governmental Organisations in the United Kingdom and their accountability*. The Democratic Audit of the United Kingdom. London, Charter 88 Trust.

Weiss, J.A. & Piderit, S.K. (1999). The value of mission statements in public agencies. *Journal of Public Administration Research and Theory*, *9*, 193-223.

WEB: Wet Educatie en Beroepsonderwijs. (1995). Wet van 31 oktober 1995, houdende bepalingen met betrekking tot de educatie en het beroepsonderwijs. *Staatsblad*, *176*, nr. 501. Den Haag, Sdu.

Wet Verzelfstandiging Informatiseringsbank: regeling van de bestuurlijke verhouding tussen de Minster van Onderwijs en Wetenschappen en de Informatie Beheer Groep, voorheen Informatiseringsbank. Tweede Kamer, vergaderjaar 1992-1993, 23 073, nr. 10. Den Haag, Sdu.

White, H.C. (1991). Agency as control. In Pratt, J.W. & R.J. Zeckhauser (eds.), *Principals and agents* (pp.187-213). Boston, Massachusetts & Harvard Business School Press.

Wiebrens, C. & Essers, S. (1999). Schaf het ophelderingspercentage af. *Het Tijdschrift voor de Politie*, *61*, 27-34.

Williamson, O.E. (1981). The economics of organization: the transaction cost approach. *American Journal of Sociology*, *87*, 548-577.

Williamson, O.E. (1989). Transaction cost economics. In R. Schmalensee & R.D. Willig (eds.), *Handbook of Industrial Organization* (pp. 136-181). Volume I. Elsevier Science Publishers B.V.

Williamson, O.E. (1995). Transaction cost economics and organization theory. In O.E. Williamson (ed.), *Organization theory: from Chester Barnard to the present and beyond* (pp. 207-255). New York, Oxford University Press.

Wilson, J.Q. (1989). Bureaucracy: what government agencies do and why they do it. New York, BasicBooks.

Wistrich, E. (1996). *Quangos in New-Zealand.* PERC Occasional Paper No. 15. University of Sheffield.

Wistrich, E. (1999). Quangos in New-Zealand. In M.V. Flinders & M.J. Smith (eds.), *Quangos, accountability and reform: the politics of quasi-government* (pp.84-93). London, Macmillan Press.

World Bank (1997). World Development report 1997: the state in a changing world. Washington.

Wright, V. (1994). Reshaping the state: the implications for public administration. *West European Politics, 17*, 102-137.

WRR: Wetenschappelijke Raad voor het Regeringsbeleid. (1983). *Organen en rechtspersonen rondom de centrale overheid.* V35, delen 1-3. Den Haag, Sdu.

Yin, R.K. (1994). *Case study research: design and methods* (2nd edition). Applied Social Research Methods Series, Volume 5. New York, SAGE.

Zijlstra, S.E. (1997). Zelfstandige bestuursorganen in een democratische rechtsstaat. Den Haag, VUGA Uitgeverij BV.

Zon, W. van. (ed.) (1990). *Volwasseneneducatie: terreinverkenning en methodische uitgangspunten van de basiseducatie.* Basisleerboek volwasseneneducatie. Houten, Bohn Stafleu Van Loghum.

Index

accessibility, 139, 179, 191, 195, 197, 198, 222, 225, 226

accountability requirements, 13, 14, 21, 39, 40, 41, 44, 47, 64, 73, 77, 81, 86, 95, 103, 112, 115, 118, 119, 124, 127, 132, 137, 138, 139, 142, 180, 181, 183, 186, 192, 193, 210, 211, 216, 225

accountability scale, 41, 103, 104, 115, 117, 210

adverse selection, 16, 17, 68, 69, 78

alliance, 169, 224

auto-correlation, 104, 130

autonomy, 6, 7, 11, 12, 16, 19, 66, 70, 86, 139, 143, 144, 150, 151, 166, 167, 174, 175, 183, 184, 187, 194, 196, 198, 219, 220, 223, 226, 228, 229, 232

bounded rationality, 62, 75, 97, 112, 113, 119, 213, 216, 221

bureaucratization, 1, 25, 180, 206, 208, 211

bureaucrats, 4, 16, 17, 47, 56, 65, 66, 67, 68, 70, 86, 209, 218

bureau shaping, 56

capture, 86

cartels, 191

civil servants, 7, 25, 32, 47, 52, 74, 98, 100, 137, 146, 147, 150, 153, 194, 131, 207, 208, 218, 232

closeness, 74, 83, 136, 228

cluster, 22, 50, 72, 96, 113-115, 118, 132, 136, 141, 142, 146, 190, 131

collective goods, 2, 3, 4, 13, 15, 16, 60, 63, 101, 103, 104, 111, 114, 118, 124, 125, 127, 209, 212, 213, 215, 216, 218

collectiveness, 101, 104, 109, 110, 114-117, 125, 126

commercial activities, 14, 136, 142, 146, 150, 153, 157, 159, 160, 162, 164, 169, 173, 175-177, 179, 181, 185, 193, 194, 196, 226

competition, 4, 5, 11, 12, 59, 66, 72, 80, 81, 87, 88, 99, 111, 122, 123, 136, 146, 147, 163, 168, 169, 180, 190, 191, 212, 214, 224, 226, 227, 230

compliance, 39, 40, 68, 69, 72, 73, 74, 83, 84, 85, 194, 206, 220, 224

corporatism, 59, 100, 101, 102, 103, 104, 109, 110, 111, 116-118, 124, 130, 137, 192, 213, 218

cost prices, 185, 187, 196

customer service, 151, 156, 159, 160, 162-164, 187, 192, 194, 196, 198, 223-226

deviance, 68, 69, 73, 74, 80, 83-85, 220

down-swing, 58, 99, 121, 122, 214

electoral competition, 59, 99, 104, 118, 123, 124, 130, 213

fringe benefits, 54, 67, 68, 169, 220, 232

free-rider problem, 2, 13, 71, 86

hiving in, 10, 55, 57, 58, 72, 99, 120, 121, 211

hiving off, 10, 32, 57, 58, 74, 86, 99, 120, 121, 130, 137, 144, 152, 159, 210, 211, 214, 219, 224

hidden action, 69, 74

hidden information, 68, 69, 73, 80

ideology, 53, 54, 57, 58, 85, 88, 98, 104, 107, 118, 120, 121, 213, 216

imitation, 62, 63, 64, 97, 103-106, 112, 117, 119, 126, 128, 213, 216, 217, 219, 231

information asymmetry, 69, 71, 77, 78, 79, 127
interest groups, 9, 10, 52, 55, 59, 64, 70, 72, 73, 81, 86, 51, 118, 123, 124, 126, 127, 137, 168, 191, 192, 208, 211, 212, 218, 219
isomorphism, 62, 217

management contracts, 7, 144, 150, 152, 162, 175, 183, 192, 193
market mechanism, 5, 11, 19, 53
market position, 136, 142, 190, 221, 224
measure fixation, 78, 82, 163
ministerial accountability, 6, 50
ministerial responsibility, 7, 9, 39, 57, 144, 150, 151
monitoring, 56, 57, 60, 62, 64, 65, 72-79, 81, 86, 88, 97, 104, 112-119, 127, 173, 175, 210, 211, 213, 216-219, 229
monitoring costs, 56, 60, 64, 65, 77, 79, 112, 127, 210, 213, 216
monopoly, 13, 56, 61, 71, 72, 81, 146, 169, 190, 131, 219
moral hazard, 16, 68, 69, 78
motives, 5, 7, 9, 10, 11, 12, 14, 18, 19, 33, 38, 47, 53, 205, 231

over-dispersion, 105, 113

patronage, 9, 55, 57, 59, 63, 64, 86, 118, 123, 212, 219
perceptions, 136, 138, 142, 225
performance assessment, 48, 75-79, 81, 83, 135, 138, 152, 163, 164, 173, 175, 178, 181-185, 192-198, 221, 224-226, 229
performance indicators, 45, 46, 75-77, 81-83, 134, 150-152, 159, 160, 175, 181-184, 196, 197, 209, 221, 225, 229, 230
performance paradox, 75, 76, 77, 78, 79, 80, 81, 82, 83, 84, 85, 86, 88, 89, 131-138, 140, 143, 160, 163, 165, 181, 185-187, 190-200, 221-230
perquisites, 54, 66, 69
perverse learning, 75, 76, 78, 80, 82
physical well-being, 52, 53, 54, 62, 66, 68, 69

policy objectives, 13, 67, 82, 83, 89, 134, 135, 138, 142, 197, 200, 225, 230
positive learning, 75, 77, 82, 135
practitioner theory, 9, 10, 12, 13, 18, 25, 58, 71, 119, 122, 130, 131, 205, 208, 209, 214, 220, 227, 228, 231
principal agent theory, 16, 17, 56, 220
privatization, 1, 5, 6, 11, 12, 14, 15, 50, 207, 210, 232
production rights, 5, 7, 12, 16, 55, 61, 64, 66, 69, 70, 71, 80, 89, 136, 142, 186, 187, 196, 200, 221, 223, 228
programme costs, 32, 133, 148, 150, 152, 156, 157, 160, 162, 164, 172, 192
programme revenues, 150, 156, 160, 175
property rights, 1, 4, 15, 16
public choice, 16, 17, 18, 51, 53, 66, 72, 51, 212, 220

quango-drift, 6, 211

rational actor model, 17, 18, 97, 111, 113, 212, 213, 216
rationalization, 4, 5, 19, 206, 208, 209, 232
regulator, 84, 51, 137, 142, 199
rent-seeking, 51
reversal of control, 61, 65, 79, 125, 127, 226, 227
rights of production, 4, 6
running costs, 32, 133, 148, 150-157, 159, 160, 162, 164, 172

scrutiny, 39, 41, 44
self-regulation, 9, 10, 11, 102
semi-monopoly, 72, 136
separation of policy and administration, 5, 11
shirking, 232
size, 4, 12, 25, 47, 58, 67, 69, 70, 74, 83, 97-99, 106, 107, 112, 117, 118, 119, 133, 137, 142, 144, 147, 157, 162, 168, 186, 193, 131, 208, 211, 213, 223
social approval, 52, 53, 54, 62, 66, 67, 68, 69, 74, 51, 220
social production function, 52
specific assets, 72, 125, 190, 215

specific investments, 16, 60, 61, 63, 65,
72, 81, 101-104, 114, 118, 125, 126,
136, 142, 213, 215, 216, 218
sunk costs, 65, 127, 190, 215
supervision, 7, 29, 55, 83, 101, 102, 150,
180, 186, 199, 207, 210, 215
supervisor, 84, 85, 137, 173, 199
suppression, 75, 76, 77, 78

transaction cost analysis, 15, 16, 61
trend, 17, 47, 97, 107, 118, 119, 121, 126,
127, 144, 177, 190, 205, 217
triangulation, 140
trust, 56, 64, 65, 124

uncertainty, 62, 63, 65, 97, 103, 119, 128,
216
unintended consequences, 75, 227
up-swing, 58, 99, 121, 122, 214
utility, 16, 17, 52

weighting formula, 98, 100, 102, 218

For Product Safety Concerns and Information please contact our EU
representative GPSR@taylorandfrancis.com
Taylor & Francis Verlag GmbH, Kaufingerstraße 24, 80331 München, Germany

www.ingramcontent.com/pod-product-compliance
Lightning Source LLC
Chambersburg PA
CBHW071852270326
41929CB00013B/2201